HOW TO MANAG
STRATEGY

THE FUTURE OF DEVELOPMENT AID

Derek Fee

Zed Books
LONDON | NEW YORK

How to manage an aid exit strategy: the future of development aid was first published in 2012 by Zed Books Ltd, 7 Cynthia Street, London N1 9JF, UK and Room 400, 175 Fifth Avenue, New York, NY 10010, USA

www.zedbooks.co.uk

Copyright © Derek Fee 2012

The right of Derek Fee to be identified as the author of this work has been asserted by him in accordance with the Copyright, Designs and Patents Act, 1988

FSC
www.fsc.org
MIX
Paper from
responsible sources
FSC® C013604

Set in FFKievit and Monotype Plantin by Ewan Smith, London
Index: ed.emery@thefreeuniversity.net
Cover designed by Rogue Four Design
Printed and bound by CPI Group (UK) Ltd, Croydon, CRO 4YY

Distributed in the USA exclusively by Palgrave Macmillan, a division of St Martin's Press, LLC, 175 Fifth Avenue, New York, NY 10010, USA

A catalogue record for this book is available from the British Library
Library of Congress Cataloging in Publication Data available

ISBN 978 1 78032 030 4 hb
ISBN 978 1 78032 029 8 pb

About the author

Derek Fee holds BE, MSc and PhD
degrees from University College Dublin
and an MBA from Trinity College
Dublin. He is the author of six non-
fiction books and one novel. He was
the EU Ambassador to Zambia and the
EU Representative to COMESA. He
is currently the Managing Partner of
DevAid Partners.

CONTENTS

FIGURES, TABLE AND BOXES

Figures

Table

Boxes

ABBREVIATIONS

ABC	Agencia Brasileira de Cooperaçao
ACP	African, Caribbean and Pacific
ADB	Asian Development Bank
AGOA	African Growth and Opportunity Act
ARA	Autonomous Revenue Authority
ARF	African Renaissance and International Cooperation Fund
BRICS	Brazil, Russia, India, China, South Africa
CIDA	Canadian International Development Agency
COMESA	Common Market for Eastern and Southern Africa
CSO	civil society organization
CSP	country strategy paper
DAC	Development Assistance Committee
DfID	Department for International Development (UK)
DRC	Democratic Republic of Congo
DTIS	Diagnostic Trade Integration Study
EAC	East African Community
EBA	'Everything but Arms' (European Council Regulation)
ECA	Economic Cooperation Administration
ECOWAS	Economic Community of West African States
EITI	Extractive Industries Transparency Initiative
EPA	Economic Partnership Agreement
EU	European Union
FDI	foreign direct investment
FOCAC	Forum of Chinese Africa Cooperation
GATS	General Agreement on Trade in Services
GATT	General Agreement on Tariffs and Trade
GAVI	Global Action for Vaccination and Immunization
GBS	general budget support
GDP	gross domestic product
GNI	gross national income
GSP	Generalized System of Tariff Preferences
HIPC	Highly Indebted Poor Countries
IBRD	International Bank for Reconstruction and Development

ICT	information and communication technologies
IDA	International Development Association
IF	Integrated Framework
IFC	International Finance Corporation
IGAD	Intergovernmental Authority on Development
IMF	International Monetary Fund
ITEC	Indian Technical and Economic Cooperation
JITAP	Joint Integrated Technical Assistance Programme
LDC	less developed country
LIC	lower income country
LMIC	lower middle income country
MDG	Millennium Development Goal
MDRI	Multilateral Debt Relief Initiative
MEA	Ministry of External Affairs (India)
MERCOSUR	Mercado Común del Sur (Common Market of the South)
MFN	Most Favoured Nation
MIX	Microfinance Information Exchange
MTS	Multilateral Trading System
NEPAD	New Partnership for Africa's Development
NGO	non-governmental organization
ODA	official development assistance
OECD	Organisation for Economic Co-operation and Development
OPEC	Organization of the Petroleum Exporting Countries
PAF	performance assessment framework
PRSP	Poverty Reduction Strategy Paper
PSBS	programme sector budget support
RIO	regional integration organization
SACU	Southern Africa Customs Union
SADC	Southern African Development Community
SAL	structural adjustment loan
SDT	Special and Differential Treatment
SWAP	sector-wide approach
TRIPS	Trade Related Intellectual Property Rights
UMIC	upper middle income country
UNDP	United Nations Development Programme
USAID	US Agency for International Development
WGI	Worldwide Governance Index
WTO	World Trade Organization

PREFACE

This book is the product of a series of reflections I have made stemming from the experience gained during the years that I have been involved in development projects at different levels. While the geographical spread of these projects has been considerable, covering Europe, Asia and Africa, the similarities of the methodologies and the chosen initiatives aimed at creating either institutional change (sometimes called large-D development) or simply change at the local or national level (sometimes referred to as small-d development) are very alike. I have followed very closely the evolution of the processes involved in development and have been somewhat taken aback at the lack of innovation in the sector. If the computer sector mirrored the development sector, we would still be inputting cards into a machine which took up the space of a large room. There are of course reasons for this lack of innovation, mainly associated with the nature of development, which is not a consumer product and is therefore inconsistent with the continual level of improvement which has characterized the consumer electronics sector. Nevertheless, it is a sad reflection on a sector which has been (effectively) in operation for the past forty years that today's exponents are using the same methodologies as the previous generation.

The past decade has seen a large body of literature aimed at showing that development aid does not work. Some of the work associated with the ineffectiveness of development aid has been highly academic, while some has eschewed the academic approach and pointed out the simple fact that while Africa has received many billions of dollars of development aid, living standards had been dropping until the improvement in growth rates witnessed in recent years. So, much as the world needs another book on why development aid does not work, this book intends to steer clear of that particular debate. I have huge respect for those who spend their days in an ivory tower poring over complicated economic equations which prove or disprove the validity of development aid initiatives. However, it is equally important in the understanding of aid to stand in a field in Africa and watch the inhabitants of a village celebrate their new school or new clinic. Therefore my purpose is to examine, from the viewpoint of the practitioner, the business which I was part of for such a long period of time. The approach I have adopted will lie somewhere between the academic and the practical. So those readers who like to see lots of citations will not be disappointed.

This book is primarily an examination of why development aid is alive and kicking despite calls from both Africa (the continent demanding the highest level of aid) and donor country leaders to bring the business to a logical conclusion.

The book begins with a chapter examining the situation of Africa in relation to aid. The past decade has shown a marked decrease in the need for aid in South East Asia and Latin America, so Africa today represents the hotspot for development aid activities. Chapter 2 looks at the history of development aid, and is to some extent an examination of why an activity that was supposed to be time-bound has expanded way beyond its initial remit. Chapter 3 looks at aid from a business perspective by considering both those on the supply side and those on the demand side of aid. It also examines the processes and the methodologies associated with development aid. In essence this chapter answers many of the 'what' and 'how' questions associated with the aid business.

The seven chapters that follow examine in some detail several of the initiatives which have been hyped as the 'magic bullet' that will solve the development dilemma. The initiatives I discuss are domestic resource mobilization, trade liberalization, the BRICS, regional integration, microfinance, remittances, and NGOs and philanthropic institutions. These seven initiatives have the ability to supplant or augment official (or unofficial) development aid. In some cases they represent policy options for replacing development aid and therefore may denote elements of a withdrawal from development aid or an aid exit strategy.

The final chapter asks what constitutes an aid exit strategy, how can it be implemented, and, more important, can such a strategy counteract the pressures which wish to maintain aid dependency?

This book represents a distillation not only of my own experience of managing development aid projects in all their facets but also of discussions with governments and other concerned actors on the broader subject of development aid. It also benefits (as I have) from the many hours I have spent discussing the dilemmas associated with development aid with my colleagues whose collective experience in the subject is incomparable.

ACKNOWLEDGEMENTS

I would like to thank my editors at Zed Books, Tamsine O'Riordan and Jakob Horstmann, for their help and encouragement, my daughter Bairbre for reading and correcting drafts, and Kay Sheedy for Maria's story in Chapter 9. I would also like to thank the many colleagues who have helped formulate my ideas: they are far too numerous to name. Most of all I would like to thank my wife Aine for her patience.

For Aine, Bobbie and Sean

1 | THE STATE OF AID

There is an unprecedented resolve on the continent to turn away from the begging bowl and engage in new efforts to build a better life. (Thabo Mbeki)

Development aid cannot continue indefinitely. The task is therefore to use limited resources as effectively as possible. This can only work through good governance which taps that country's economic potential. (Angela Merkel, at the High Level Plenary Meeting of the UN General Assembly on the Millennium Development Goals, 21 September 2010)

Development aid is in trouble

The above statement by the German Chancellor might be considered to contain both a heresy and an aphorism. It simply depends from what side of the development debate the comment is viewed. The statement that development aid cannot continue indefinitely is viewed as heresy by those who have continually petitioned the developed world to honour their moral commitments to the developing countries by increasing the level of resources which they commit to development assistance. On the contrary, the statement will be seen as an aphorism by those who view development assistance as a black hole into which developed countries, principally those who are members of the Organization for Economic Cooperation and Development (OECD), have for almost four decades poured trillions of dollars without any appreciable result in terms of development and consequently poverty reduction. It has been estimated that the total resource transfers from the developed countries during the four decades is the equivalent of five Marshall Plans (the large-scale US programme of monetary support to help rebuild European economies after the end of World War Two).

It is now more than twenty-five years since Bob Geldof did not say 'give us your ****ing money'. In the intervening period Geldof, assisted by Bono and academics such as Jeffrey Sachs, have continually lobbied Western governments to relieve developing countries' debt, mainly through the Jubilee Debt Campaign, and increase the volumes of aid. This moral crusade to alleviate poverty in developing countries led to the Highly Indebted Poor Countries (HIPC) initiative and indeed to the result of the Gleneagles Summit of the G8 forum of eight of the world's largest economies. The Gleneagles Summit launched the Multilateral Debt Relief Initiative (MDRI) and called on the OECD donors to double their aid commitments in the period 2006 to 2015. Sachs established the philosophical background of the campaign to relieve debt and the campaign to increase funding levels (Sachs 2005). However, he was writing in 2005, the year in which the Gleneagles Summit took place. Those halcyon days are long past, and one wonders how the leaders of the developed world would respond in today's post-economic crisis time of austerity to calls for increased development aid. Budget deficits in the OECD countries have led to increased pressure on all elements of the national budgets, and development aid, even with its high moral standing, may escape in the short term but will inevitably come under increased pressure. With the further fact that the developing countries appear to have weathered the economic storms better than their developed counterparts, the future of aid flows can be considered to be highly uncertain.

These factors certainly have not escaped the attention either of the political classes in the developing world, or of many of their better-educated citizens. There is therefore a case for most developing countries to begin plotting their future course in an era of diminishing aid flows. Some leaders, as can be seen by the quotation from Thabo Mbeki at the head of this chapter, have already drawn this conclusion. The economic crisis, which has not abated since its inception in 2008, has already claimed many casualties. It is not beyond the realms of possibility that development aid will be included in their number in the near future.

The aid crisis is deepening

It cannot be contested that despite the very large increases in the volume of official development aid and the proliferation of new organizations assisting the developing world, the aid 'business' is in crisis. There is nothing new in this. Aid has been in crisis before, especially during the 1980s and 1990s when aid volumes fell. But this time is different. Prominent Africans, including Paul Kagame, President of Rwanda, Arthur Mutambara, the leader of the Movement for Democratic Change (MDC) in Zimbabwe, and Dambisa Moyo, have indicated their desire to see the end of aid as we know it to African countries (Kagame 2009, Mutambara 2009, Moyo 2010). They therefore align themselves with other commentators, such as Easterly (2007) and Riddell (2007), who from the donor side have called for a radical rethink of how aid is delivered. There is therefore a confluence of donor and recipient opinion that aid is not accomplishing its aims. The question remains whether the current aid model is simply broken and can be fixed or whether the model is redundant and must be replaced with a model that assists developing countries to exit from aid in a regulated manner. Simply ringing up leaders and telling them that aid will end on a specific day will not solve the problem.

Although the moral imperative of aid, which has been the cornerstone on which aid has been built and which will be examined later in this book as we look at the history of aid, still exists, the pressure on Development Assistance Committee (DAC) donors,[1] many of whom face massive debts themselves, will inevitably lead their citizens to question the continuation of a system of aid which has not succeeded despite forty years' existence. Angela Merkel has already voiced this opinion, and although she couched it in diplomatic terms the conclusion is clear. A modern aid system or model must be one which incorporates a time-bound approach – in other words the end of aid as we know it. Even within the UK, which has a historical commitment to assisting Africa,[2] there is some apprehension at the continuation of aid. The House of Commons International Development Committee reported:

> UK support for development has been regarded as strong. Some 74 per cent of respondents to DfID's [Department for International Development] latest Attitudinal Tracking Study claimed to be concerned about poverty in developing countries. However, there are indications that the economic downturn could be undermining

1 The DAC has 24 members (year of joining in parentheses): Australia (1966), Austria (1965), Belgium (1961), Canada (1961), Denmark (1963), Finland (1975), France (1961), Germany (1961), Greece (1999), Ireland (1985), Italy (1961), Japan (1961), Korea (2010), Luxembourg (1992), Netherlands (1961), New Zealand (1973), Norway (1962), Portugal (member 1961–74; rejoined 1991), Spain (1991), Sweden (1965), Switzerland (1968), the UK (1961), the USA (1961), and the European Union Institutions (1961).

2 Morris (2003a and b) gives a good perspective on the involvement of the UK in aid to Africa in the nineteenth century.

the public's willingness to support Government aid expenditure. The Secretary of State told us that he was 'worried' about how to maintain this during difficult economic times. (International Development Committee 2009)

Development aid has suffered from three major problems. The first is a phenomenon that has only recently been recognized after the US-led adventures in Iraq and Afghanistan. This new phenomenon is called 'mission creep', and development aid can be seen as one of its prime examples. The DAC donors, a plethora of non-governmental organizations and an equally large number of philanthropic bodies have poured hundreds of billions of dollars into the developing world over a period of more than forty years. Despite all this effort, many countries are still dependent on aid, with stagnating economies. This leads to the continual call for increased resources to add to the already disbursed funds which did not have the desired result. This is typical of the 'it will be different this time' kind of thinking that has permeated the development space. Advocates for the 'big push' are living more in hope than in the reality that the current development model is simply a black hole into which financial aid disappeared. As results did not correspond to efforts (particularly financial efforts), increased volumes of aid were seen as the answer. And so the mission crept forward, sometimes suffering from donor fatigue as those professionals on the ground despaired of ever arriving at the end of their mission. We are now into the second generation of professionals who have dedicated their working lives to development aid and yet we are still on the original mission.

However, there is another aspect of mission creep that is more invidious than the constant clamour for additional resources. Development aid started its life as an effort to assist nascent countries to establish working economies and to provide basic services to their people. Somewhere along the line (possibly around the time of the Live Aid events of 1985) this rather simplistic initial mission suddenly became the 'fight against poverty'. It is widely accepted (even by Jeffrey Sachs) that the elimination of poverty is beyond our capacity. In 2011, 16.4 million children in the US were living in poverty. Extending the mission of development aid to combating poverty instead of concentrating on assisting developing countries to put their economies on a sound footing was a serious reorientation of the original mission. The Chinese 'miracle' used economic growth to move millions of its citizens out of poverty; there are no examples of the inverse relationship. Reorienting the development aid mission towards poverty alleviation may have succeeded in keeping people in poverty rather than the opposite.

The second problem is the lack of an exit strategy in the thinking of the major donor organizations. Go to the website of any donor (or cooperating partner, as they are now called) and download the strategy for country X. You will find an excellent analysis of the economic, political and social situation in country X along with the donor's response to the needs identified in the analysis. If the country is deficient in infrastructure then the obvious solution is to build a road from the capital A to a point B on the border that will assist exports. This is all very well in and of itself but the strategy document generally misses the big picture. In other words, there is not a single word on how the donor intends to exit country X. Developing this 'exit strategy' is not easy but it should be an element of any development aid policy. The professionals on the ground often define their mission as 'making themselves redundant', yet the combined effects of mission creep and the lack of a clearly defined exit strategy have led us to the point where many in the donor community are saying that we cannot go on for ever.

The third problem that development aid poses is the symbiotic relationship between the donors and the recipients of aid. Development aid strategy has progressed from the situation in which the donors told the recipients what kind of development aid they needed to a more appropriate relationship where the recipient plays a full part in the decision on where the aid will be used (in a later chapter we will look at how aid is delivered). This marked the shift from the supply-driven approach to the demand-driven approach. This shift had a positive impact in making aid more efficient. But it lacked the concentration on results that would have justified the financial flows involved. The large number of professionals, volunteers and downright amateurs who form the development aid cadre are totally dependent on aid for their living. For the most part these participants in the aid game are judged on their ability to dispense aid and not on the results they may obtain. International organizations such as the World Bank, the United Nations Development Programme (UNDP) and the European Union (EU) regularly rotate their personnel so that the person who begins a particular project is unlikely to be the person who is in charge at the finish. Berkman (2008) and Hancock (1994) have denigrated the efforts of the international staff of development organizations, pointing out how staff have undermined development by lack of attention to results, and Hancock has demonstrated how international development staff have looked after themselves to the detriment of their African charges. The examples given by Berkman and Hancock represent the extremes of those working for aid agencies, and it is clear that most development aid workers are consummate professionals committed to the mission of their organization. However, it is not simply the international staff who have 'the spend at all costs' bug. African treasury and ministerial officials spend a good deal of their time searching for grant funding for their pet projects. Also, donor funding is an attractive method of supplementing their official salaries. The ubiquitous 'sitting allowance' allows government officials to charge donors for attending workshops, seminars and training events. There are also the opportunities for international travel as donors pay officials' travel and other expenses to attend training courses or conferences held in interesting locations, with a distinct preference for Washington and London. The spring and autumn meetings of the Bretton Woods institutions offer an opportunity for hundreds of African ministers and government officials to get together with the hierarchy of the World Bank and the International Monetary Fund (IMF) to discuss issues of mutual interest. It is considered a plum to be added to the sometimes large delegations which descend on Washington's hotels twice yearly. Then there are the annual meetings of the African Development Bank, the 'development days' organized by the European Commission and the regular meetings in New York of the UNDP.

Easterly (2007) has rightly pointed out the enormous pressure placed on the ministries of any individual African country by the donor community by way of reporting. Recipients must also accommodate dozens of aid delegations; the Tanzanian authorities have been forced to establish a three-month moratorium on contacts with donors in order to get ministry work done. However, in-country donor representatives and indeed government officials exist on their ability to interact with each other. Development aid is a two-way street which requires both parties to be in more or less constant contact. Thereby hangs the symbiotic relationship. Each side needs the other so that the aid dance can continue. Both see advantages, both commercial and political, in maintaining the flow of funds and a constant pipeline of fundable projects.

These three elements of development aid – mission creep, lack of an exit strategy, and the symbiotic relationship – militate against an early end to aid. Moreover, despite the body of literature about the improvement of aid, whether in terms of effectiveness or efficiency, the proscriptions always look like business as usual – otherwise known as reshuffling the deckchairs on the *Titanic*. However, pressure is growing in both donor and recipient countries for a revised approach to aid.

Some commentators, particularly Hubbard and Duggan (2009), have called for a Marshall Aid approach to development aid. There is some merit in considering this proposal. There is no doubt that Marshall Aid was successful in revitalizing a shattered Europe in the years after the Second World War. But Marshall Aid lasted only for three years and dispensed on average only 3 per cent of the gross national product (GNP) of the countries being assisted. This compares with development aid to Africa, which has a lengthy history and which makes major contributions to the budgets of some countries including a massive 30 per cent to the budget of President Paul Kagame of Rwanda. One is forced to ask why, given the level of dependency on aid, does Kagame lead the charge to end aid in Africa? It appears illogical for a leader to propose cutting off aid totally without at the same time presenting an alternative source of budget funding. One can only conclude that Kagame's approach has both a political and a practical aim. Politically he is aligning himself with those calling for an end to the 'begging bowl' politics of the past and practically he is preparing his people for a budgetary process with a heavily reduced aid component. That being said, there is an attraction in a plan that is time-bound, which has a limit on its financial resources, which has a light administration and which places the onus on the recipient to implement the plan and makes that recipient responsible for the results.

Who has exited from aid, and how did they do it?

Despite the negative perception of development aid espoused by several commentators and the undoubted difficulty in showing positive results for the considerable financial outlay in aid, several geographically dispersed countries have managed to extricate themselves from aid dependency. In order to understand what might form the basis of an effective aid exit strategy we should first look at the experience of those who have already accomplished this feat. The following examples show how several countries in different continents have managed to extricate themselves from a dependency on aid.

South Korea In 1960, the gross domestic product (GDP) of the Republic of Korea was $3.73 billion. The population at that time was 24.7 million and the income per capita was $150. The Government of the Republic of Korea launched a series of reforms during the late 1950s which bore fruit in terms of a significant increase in economic growth. The economy grew by 6 per cent in 1960, 2 per cent in 1961 and reached 9 per cent in 1962. During this period of high growth, Korea continued to receive significant amounts of assistance. In 1960, for example, grants were equivalent to 56 per cent of government expenditure; for 1962 and 1963 the corresponding amounts were 42 and 45 per cent. This represented a high in terms of grants. By 1970, grants represented only 6.5 per cent of government expenditure. Grants ceased altogether in 1977, at which point Korea's GDP was $37.3 billion and the income per capita was approximately $1,050. The main reason for this impressive performance was the series of policies adopted by the Korean Government aimed at promoting shared economic growth. An added advantage of the policies adopted by the government was their ability to adapt to changes in the political or economic environment. This was displayed during the 1980s when the balance of payments was severely distorted and foreign debt increased precipitously. The government reacted with harsh measures aimed at rebalancing the economy. These measures were effective and economic growth continued. The Asian Crisis was another occasion when the government displayed its ability to respond effectively. In 1998, real GDP fell by 9.3 per cent. The government responded to ease the impact of the crisis and quickly succeeded in restoring growth. In 1999, real GDP increased by 11 per cent; it has been growing since then. In 2006, Korea's GDP was $888 billion and its income per capita was $17,700.[3]

Mauritius The Commission headed by James Meade in 1961 was pessimistic about the country's possibilities. In that year, GDP was $160 million or approximately $250 per capita. By Independence in

---

3 Economist Intelligence Unit country reports, 2000–2010.

1967, GDP had risen to $175 million and per capita income had fallen to $225. Although data is difficult to find it is apparent that Mauritius received substantial aid during the period 1978 to 1985, a period in which the economy stagnated. The price of sugar, Mauritius's principal export crop, had slumped and the second oil crisis with its attendant increase in oil prices raised costs substantially, thereby cutting the economy's competitiveness. The rapid expansion of tourism in the mid-1980s helped revive the economy, and limited economic growth ensued. Aid flows during this period mirrored the general trend, and Mauritius only received limited aid. Aid as a percentage of GDP was 3 per cent in 1980, 0.4 per cent in 1994 and 0.3 per cent in 2006 (World Development Index 2008). Grants from official sources amounted to $3 million in 1970 and $19 million in 1989. Essentially when Mauritius could have used additional aid in the late 1960s to the mid-1970s the flows were small. By the end of the 1980s, the country was growing rapidly and aid was not required. In 2006, per capita income was $5,430.

Botswana At Independence in 1966, the GDP of Botswana was $50 million and the income per capita was approximately $100. Exports were approximately $14 million. The discovery of Botswana's diamond resources lay in the future. Diamond production began in 1968 and it took more than a decade for the industry to begin to dominate the economy. In the interim, Botswana received sizeable grants that in 1978 were equivalent to 18 per cent of government spending. Grants continued but by the turn of the century they amounted to only 0.4 per cent of government expenditure. Macroeconomic stability was achieved through a conservative fiscal stance (with budget surpluses continuously from 1983 to 1998), a competitive exchange rate, and the regular setting aside of reserves (currently in excess of $6 billion). This provided the background for rapid economic growth. By 2006, the income per capita was $5,570. The only cloud on the horizon for Botswana is that country's very elevated level of HIV/AIDS which has serious effects on human resources.[4]

Costa Rica In 1960, the GDP of Costa Rica was about $510 million and per capita GDP was $400. Over the next decade and a half,

---

4 Economist Intelligence Unit country reports, 2000–2010.

GDP grew relatively rapidly with income per capita rising to around $1,000 by 1975. Economic growth had been fostered by relatively modest government expenditure (less than 20 per cent of GDP) and high rates of investment. The majority of the growth resulted from the expansion of banana, coffee and beef exports. The oil crisis of the mid-1970s destabilized the economy. Inflation rose and the rate of economic growth dropped sharply. For the entire decade 1975 to 1985, real GDP increased by only 31 per cent, barely ahead of the growth in population. The government made increasing use of exceptional financing. With export growth low, and, based on projected world market trends, unlikely to increase dramatically, a new direction was needed. The government reformed its economic policies with the explicit intention of attracting foreign investment and moving the country's competitiveness 'up the value chain'. That strategy paid off when Intel decided to set up a manufacturing and testing facility. Foreign aid, never very large, has been overtaken by foreign investment. In 2006, Costa Rica's income per capita was $4,980.[5]

These examples could easily be augmented by many others, particularly Tunisia, Morocco, Malaysia, Singapore, Colombia, Jamaica, Dominican Republic, Sri Lanka and Peru as examples of countries which have policies which have allowed them to move beyond aid as a substantial element of their development. This is not to say that these countries receive no aid. They do receive some, but that aid is generally targeted at specific projects or activities. Moreover, since aid forms such a small share of income, investment, imports and the budget of these countries, they have effectively moved beyond aid. The examples abound and the list of countries already cited shows that gaining independence from aid is not a geographical or indeed a resources issue. The countries are geographically dispersed and nobody can say that Mauritius is particularly resource rich. It is also apparent that all the countries cited above started from very low levels of GDP and income per capita, and all have been the subject of severe economic shocks. The governments of these countries were of every political persuasion but the one point they have in common is that government policy is aimed at using all resources for the benefit of the nation.

The foregoing demonstrates that countries in South East Asia,

---

5 Economist Intelligence Unit country reports, 2000–2010.

Africa and the Caribbean have managed to develop policies which have significantly reduced their aid dependency. While the sample is small, we can possibly draw at least one conclusion from the cursory examination above. In all cases, the process was led by a government committed to implementing policies which had the ultimate aim of exiting aid. In the context of the discussion on the lack of aid exit strategies in the donor approach, it is clear that not only must the donors be committed to an aid exit strategy but the recipient government must have such a strategy as a cornerstone of its own development policy.

Africa and development aid

Although eclipsed by aid flows to Afghanistan and Iraq, Africa is still the epicentre of the development aid business. South East Asia and Latin America have greatly reduced their dependence on aid over the period 1990–2010, leaving Africa as the laggard in the development process. Therefore Africa can be used as the barometer of the aid business as a whole.

Africa has been a significant recipient of aid since most African countries gained their independence from 1965 on. Figure 1.1 shows the aid flows between 2001 and 2009 established by the Development Assistance Committee (DAC) of the OECD. While this graph presents the situation of official development assistance as defined by the DAC, it does not represent the full volume of aid flows.[6] Severino and Ray (2009) have pointed out the shortcomings of the ODA approach, but the DAC is possibly the only source of reliable data on the trends in the provision and use of aid. The graph shows that aid flows to Africa follow almost exactly the overall aid flows with Africa receiving about one third of overall aid flows. This is despite the recognition that Africa requires the most effort in terms of both development and poverty eradication. It is also despite the efforts of high-profile interventions

---

6 'Flows of official financing administered with the promotion of the economic development and welfare of developing countries as the main objective, and which are concessional in character with a grant element of at least 25 percent (using a fixed 10 percent rate of discount). By convention, ODA flows comprise contributions of donor government agencies, at all levels, to developing countries ("bilateral ODA") and to multilateral institutions. ODA receipts comprise disbursements by bilateral donors and multilateral institutions.' OECD Glossary of Statistical Terms (http://stats.oecd.org/glossary/detail.asp?ID=6043)

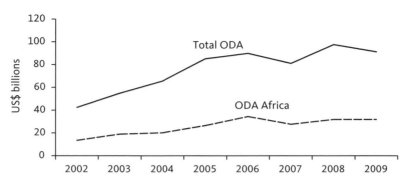

1.1 Total ODA and ODA to Africa (*source*: DAC database)

on Africa's behalf. Having risen somewhat in the 1980s probably due to increased awareness surrounding the plight of individual countries as pointed out by initiatives like Live Aid, aid was stagnant or fell slightly during the period 1990–2000. The take-off in aid flows from year 2000 was spectacular and ODA flows continue to increase (they reached more than $127 billion in 2009). Africa's share of this increased flow was $47 billion or almost one third of all ODA.

Africa in an aid exit scenario

Africa is currently the 'hot spot' for development aid. Despite trillions of dollars spent over a period of forty years or more, the continent still languishes in the economic wilderness with a history of falling standards of living. While it is not typical of the case, the GDP per capita of Ghana at independence in 1957 was higher than that of South Korea. In 2011, South Korea's GDP was ten times that of Ghana. There are of course reasons for Africa's appalling economic performance. A history of sometimes violent struggles for independence including proxy wars fought by the Cold War parties has left a legacy of destruction in its wake. No corner of the continent has escaped either political or ethnic conflict. The lines drawn by the colonial powers establishing countries where none existed have proved to be the grist of war. Corruption and administrative incompetence have also played a part in stunting growth rates. Predatory regimes have pilfered, and continue to pilfer, the wealth of individual nations and beggar their peoples. The era of the 'Big Man' is in its last throes although many African countries are still run as fiefdoms for a particular family or a particular tribe. The effect of demographics should also not be ignored. Africa is a young continent in terms of its population. The increasing population is a double-edged sword. On the one hand it produces a larger workforce and a larger consumer base which can contribute to economic growth but it also puts pressure on government services like education and health. Demography also puts pressure on the environment with increased need for fresh water resources and has led to conflict between pastoralists and cultivators in the drought areas of the Somali eco-system.

Africa therefore represents the real challenge for the development of an effective aid exit strategy. The examples of Mauritius and Botswana in succeeding in exiting from aid are encouraging but as yet they represent only a minuscule set. Given the exceptionally high levels of aid dependency in sub-Saharan Africa, no one should underestimate the challenge of developing aid exit strategies.

A recent report by the McKinsey Global Institute gives the most complete analysis of the potential for the economies of Africa (McKinsey Global Institute 2010). Some of the figures established by McKinsey for Africa are: the collective GDP in 2008 was $1.6 trillion, roughly equal to Brazil or Russia; Africa's combined consumer spending in 2008 was $860 billion; 316 million new mobile phone subscribers have signed up in Africa since 2000; Africa has 60 per cent of the world's uncultivated arable land; Africa has 52 cities with more than 1 million people each; and there are 52 African companies with revenues of at least $3 billion. The study shows that the recent acceleration in growth rates in Africa, which are in the region of 5 per cent to 6 per cent for most of Southern Africa (with the notable exception of Zimbabwe), is not simply a resource boom. Growth has taken place in all sectors including agriculture (5.5 per cent compound annual growth rate), transport and communications (7.8 per cent compound annual growth rate), manufacturing (4.6 per cent compound annual growth rate) and the financial sector (8 per cent compound annual growth rate).

There are undoubtedly problems in maintaining, or indeed increasing, Africa's growth rates. McKinsey concluded that 'Africa's future growth will continue to be supported by external trends such as the global race for commodities, Africa's increased access to international capital, and its ability to forge new types of economic partnerships with foreign investors.'

The conclusions drawn by McKinsey on the internal and demographic trends are less convincing. Undoubtedly the rise of a new middle class will have a significant impact on economic development; however, the increase in the population of mainly uneducated and unskilled labour will increase both the pressure on job creation and social ills such as drunkenness.

McKinsey makes several further projections for the future: $2.6 trillion as Africa's collective GDP in 2020; $1.4 trillion as Africa's consumer spending in 2020; 1.1 billion as the number of Africans of working age in 2040; and 128 million as the number of African households with discretionary income in 2020; according to McKinsey, 50 per cent of Africans will be living in cities by 2030.

The methodology behind these projections is impressive but McKinsey is quick to point out that there is a wide range of impediments which need to be overcome before these impressive figures can be attained. The primary constraint will undoubtedly be the development of diversified economies. On the entire continent only South Africa can be considered to have a diversified economy. Other countries endeavouring to produce a diversified economy are Egypt and Kenya. Most other economies (including that of Nigeria, a continental economic giant) are still commodity-based. The investment requirements in the area of infrastructure have been estimated at $72 billion per year and cannot be attained without a very serious engagement by the private sector. Africa's infrastructure is half to a fifth of that of the leading emerging economies, the BRICS (Brazil, Russia, India, China and South Africa). For example the road density (measured in kilometres per thousand square kilometres) is 39 for the BRICS and 8 for Africa, a factor of 4.9 in favour of the BRICS; the corresponding figures for power (measured in kilowatt-hours per person) are 1,627 for the BRICS and 682 for Africa, a factor of 2.4 in favour of the BRICS (McKinsey Global Institute 2010: 19). This power problem inevitably feeds back into the lack of economic development in Africa. The lack of investment has already been exposed in Southern Africa, where the power deficit has brought the mining sector in South Africa to a standstill on several occasions. However, the power sector alone is not responsible for putting a brake on African development. Roads, airports and ports all need significant investment if Africa is to accomplish the economic projections that have been developed by McKinsey. Infrastructure development will be central to the expansion of intra-African trade which will be the key to the creation of regionally based markets (this will be examined later in terms of aid for trade and regional development), producing economies of scale for manufacturers or service providers.

The investment in hardware will need to be augmented by a corresponding commitment on behalf of governments to implement changes in the software of trade. Commitments made at summits of COMESA (Common Market for Eastern and Southern Africa), SADC (Southern African Development Community) and ECOWAS (Economic Community of West African States) regarding the improvement of trade through the establishment of free trade areas (FTAs) still have not been implemented at country level. The issue of trade facilitation is important on a continent like Africa where countries are inextricably linked. On average it takes 39 days to import goods into Africa compared with 25 days in Brazil, China, India and Russia. African companies are not only hamstrung by increased transportation costs caused by poor road conditions but also suffer because of long delays at border crossings caused by slow and inefficient bureaucracy. The recent opening of the one-stop border post at Chirundu between Zambia and Zimbabwe needs to be replicated throughout the continent, and soon.

McKinsey is honest in pointing out that many of its projections for African economies are dependent not only on economic issues but also on government actions aimed at removing bureaucratic or traditional obstacles to growth. For example, the projections for growth in the agricultural sector are impressive (McKinsey reckons that an African 'green revolution' could increase the annual agricultural output from the current $280 billion to $880 billion by 2030), and the methodology used to establish these figures appears sound, but the challenges in moving from a traditionally based land system with a large number of subsistence farmers to an economic-based agricultural industry are substantial. A large body of work – particularly the World Bank/ Food and Agriculture Organization report (World Bank/FAO 2009) – already exists to guide policy makers, but as yet agriculture is still concentrated on subsistence farming.

While McKinsey paints an optimistic picture of the economic future, some commentators point out a range of possible pitfalls. Von Drachenfels and Krause (2009) show that 18 out of 45 sub-Saharan countries export just four or even fewer products (mainly oil, mineral resources and some agricultural products) which accounted for 75 per cent of total sub-Saharan exports in 2007. Diversifying an economy is never easy but it becomes impossible if the government does not invest in the diversification process. Von Drachenfels and Krause point out that sub-Saharan countries failed to use windfall gains from the commodity sector to make strategic investments and enhance structural change.

Because of its low developmental level Africa tends to finish in the bottom quartile of most of the indices produced by relevant organizations. For example, the Global Competitive Index 2010–11 produced by the World Economic Forum covers 139 economies in the world including 34 African countries. Some 24 African countries can be found in the bottom quartile. The highest African country is Tunisia at number 32, followed by South Africa at 54 and Mauritius at 55. The top-ranked sub-Saharan country was Namibia at number 74, followed by Botswana at 76 and Rwanda a credible 80 (World Economic Forum 2011).

The *Doing Business 2011: Making a Difference for Entrepreneurs* report compiled by the World Bank examines 183 countries on their openness to business (World Bank 2011a). Sub-Saharan Africa has the lowest score with an average of 137, while the OECD economies are at the other end of the scale with an average of 30. In terms of individual countries, South Africa ranks highest of the African nations with a rank of 34, two places behind its 2010 ranking, Botswana is next at 52, also two places off its 2010 standing, Rwanda was the big climber, coming in at 58, up twelve places from the 2010 rank, while Zambia improved from 84th in 2020 to 76th in the 2011 ranking. There are 30 African countries in the bottom quartile so the *Doing Business* report mirrors the results of the *Global Competitiveness Report* by showing Africa to be the weakest of the world's areas in terms of business promotion.

Africa also performs badly on most other surveys. The Environmental Performance Index for 2010 reviews 163 countries, with the highest African country being the Maldives in 48th place followed by Morocco in 52nd place.[7] The highest sub-Saharan country is Djibouti at 75th, but again the majority of African countries find themselves in the bottom quartile.

The Report by Transparency International on corruption perceptions places 21 African countries in the bottom quartile.[8] Only four

---

7 See http://epi.yale.edu

8 Corruptions Perception Index 2010, Transparency International, www.transparency.org

countries appear in the top 50: Botswana, Mauritius, Cape Verde and Namibia. It is perhaps significant that two of these countries (Botswana and Mauritius) are among those countries that have already significantly reduced their aid dependency.

Similarly, the Press Freedom Index established by Reporters without Frontiers reviews 175 countries and has Mali at 30 as the highest African nation, followed by South Africa at 33. However, again the majority of African nations find themselves in the bottom quartile.

The only survey where Africa outranks the world is the United Nations Total Fertility Rate (TFR, the expected number of children born per woman in her childbearing years) that surveys 195 countries. Here Africa leads the list with the majority of countries having TFRs of 3 or more. Niger leads the list with a TFR of 7.19, while Macau has the lowest TFR at 0.91.

Foreign direct investment (FDI) in Africa

FDI in Africa has increased from $11 billion in the year 2000 to $55 billion in 2010, having reached a high of $74 billion in 2008 (see Figure 1.2). For comparison, the state of Singapore received FDI of $39 billion in 2010, or 71 per cent of the total African amount.

Africa receives only a very minor share of FDI, usually around 14–15 per cent of the world total (see Figure 1.3). This is hardly sufficient to spur development. Additionally, the investment is concentrated

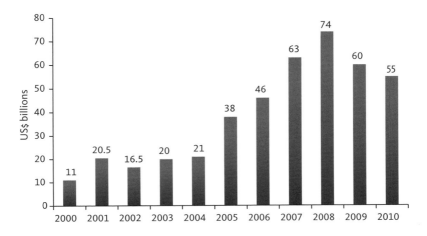

1.2 FDI inflows to Africa, 2000–10 (*source*: UNCTAD 2010)

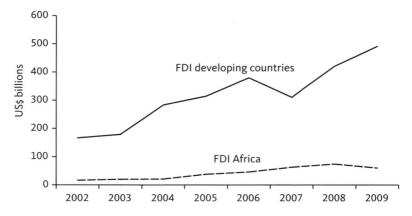

1.3 FDI developing countries and Africa (*source*: World Bank)

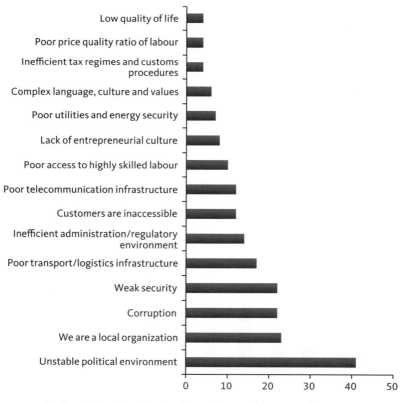

1.4 Barriers to investing in Africa (*source*: Ernst and Young 2011)

both in terms of sector and country. Only those countries with a significant resource base are recipients of FDI, and in their cases the investment is concentrated in the resource exploitation sectors, principally oil and gas and mineral extraction.

There are obviously reasons for the very limited FDI to Africa. Ernst and Young carried out a survey of investment managers in major transnational corporations (TNCs) in order to discover why Africa receives so little FDI. The main reasons are summarized in Figure 1.4: they relate in general to the poor state of overall governance and security. While issues of overall governance are important, of equal importance are laws protecting investment and adherence to the rule of law.

The search for FDI is a competitive one at an international level. It is important that countries position themselves correctly to attract FDI. The history of Africa, which includes war, social unrest, expropriation of property, rampant corruption, poor protection of investments, and insecurity, does not lend itself to attracting FDI. While FDI will not solve the development dilemma, it is important in terms of job creation, the development of local suppliers, technology transfer and as a catalyst for economic diversification. The onus here is for governments to ensure that the barriers to FDI are eliminated as much as possible.

Conclusion

Development aid has been treated for almost its total life of four decades as some kind of altruistic endeavour staffed by do-gooders – a Cinderella business par excellence. However, these do-gooders and the organizations they work for are responsible for an annual budget of $120 billion – and that is only the official development assistance figure of the OECD donors as produced by the DAC. The actual aid figure is much higher and could indeed reach $200 billion. This is of itself a very large industry: the $200 billion figure is higher than the annual revenues of the four largest pharmaceutical companies (Novartis, Pfizer, Bayer and GlaxoSmithKline). While there is no data on the actual number of individuals involved in the aid 'business', the figure will surely be somewhere between 90,000 and 100,000. The organizations involved in development aid rank from the 10,000 employees of the World Bank, and the 4,414 overseas employees at USAID to the three employees at the small NGO Build It and everything in between. These organizations draw their funding from governments, business, philanthropists and the person in the street. Virtually every individual in the developed world has viewed a commercial on television requesting assistance for the poor of the Third World. Aid touches us all because aid is about our very humanity. However, far from being Cinderellas, development aid organizations are real businesses which should be required to show results for the inputs they receive and disburse. To date those results have been lacking. According to Per Tjernberg, Director of BearingPoint, the development sector can learn from business. 'In the business sector, we work with transparency, accountability, efficiency and results-based management – we face the same challenges as the development sector. The point of departure is the customers' needs. In the development context, this means the needs of the poor citizens to whom the aid is directed.'

This feeling that aid cannot continue indefinitely is certainly a function of donor fatigue and possibly of recipient country fatigue also. One of the issues driving donor fatigue has been the lack of results to date. As the Director General of the European Commission's Cooperation Office, Koos Richelle, has noted: 'Donors should put their practices where their policies are, because this is a big problem at the moment. We in the donor community are not very good at deliverables.'

So maybe the first point to bear in mind, and considering that aid professionals themselves are dissatisfied with their own business, is that the development aid business is in need of some re-engineering. Although the business community during the 1990s and the 2000s launched major programmes aimed at making their industries more efficient, only minimal efforts were made by the development aid business to put its house in order.

The state of aid is therefore precarious. The financial crisis and the attendant deficit problems being experienced in the major world economies allied to the widespread belief that the current aid model has not worked will certainly constitute the 'perfect storm' for the aid business. Developing an orderly retreat from a redundant model is somewhat like changing the direction of a tanker. It will take time and will require a strong pull on the tiller.

2 | A SHORT HISTORY OF DEVELOPMENT AID

Only understand the origins of an institution or instrument and you will find the present-day role much easier to grasp. (Niall Ferguson, *The Ascent of Money*)

Several days after the new coalition government of the Conservative and Liberal Democrat parties took office, the British government announced that the British economy was in such poor shape that cuts would be required in public services and that only two areas would be ringfenced in terms of exemption from cuts, namely the National Health Service and development aid (Brennan 2010). It is therefore worth examining how development assistance has reached the situation that despite swingeing cuts being applied to many public services it is considered untouchable. This declaration by the government was in direct opposition to the stated objectives of the Conservative Party prior to the election of 2010 (Elliott and Stewart 2009). So how did development aid gain this privileged position? How can a Conservative government cut government programmes by 19 per cent but leave development aid untouched? Is the issue security, the fight against terrorism, or protection of overseas markets? The colonial histories of Great Britain, France, Spain, Portugal and Holland obviously play a part in the relationships which were established during the colonial period. But that does not explain why countries as diverse as Ireland, Estonia, and Hungary, and many other non-traditional development aid donors, are so committed to development aid.

Rist (2008) has examined the philosophical background behind the question of development. He charts the history of development from the time of the Greeks until the recent past and his work is a standard for anyone wishing to understand the philosophy of development as a concept. For the sake of this book we will look at development from a more recent perspective beginning with the colonial expansions of the nineteenth century. The presentation here will be aimed more at the evolution of development aid as a tool of international foreign policy both for the donors and for the recipients.

The genesis of development aid

Morris (2003a and b), in the middle book of her Pax Britannica trilogy, set forward the general thesis that a major element of Britain's colonial expansion was not only the economic development of the empire but also the belief that the European model, and in particular the British Protestant model of government and morality, were superior and needed to be propagated throughout the world. This idea came several centuries after the Spanish and Portuguese colonial expansion which had elements of proselytization of Catholicism on top of a predatory need to collect gold and other precious metals and stones. While the Spanish, Portuguese and Dutch colonial adventures were concentrated on trade and the economic expansion of the mother country, the British and French colonial ventures had a more cultural and religious aspect. This was the genesis of development as a moral imperative. The improvement of the colonies was predicated on the establishment of the rule of law already in place in the mother country and the suppression of local religious practices and the establishment of the Protestant and Catholic faiths.

This moral crusade had already yielded results with the passing of the Slavery Abolition Act in 1833. The adoption of the Act was the result of the work of William Wilberforce in opposing slavery. Wilberforce was an evangelical Christian who also established the Church Mission Society and promoted missionary work in India.

Despite the moral aspects of the colonial era, the roads, railways and ports were developed with the expansion of trade in mind. Moving commodities from the centre of a colony to the coast via a railway or a road system led to development in the larger sense. The establishment of schools for the natives was devolved to missionaries and set off the great era of missionary activity not only in Africa but throughout the under-developed world.

The nineteenth century witnessed a major expansion of European power throughout Africa and a major expansion of the British Empire throughout the world. Major economic players such as Cecil John Rhodes pushed the boundaries of British influence from South Africa northwards: his dream of a Cape-to-Cairo railway would have opened the entire continent to economic exploitation. Meanwhile the French concentrated their expansion on West Africa, the Indian Ocean and South East Asia.

The colonial system was not all beneficent. Local populations were physically and politically abused. Slavery had been abolished but indigenous peoples were still required to work on plantations and in mines in conditions which were at the time being outlawed in Europe. The concept that all things European were superior to the traditional ways of the colonies continued to dominate colonial thinking despite a sometimes enlightened clergy who continued their work of Christianizing the population but at the same time provided the schooling and health facilities which the colonial powers neglected.

Administration remained in the hands of the nationals of the 'mother country'. Taxes could be collected by the village headmen and tribal chiefs but the national tax collector was a colonial officer. The role of the regional administrator came about in the later part of the nineteenth century and remained intact until the surge of independence.

The legacy of the colonial era was not fully crystallized until many African countries obtained their independence, in the sixth decade of the twentieth century. The early political leaders lacked the education and background to take the reins effectively. Meredith (2006) has charted the problems of the nascent African states from their date of independence and demonstrates how the legacy of the colonial system impeded the establishment of an effective local administration. The promise of the colonial system to create societies that mirrored the European colonial powers while at the same time ensuring the development of the colony was never fully achieved. The mix of religion and race plus the requirement to repatriate to the colonial power the benefits that should rightly have been used to spur development failed to create nations which could manage their own affairs once they had been set free.

The period 1900–1955

While the period 1900–1955 was not notable in terms of the history of development aid, four important events during these years had an impact on the future of aid. These were the League of Nations mandate system, the establishment of the Bretton Woods system, the Marshall Plan and the Truman Doctrine.

The League of Nations mandate system The mandate system was established under Article 22 of the Covenant of the League of Nations and took effect on 28 June 1919. The establishment of the mandate system was a direct consequence of the end of the First World War and the Treaty of Versailles. The aim was to oversee the change of administrative control over territories which had previously been under the control of the defeated Axis powers. Despite assurances to the contrary at the time, it is clear that the mandate system had a strong element of the division of the spoils of war among the victors.

The process of establishing the mandates consisted of two phases: the formal removal of sovereignty from the previous controlling state followed by the transfer of mandatory powers to individual states among the Allied powers. The system was designed as a mechanism to safeguard stability in a territory's transitional process of attaining self-governance. The importance of stability in state building and the experience of the difficulties when attempting to impose a Western understanding on societies with different histories, cultures and traditional values has been demonstrated by the arduous transition which many African countries have had in their progress to democracy. It is a sad fact that many African countries have been ruled by a single ruler or political party since independence and the existence of elections is simply a sop to democracy.

The mandate system had some of the elements of the old colonial system, particularly in relation to the overall administration of the mandated territory. The Trusteeship System of the United Nations gave to a European power the right of administering a sovereign area as an interim measure in order to have a stable progress towards self-determination. A major difference between the colonial and the trusteeship arrangements was the acknowledgement by the mandatory power that it recognized that the mandate was time-limited and that it owed obligations to the inhabitants of the mandated territory and to the League of Nations.

There were seven mandated areas in Africa: British Togoland, French Togoland, British Cameroons, French Cameroun, Ruanda-Urundi, Tanganyika and South West Africa. These areas represented the former Schutzgebiete (German territories) in the sub-Saharan regions of West, Central and Southern Africa. The other mandated areas were located in the Middle East and included Syria, Lebanon, Palestine and Transjordan.

The mandate system represented an advance on the existing colonial system. The major difference was the recognition that each mandate was held in trust and that the ultimate objective of the mandate was the establishment of a sovereign state with full self-determination. While the Mandatory Powers fully recognized the conditions of the mandate they incorporated the mandated areas directly into their colonial system. Britain incorporated its mandated areas into the Empire and the British Commonwealth. The overall administration of the mandated areas was vested in the Commonwealth Office and the mandated areas attained their independence at the same time as the other colonies.

While the concept that a post-colonial stable state system would be created as the colonial power took its leave was laudable, there appears to be no appreciable difference between the paths to statehood of the colonies and of the mandated areas. The mandate system can therefore be seen as a cynical move on behalf of the victors of the First World War to take over former German and Turkish colonies. There was no appreciable attempt to prepare the mandated areas for independence and they found themselves as unprepared as their fellow colonies when the wind of change blew through Africa in the 1960s.

The Bretton Woods system The Bretton Woods system of monetary management established the rules for commercial and financial relations among the world's major industrial states in the mid-twentieth century. The Bretton Woods system was the first example of a fully negotiated monetary order intended to govern monetary relations among independent nation-states.

Preparing to rebuild the international economic system while the Second World War was still raging, 730 delegates from all forty-four Allied nations gathered at the Mount Washington Hotel in Bretton Woods, New Hampshire, for the United Nations Monetary and Financial Conference. The delegates deliberated upon and signed the Bretton Woods Agreements during the first three weeks of July 1944.

Setting up a system of rules, institutions, and procedures to regulate the international monetary system, the planners at Bretton Woods established the International Monetary Fund (IMF) and the International Bank for Reconstruction and Development (IBRD), which today is part of the World Bank (see Box 2.1).

The establishment of the IMF and the IBRD is important in the story of development aid. These two organizations (and particularly the World Bank) are the primary organizations in the provision of developmental finance.

Box 2.1 The World Bank

The World Bank is one of the two main organizations created by the Bretton Woods Conference in 1944. In its most basic sense it is an international financial institution which provides loans to developing countries for initiatives aimed at economic and social development. In development terms the Bank consists of two entities, both of which can be involved in lending for a project or programme. The International Bank for Reconstruction and Development (IBRD) gives loans which are intended to be repaid while the International Development Association (IDA) gives finance in the form of a grant.

The Bank also has three other entities which are not directly involved with development but form part of the World Bank Group – the International Finance Corporation (IFC), the Multilateral Investment Guarantee Agency (MIGA) and the International Centre for Settlement of Investment Disputes (ICSID).

The World Bank has established itself as the primary organization in the field of international development. IBRD can deal with all member countries while IDA's efforts are concentrated on the eighty poorest countries. The World Bank differentiates itself from other development organizations through its commitment to research in development issues which has led to it being known as the 'knowledge bank'.

The stated purposes of the Bank are:

1 To assist in the reconstruction and development of territories of members by facilitating the investment of capital for productive purposes, including the restoration of economies destroyed or disrupted by war, the reconversion of productive facilities to peacetime needs and the encouragement of the development of productive facilities and resources in less developed countries.

2 To promote private foreign investment by means of guarantees or participation in loans and other investments made by private investors; and when private capital is not available on reasonable terms, to supplement private investment by

providing, on suitable conditions, finance for productive purposes out of its own capital, funds raised by it and its other resources.

3 To promote the long-range balanced growth of international trade and the maintenance of equilibrium in balances of payments by encouraging international investment for the development of the productive resources of members, thereby assisting in raising productivity, the standard of living and conditions of labor in their territories.

4 To arrange the loans made or guaranteed by it in relation to international loans through other channels so that the more useful and urgent projects, large and small alike, will be dealt with first.

5 To conduct its operations with due regard to the effect of international investment on business conditions in the territories of members and, in the immediate postwar years, to assist in bringing about a smooth transition from a wartime to a peacetime economy.

In 2010, the IBRD had a loan portfolio of $120 billion and total assets of $238 billion. IDA had $113 billion development credits outstanding and $128 billion of total development resources. In 2010, 9,000 staff were employed from 165 countries.

Source: World Bank website, World Bank Annual Report 2010

The Marshall Plan The Marshall Plan (officially known as the European Recovery Programme) was devised by the US Secretary of State George Marshall, who announced it in a speech to Harvard University on 5 June 1947.[1] The Marshall Plan is of interest because it is the first real example of a plan aimed at restoring the economic and political fabric of post-war Europe. The speech at Harvard is notable for its language, which is pragmatic and unemotional. The purpose of the plan was not only to reinvigorate the shattered industrial base of the Western European countries but to ensure that no political

---

1 George Marshall's speech is available at www.oecd.org/document/10/0,3746, en_2649_201185_1876938_1_1_1_1,00.html

dislocation occurred. Marshall related the support of European industry to issues of political stability and peace.

The Marshall Plan has several attractions in comparison to development aid today. The plan was time-limited. It would last for only
four years. It was also limited in terms of finance. Marshall initially
asked for $22 billion but President Truman provided just $17 billion.
Truman signed the Marshall Plan into law on 3 April 1948 and
established the Economic Cooperation Administration (ECA) to run
the programme. The administration was light and the staffing at the
ECA was minimal. The money was transferred to the governments
of the recipient nations. The funds were jointly administered by the
local government and the ECA.

In 1948, the participating countries (Austria, Belgium, Denmark,
France, West Germany, Great Britain, Greece, Iceland, Ireland, Italy,
Luxembourg, the Netherlands, Norway, Sweden, Switzerland, Turkey
and the United States) signed an accord establishing a master financial
coordinating agency, the Organisation for European Economic Cooperation, which later became the Organisation for Economic
Co-operation and Development.

The Marshall Plan ended in 1951 and its effectiveness can be
assessed by the fact that the fastest period of growth in European
history was recorded between 1948 and 1952. Industrial production
increased by 35 per cent. Agricultural production substantially sur-
passed pre-war levels. The poverty and starvation of the immediate
post-war years disappeared and Western Europe embarked on two
decades of unprecedented growth.

The Truman Doctrine The other main initiative of the colonial pre-
independence period was the Truman Doctrine. President Harry S.
Truman's inaugural speech of 20 January 1949 became known as
the 'four point speech'. The basis of the speech was the call to assist
people around the world struggling for freedom and human rights.

The four points were:

- We will continue to give unfaltering support to the United Nations
  and related agencies, and we will continue to search for ways to
  strengthen their authority and increase their effectiveness.
- We will continue our programmes for world economic recovery.
- We will strengthen freedom-loving nations against the dangers of
  aggression.

- We must embark on a bold programme for making the benefits of our scientific advances and industrial progress available for the improvement and growth of under-developed areas.

The Truman Doctrine established the future direction of development aid from a US perspective.

1955–2011 – the golden age of development aid?

Harold Macmillan coined the phase 'a wind of change is blowing through Africa' in his speech to the South African parliament on 3 February 1960. It was apparent by this time that many of the former colonies harboured the desire for independence; political movements to obtain independence were already established in many countries. However, relatively few of the countries that would become sovereign states in the 1960s were adequately prepared for the change. The fault for this can be laid firmly at the feet of the colonial powers, who made very minor attempts to involve local political elites in administration prior to independence. There was therefore an immediate and desperate need for a transfer of funds and knowledge from the developed world to the developing world.

The European Community launched the European Development Fund in 1958 in order to assist the African, Caribbean and Pacific former European colonies with their development initiatives. USAID was established in 1961 and the UK Department of Technical Assistance (which was the forerunner of the Department for International Development, DfID) was established in 1961. The Canadian International Development Agency was established in 1968.

Figure 2.1 shows the evolution of aid flows from the OECD donors during the period 1965–2010. Aid to developing countries rose from $5.8 billion in 1965 to almost $90 billion in 2010. The corresponding African aid flows were just over $1 billion in 1965 and $30 billion in 2010. It is noticeable that in the period immediately after independence, aid to Africa was stagnant; it rose only after 1973. This is somewhat surprising since the period prior to 1972 was the era of the expansion of development aid bodies. It appears that although the number of entrants into the aid development space was increasing, the actual volume of aid remained constant.

The enormous expansion in aid flows was not accompanied by a corresponding increase in economic growth. During the 1980s per

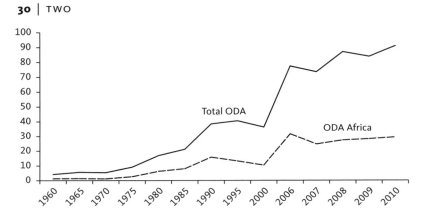

2.1 Aid flows, 1965–2010 (US$ billions constant currency)

capita GDP in Africa declined by 1.3 per cent per year. This result went totally against the development wisdom of the time which had been established by the Brandt Commission Report (Brandt 1980). The Brandt Report was the first attempt to bring the various strands of the development agenda together. The Commission looked at poverty, hunger and food, population, disarmament, trade and energy. The Commission was very much ahead of its time in considering the development question in a holistic fashion and was the first body to point out the question of mutual interests, especially in the areas of energy and environment. Despite the already growing aid flows the Commission's Emergency Programme had as its first priority large-scale transfers of resources to developing countries. This was despite the fact that Africa was moving backwards with increasing aid flows.

Several issues militated against African growth during the 1970s and 1980s, the most pertinent of which was the large number of conflicts which were taking place throughout the continent. Collier (2007) has shown the highly disruptive effects of conflict not only on the country in conflict but also on neighbouring countries.

The Brandt Commission was followed up in 1987 by the establishment of the South Commission. Where the members of the Brandt Commission had included both developed and developing countries the South Commission was made up of only developing countries under the chairmanship of Julius Nyerere, the former President of Tanzania. In its report, the Commission assessed the South's achievements and failings in the development field and suggested directions for action. Although the Commission carried out its work in the final years of a decade that had devastated many economies in the South, the report struck a note of hope and made a cogent case for self-reliant, people-centred development strategies. The main thrust of the report was a call to the South to act in concert in international negotiations, especially those related to trade, finance and technology.

The South Report marks an important moment because for perhaps the first time the role of the South in the solution of the problems it faced was highlighted. The Brandt Commission Report concentrated on what the North should do to solve the problems faced by the South, but the problems of one region cannot simply be solved by inputs from another. It is a pity that little of the advance made by the South Commission in looking for regional solutions to regional problems was incorporated into the thinking that went into the next series of 'great mind' reports. The South Report led to the creation of the South Centre, an international think-tank located in Geneva that produces research relevant to the issues raised in the report.

The Earth Summit in Rio de Janeiro in 1992 gave the world's leaders an opportunity to come together to discuss issues relating to poverty and environment and indeed the whole question of sustainable development. While the summit cannot be declared a success despite the adoption of Agenda 21, it undoubtedly raised awareness of the impact of economic development on the environment. While this had no immediate relevance in developing countries there was an immediate impact on the development community in placing the environment and energy as issues to be considered in any specific development project. One of the positive aspects of the Earth Summit was the fact that it included commitments by all states to develop their economies in a sustainable fashion.

It had by now taken twenty-five years of development activity to arrive at the conclusion that development was not simply the obligation of the donors but that there was an obligation on the recipients to develop their own economies. Donor funding was substantially increased during the 1980s and 1990s while growth rates continued to fall and Africa as a continent fell further behind in the globalized world. South East Asia and Latin America were experiencing increased growth rates, and many of the counties in these two regions were demonstrating a much lower dependency on aid. Figure 2.2 shows economic growth rates in these three areas in the period 1980–2000.

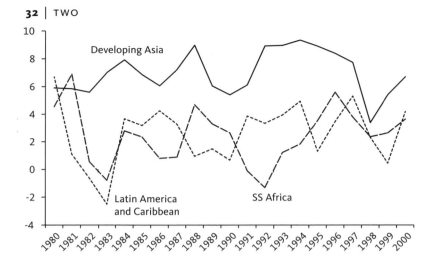

2.2 Growth rates in developing Asia, Latin America and the Caribbean, and sub-Saharan Africa (percentage) (*source*: World Development Report 2010)

Figure 2.2 clearly shows the disparity in growth rates which has seen much of developing Asia and Latin America exiting from dependency on aid while in Africa dependency has been increasing. It is of course naïve to conclude that the increasing aid flows of the last two decades of the twentieth century were the reason for the low growth rates in Africa and consequently to conclude that development aid does not work. Aid flows have not always been used to promote economic growth, and disbursements by donors have not always been based on criteria other than political expediency. The predatory government of Mobutu Sese Seko was supported by rich countries to the tune of $12 billion during the thirty-two years in which the despot ruled Zaïre. This beneficent treatment of a dictator happened not just because Mobutu was on the side of the West during the Cold War, but also because of the DRC's huge wealth of natural resources. The whole economy of Zaïre was geared towards institutional kleptomania for the benefit of Mobutu, his family and the ruling elite who controlled the army and the police. The UN has estimated that Mobutu alone embezzled $5 billion during his reign.

It was a similar story for many of the other African states that received substantial aid during the Cold War period; $5 billion has also been the figure put on the embezzlement carried out by Daniel

Arap Moi in Kenya. Countries including Nigeria and Gabon were the recipients of aid when the existence of oil and membership of OPEC, the oil producers' cartel, should have been enough to put both countries at the top of the list of those African countries ready to abandon aid dependency. The fact that this is not the case has more to do with the kleptocratic regimes of Sonny Abacha and Omar Bongo than on the efficacy of aid.

Development aid and the crusade to end poverty – the road to and from Gleneagles

The Ethiopian famine of 1984–85 opened one of the doors which has been a major driver of aid policy since that date. The Live Aid series of concerts and the advocacy the leaders of the effort used to increase awarenes of the crisis in Ethiopia ushered in the next era of development aid policy. We are still working our way through this new advocacy-by-pop-star approach and its attendant moral imperative. We should perhaps ignore the fact that the crisis which ushered in this new era, the Ethiopian famine, was not a natural event but a crisis engineered by the despotic government of Haile Miriam Mengistu and aimed at eliminating a large section of the population which he felt was resisting his efforts to implant communism in his country.

The confluence of twenty-four-hour international television news and the involvement of the entertainment industry led to the holding of charity concerts on every continent, shown live throughout the world, which involved the participation of hundreds of thousands of young people, thereby raising the profile of hunger in Ethiopia and indeed the African continent. Live Aid was a seminal event not just because it launched Bob Geldof as a future lobbyist for a series of initiatives aimed at poverty reduction in Africa but also because it showed that there was a large constituency of mainly young people who could be mobilized to influence political thinking on the plight of the poor in Africa.

Professionals working in the field at the time probably under-estimated the impact of Live Aid on the overall direction of development aid policy. Until the mid-1980s, development aid policy had two strands: the first was a political instrument to show gratitude to developing countries for their allegiance to the Western political model, while the second was aimed at improving the economic situation of the recently independent nations. Live Aid had no political or economic overtones but was simply a visceral response to the plight of people dying from hunger in Ethiopia. That response was based on morality and was in its own way the genesis both of the crusade to end poverty and of the anti-globalization movement.

The cornerstone of the new advocacy became the usurious indebtedness of many Third World countries. The Jubilee Debt Campaign brought together a wide range of NGOs with the express purpose of lobbying for the cancellation of the heavy debts incurred by Third World countries. This effort was successful with the launch of the Heavily Indebted Poor Country (HIPC) Initiative in 1996 by the IMF and World Bank, with the aim of ensuring that no poor country faces a debt burden it cannot manage. Since then, the international financial community, including multilateral organizations and governments, have worked together to reduce to sustainable levels the external debt burdens of the most heavily indebted poor countries.

In 1999, a comprehensive review of the Initiative allowed the IMF to provide faster, deeper, and broader debt relief and strengthened the links between debt relief, poverty reduction, and social policies. In 2005, to help accelerate progress towards the United Nations Millennium Development Goals (MDGs; see below), the HIPC Initiative was supplemented by the Multilateral Debt Relief Initiative (MDRI). The MDRI allows for 100 per cent relief on eligible debts by three multilateral institutions – the IMF, the World Bank, and the African Development Fund (AfDF) – for countries completing the HIPC Initiative process. In 2007, the Inter-American Development Bank (IADB) decided to provide additional ('beyond HIPC') debt relief to the five HIPCs in the western hemisphere. A country wishing to avail itself of the HIPC and the MDRI debt relief must first meet HIPC's four threshold requirements, which are: be eligible to borrow from the World Bank's International Development Agency and from the IMF's Extended Credit Facility; face an unsustainable debt burden that cannot be addressed through traditional debt relief mechanisms; have established a track record of reform and sound policies through IMF- and World Bank-supported programmes, and have developed a Poverty Reduction Strategy Paper (PRSP) through a broad-based participatory process in the country.

The establishment by the United Nations of the Millennium Project and the adoption of the Millennium Development Goals at the special UN Development Summit in 2000 set the objectives for the

---

Box 2.2 The Millennium Development Goals

1 Eradicate extreme poverty and hunger
2 Achieve universal primary education
3 Promote gender equality and empower women
4 Reduce child mortality rates
5 Improve maternal health
6 Combat HIV/AIDS, malaria, and other diseases
7 Ensure environmental sustainability
8 Develop a global partnership for development

---

development community for the fifteen years to 2015. The eight goals were chosen as a series whose attainment would have a significant effect on world poverty (Box 2.2).

At the 2000 UN Summit, both developed and developing countries agreed to work towards the attainment of the eight goals and to review regularly progress on a national and regional basis in the attainment of the goals. The MDGs mark the culmination of the movement away from setting purely economic growth criteria for under-developed countries. Despite evidence that economic growth was the single most important engine in poverty reduction, the movement towards a more moralistic approach to development was firmly established by the MDGs.

This move from a concentration on economic growth to a more moralistic approach with a much higher-level objective may in some way explain some of the issues of mission creep and lack of a definite exit strategy which were discussed in Chapter 1. Setting economic criteria as part of an exit strategy is fairly straightforward. If country X reaches a level of $1,000 (say) per capita gross national income (GNI) it then becomes a candidate for an aid exit strategy. If, on the other hand, one sets poverty reduction goals as the basis for the adoption of an aid exit strategy the process becomes more complicated. A comparison can be made to the war on terror, which will end only when all terrorists have been eliminated.

The adoption by the international community of the MDGs indicates the direction in which the development aid community was being drawn. This movement was about to accelerate with the involvement of the G8 group of major economies for the first time.

The MDGs UN Summit was followed by an International Conference on Financing for Development held in Monterrey, Mexico, from 18 to 22 March 2002. Its purpose was to obtain pledges from the international community which would lead to the financing of initiatives aimed at achieving the MDGs. Its outcome, the so-called Monterrey Consensus, proposed a series of financial operations which could be used to finance development activities (United Nations 2003). Among the initiatives considered were the mobilization of domestic financial resources – particularly taxation, and the use of capital markets, micro-finance and public–private partnerships. The cornerstone of the Monterrey Consensus was, however, a commitment by the international donor community to make concrete efforts to increase official development assistance towards a target of 0.7 per cent of GNP to developing countries, including at least 0.15 to 0.2 per cent of GNP going to least-developed countries. The Consensus also called for efforts by both donors and recipients to make ODA more effective. Finally, the Consensus called for a redoubling of debt relief, especially within the context of the HIPC Initiative.

The calls made at Monterrey to improve the effectiveness of aid, the declaration made at the High Level Forum on Harmonization held in Rome in 2003, and the fundamental principles achieved during the Round Table in Marrakesh on Aid Management aimed at development results in 2004 led directly to the High Level Forum on the Efficiency of Development Aid held in Paris in March 2005. The commitments made at Monterrey by the Development Assistance Committee (DAC) of the OECD donors, plus the return of non-traditional donors and the proliferation of new NGOs including religious and philanthropic organizations, led to calls for a rationalization of aid within each recipient country. At the core of the Paris Declaration on Aid Effectiveness was the setting up of Partnership Commitments that would define the relationship between the donors and the recipient country. The Partnership Commitments would be based on three areas – ownership, alignment and harmonization – with all three areas being coordinated at achieving concrete results. The purpose of the Paris Declaration was to make development aid more results-oriented rather than funding-oriented, with a concentration more on outputs rather than inputs. The commitments made at Monterrey covered only the amount of funding that would be made available, while the outcome of the Paris conference aimed to align donors to support specific sectors. The concept of a division of labour was central to the implementation of the Paris Declaration. A large number of donors present in a particular sector complicate relations between this large donor group and the government ministry involved. In complying with the Paris agenda donors agreed to limited their participation in sectors and to concentrate their efforts on their chosen sector. Therefore in a specific country donor X might have been active in the health and education sector as well as the road sector. In complying with the Paris Effectiveness Agenda donor X might retire from the education sector to concentrate on health while his colleague donor Y would retire from health and take up the slack in education casued by donor X's departure.

G8 meeting at Gleneagles 2005

The British prime minister Tony Blair and his Chancellor of the Exchequer Gordon Brown set out their stall early for the UK's tenure of the chair of the G8 for 2005. It was no coincidence that the Blair Commission on Africa established by the British prime minister, and following in the line of the Brandt Commission and the South Commission, was due to make its report in the same year. Like earlier reports, *Our Common Interest* concentrated on the relationship between the developed countries of specifically the G8 and the developing countries of Africa (Commission for Africa 2005). Issues of peace and security, investing in people, growth, trade, aid and the reform of the international institutions were addressed by the report. In this respect it might be considered as the Brandt Report revisited, but the international context had changed in the intervening thirty years and the Commission for Africa Report was based much more on establishing a mature relationship between the two groups in order to face up to the international problems of the day, namely terrorism, migration, the environment, and energy. The report was therefore a call for combined action by the developed world and the developing world for a common front to combat common threats. It was presented at a time when growth rates in Africa had been rising over several years and when many African countries were benefiting from substantial rises in commodity prices on international markets.

Blair and Brown decided to make Africa and its development the central theme of the G8 Gleneagles summit. This was the first time that the G8 had involved itself in the question of African development. The G8 itself had grown from a 'fireside chat' type of organization into a decision-making body which committed the economically most powerful countries in the world to follow a commonly agreed approach to international problems. Among the invited attendees were Luiz Inácio Lula da Silva, the President of Brazil, Meles Zenawi, prime minister of Ethiopia, Manmohan Singh, prime minister of India, Vincente Fox, president of Mexico, Hu Jintao, president of China, and Thabo Mbeki, president of South Africa. The failure of development aid to fulfil its promise was the central issue of discussion at the Gleneagles summit, which thus demonstrated the arrival of development aid as an issue at the highest level in world politics. The confluence of the Make Poverty History Campaign with the Millennium Project and the report of the Commission on Africa plus the very high-profile lobbying had managed to push Africa to the top of the political agenda. Gleneagles would also discuss global warming, but the emphasis on Africa's development problems was clear.

The major outcomes of the meeting in relation to development aid were:

- US$50 billion (some of it previously announced) was pledged in aid to developing countries by 2010, of which US$25 billion was to go to Africa, on top of the ministerial-level agreement to forgive debt to countries reaching the HIPC point;
- agreement to full debt cancellation for eighteen countries (despite a call by African countries for debt relief for the whole of Africa);
- universal access in Africa to anti-HIV drugs to be achieved by 2010;
- a commitment to train 20,000 peacekeeping troops for Africa in exchange for African commitments to good governance and democracy;
- G8 members from the European Union committed themselves to a collective foreign aid target of 0.56 per cent of GDP by 2010, and 0.7 per cent by 2015;
- the signalling of a new deal on trade with a stated commitment to reduce subsidies and tariffs that inhibit trade.

These political commitments were impressive at the time. The doubling of aid plus the comprehensive package of debt reduction represented a heavy financial commitment on behalf of the G8. The package was very much in line with what high-profile lobbyists and the leadership of the Millennium Development Goals project were requesting. Despite evidence to the contrary, the solution of throwing money at the problem had now been accepted at the highest political level. While it is easy to make political commitments with respect to the doubling of development aid, it is another matter to make such political commitments real at ground level. The question of absorption capacity had never been considered at Gleneagles but had been a well-known impediment among development aid agencies. The governments of developing countries have only a limited capacity to absorb financial assistance. Piling additional assistance on will not solve the problems and may indeed exacerbate them by diverting government human resources away from priority areas.

Gleneagles was important in raising the political profile of Africa but it is interesting to look at the reactions of the various parties to the outcome of the meeting. Tony Blair declared, 'We do not, simply by this communiqué, make poverty history.'[2] The Gleneagles communiqué received limited approval from Bob Geldof and Bono while Kumi Naidoo, the chair of the Global Call to Action against Poverty declared, 'The People have roared but the G8 has whispered.'[3]

The reaction from Africa was more muted. Andrew Mwenda, a Ugandan radio journalist, opined that 'Uganda was forgiven its debts, as a consequence, government indulged itself in very luxurious expenditure ... and invaded Congo and Sudan.' He added that the Gleneagles approaches 'do not work and will not work'.[4] Allen Kagina, the Commissioner General of Uganda's tax authority, acknowledged that Uganda collects only a fraction of the tax it could because aid makes up the difference. As with the Live Aid initiative, Gleneagles marked an important milestone in the progress of development aid. The most powerful club in the world had now brought what was considered by many to be an adjunct to foreign policy to centre stage, and they had committed themselves to the solution of this thorny problem.

The impetus of the Gleneagles G8 meeting continued with the Heiligendamm summit held in 2007 under the chairmanship of Germany. Again the discussions were enlarged to include the leaders of

---

2 'Government defends G8 aid boost', BBC News, 9 July 2005, http://news.bbc.co.uk/1/hi/business/4666743.stm

3 Ibid.

4 See 'Africans on Africa: Debt', at http://newsvote.bbc.co.uk/mpapps/pagetools/print/news.bbc.co.uk/2/hi/africa/4657139.stm

China, Ethiopia, India, Mexico, South Africa and Brazil. The communiqué on Africa and development concluded:

> We reiterate our commitment to the Millennium Development Goals (MDGs), the eradication of poverty and sustainable global development. In view of our responsibility regarding the challenges of development we shall strengthen cooperation and coordination between us to achieve these goals.
>
> We commit to embark on a high-level dialogue on specific challenges as proposed by the G8 (Heiligendamm Process) as a follow up to continue our discussion in a more structured manner for a period of two years until the G8 Summit in 2009 where we will review the progress made on the following issues: Promoting cross border investment to our mutual benefit; Promoting Research and Innovation; Development, particularly Africa; and Sharing Knowledge for improving Energy Efficiency.[5]

Two issues were about to impact on the G8 which would drastically affect the picture: the first was the impending financial crisis which broke upon the world in 2008 and the second was the move from the G8 to the G20. The financial crisis has inevitably impacted on the ability of the G8 to comply with its financial commitments, while the move to a wider G20 with significant input from large emerging economic powers will change the strategic relationships that have existed between developing and developed countries. This change in the strategic relationship will affect not only the economic relations but also the social and political relations. Such a change in the strategic relationship represents a seismic shift in the way the aid business is managed. A recent report from the Chatham House think-tank (Cargill 2010) has underlined that the old aid relationship is already on the wane and that the new relationship will be based more on political and diplomatic engagement which will lead not to increased aid but to higher foreign direct investment in wealth creation in Africa with consequent reduction in poverty levels. This new relationship will be predicated on some changes in the political

---

5 'Joint Statement by the German G8 Presidency and the Heads of State and/ or Government of Brazil, China, India, Mexico and South Africa on the occasion of the G8 Summit in Heiligendamm, Germany, 8 June 2007'. See www.g-8.de/Content/ EN/Artikel/__g8-summit/anlagen/o5-erklaerung-en,templateId=raw,property= publicationFile.pdf/o5-erklaerung-en.pdf

landscape within Africa. While there will inevitably be some differences between the strategic outlook of the old G8 on development processes and the strategic outlook of the emerging G20, the question of good governance and the strict application of democratic principles within Africa will be the cornerstone of a partnership between the economic powers of the old G8 and the emerging G20. The new economic and diplomatic relationships which are emerging can only be based on the rule of law and trust of the partners.

The financial crisis was beginning to unfold by the time the L'Aquila and Seoul G8 summits rolled around, and consequently development issues were relegated in the face of the emerging global financial meltdown. L'Aquila recognized the possible impact of the financial crisis on African economies and was particularly concerned with the spectre of rising food prices. The major commitment for Africa at L'Aquila was the creation of a $20 billion fund for farm investment in the world's hungriest countries.[6] By 2010, the G8 officials at L'Aquila were admitting that the G8 would fail to meet the pledges which had been made at Gleneagles five years earlier (Grice 2009). It will be interesting to follow the evolution of the L'Aquila commitments of $20 billion. By Seoul the G8 had morphed into the G20 and the Summit held on 11–12 November 2010 naturally concentrated on the aftermath of the financial crisis. The developing countries were naturally not excluded from the discussion on how to stabilize the world's economy. The meeting launched the Seoul Development Consensus for Shared Growth that

> sets out our commitment to work in partnership with other developing countries, and LICs in particular, to help them build the capacity to achieve and maximize their growth potential, thereby contributing to global rebalancing. The Seoul Consensus complements our commitment to achieve the Millennium Development Goals and focuses on concrete measures as summarized in our Multi-year Action Plan on Development to make a tangible and significant difference in people's lives, including in particular through the development of infrastructure in developing countries.[7]

---

6 Final Communiqué L'Aquila G8 Summit. Accessed at www.g8italia2009.it/static/G8_Allegato/G8_Declaration_08_07_09_final,0.pdf

7 The G20 Seoul Summit Leader's Declaration, November 11/12, 2010. See www.g20-g8.com/g8-g20/root/bank_objects/EN_declaration_finale_seoul2010.pdf

The Accra Agenda for Action recognized that many countries would fall short of achieving the MDGs and that increased efforts would be required from both donors and recipients to rectify this situation.[8] Three areas were outlined: recipient country ownership is key, effective and inclusive partnership would need to be built, and the process would have to be results-oriented. The purpose of the Accra Agenda was to keep up the momentum which had been created in terms of aid effectiveness by the Paris Declaration. It is also probable that many donors envisaged a future in which development aid volumes would be limited because of the residual effects of the financial crisis on the indebtedness of the donor countries.

Conclusion

What have we learned on this rather short trawl through the history of development aid? The development process of the nineteenth century was high-concept – Africans were being prepared to meet their maker, who was the Christian God of the European powers. The schools and hospitals were primarily run by missionaries and were oriented towards the production of good Christians who would continue to propagate the word of God.

The early twentieth century had a purportedly lower concept – the preparation of Africans to take over the running of their own countries. This was in fact a lie and led to the unenviable situation (for Africans) that on independence there were very few nationals with the capacity to take over from the departing European powers. In the Congo there were thought to be only sixteen people at independence who had completed a university degree; in Burundi the figure was said to be two (Bolton 2008). The sham that was the Mandate system lasted only forty years but the negative effects of this preparation of African countries for their independence is still being felt today.

Almost every commentator points to the Marshall Plan as the example of a development initiative that worked brilliantly (Hubbard and Duggan 2009). But nobody in the subsequent forty years followed its example. It was low-concept (aimed as it was on simply rejuvenating the shattered economies of Europe), it was time-bound, it had limited finance and the administration was just about as simple as one could get. The behemoth of the development aid business

---

8 Accra Agenda for Action, Communiqué of the 3rd High Level Forum on Aid Effectiveness, 4 September 2008.

which grew up in the years after African independence is virtually the opposite of the Marshall Plan. It continued to grow rather than being a plan with a built-in exit strategy. However, at least the early years of independent Africa were low-concept, with a concentration on improving the infrastructure along with education and health facilities.

The twenty-first century has seen a return to high-concept development aid. The mission became the 'end of poverty', and like all high-concept missions this one could not be accomplished quickly and certainly not without throwing billions (perhaps even trillions) of dollars at it.

The financial crisis and its aftermath has, at the least, inspired somewhat cooler reflection among the political elite on what should and could be done to bring Africa not only into the world trading system but also into the world economic system. Aid is not as indispensable as some of the high-profile lobbyists would have you believe. But it is also important not to throw that baby out with the bathwater. Africa is not a homogeneous continent: some countries are prepared to slough off their aid dependence immediately while others will have to go through a more lengthy process.

We have looked briefly at how we got here and maybe it has helped us to understand where we find ourselves today. We have some idea of where the mission creep has come from and why aid exit strategies have not been the flavour of the month. It is now time to look at the structure of the aid business. Who are the players and how do they do their business?

3 | THE DEVELOPMENT AID BUSINESS

Development aid is a multinational business. Like any business it has its suppliers and its demanders. The funds that oil the development business come from a wide range of sources but most are in the OECD countries. The main actors on the supply side are the multinational organizations such as the World Bank, the IMF and the European Union, bilateral agencies that have been set up by national governments, development banks, NGOs, and more recently major philanthropic organizations.

Added to these organizations are the many missionary societies which through the founding of missionary schools and hospitals formed the backbone of assistance in the education and health sectors in developing countries. A trip through Africa today shows that these societies are still alive and well. Missionary schools, hospitals, clinics and particularly churches can be found in most reasonably sized towns, and even in the bush one can stumble across an imposing church totally out of context with the surroundings.

Most of the major aid agencies have a fairly recent history and have evolved from ministries of foreign affairs of the OECD countries. As aid increased in importance, separate agencies were created to concentrate on the disbursement of aid. The UK and the USA both followed this course, creating the Department for International Development (DfID) and USAID respectively as operational agencies responsible for development aid activities but housed within their diplomatic missions. There are 24 donor country members of the Development Assistance Committee of the OECD which are active throughout the world. The aid agencies of the large donor states were mainly established in the 1960s. Canada was perhaps the first to set up an official aid agency by creating an External Aid Office in 1960, which in 1968 became the Canadian International Development Agency (CIDA). France was the first country, in 1961, to establish a Ministry for Co-operation to be responsible for assistance to independent, mainly African, developing countries. This was the predecessor of the Agence Française de Développement (AFD). Enactment in the

USA in 1961 of the Foreign Assistance Act as the basic economic assistance legislation established the US Agency for International Development (USAID).

The existence of so many official aid organizations which effectively do the same work has long been a complication in the development aid sector and has led to one of the perennial problems of development aid, namely the concentration on inputs rather than outputs. As in any business, there is competition among the suppliers in order to meet the demand. Since in the development aid business the suppliers (that is, the aid agencies) all supply the same commodity – money – the competition to be the preferential supplier has been part and parcel of the business. The desire to be the preferential supplier is governed by the diplomatic or political approach of the home country of the development agency. Thus the Agence Française de Développement has been active in countries which were former French colonies, while the UK's DfID has concentrated on former British colonies. Aside from this colonial and perhaps linguistic demarcation there is little to distinguish between the offerings of the various agencies. During the period of tied aid (when aid was inextricably connected to the purchase of goods and services from the donor), competition between donors had some level of technological differentiation. However, in the current state of a general acceptance that untied aid represents better value for money, there is little to differentiate between the various agencies. The situation is exacerbated by the return to the market of many non-DAC donors which have little or no apparent competitive advantage aside from supplying additional funding. In contrast to the lack of differentiation between the DAC donors, the BRICS present a totally different development model. This is a South–South model which eschews any requirement for the recipient government to improve either its overall governance or indeed its financial administration. Both of these requirements form the cornerstone of the current DAC donor approach that I will discuss below.

Therefore, the first point of note on the supply side is that the bilateral and multilateral aid agencies are providing the same good, namely money. Second, there is little or no differentiation between them in terms of what they have to offer beyond the primary good. Third, none of the agencies demonstrates a competitive advantage beyond a linguistic or colonial one. Finally, the only *raison d'être* for such a large array of aid agencies is the need for visibility and the promotion of a particular foreign policy stance. Each of the DAC aid agencies has evolved its own tendering and contract procedures and its own programme timetables which are inevitably out of phase with those of others. The question on the supply side therefore becomes, why do the aid agencies maintain their existence when there has been a recognition among the development community that aid coordination eats up a large amount of human resources?

The aid coordination issues which are already difficult when considering the DAC agencies alone become extreme when one adds in the plethora of programmes being undertaken by the various NGOs and philanthropic bodies. A count of the NGOs active in the Kenyan health sector produced a list of some forty individual NGOs pursuing their own special-interest programmes alongside the programmes supported by the DAC agencies.[1] Although many of the NGOs are small in relation to the DAC agencies, they cannot be discounted. The entry of the philanthropic institutions such as the Bill and Melinda Gates Foundation has brought in very significant levels of funding. The Gates Foundation alone had assets of \$33.9 billion in 2009.[2]

Recently there has been a change in emphasis from the input, or money, side of the equation to the output, or results, side. The concentration on the visibility aspect of development aid has undoubtedly led to a concentration on the disbursement of funds rather than the achievement of objectives. A change to a results orientation would need to be accompanied by a more or less total rethink of the supply side of the business. Reduction of the number of actors on the supply side would seem to be appropriate and would assist the new results orientation.

The demand side of the aid business has an equally difficult situation. Government officials are faced with a range of suitors all willing to assist in the development process. In each country it is normal for a parade of donors to pass through the office of the minister of finance as they pitch their wares. The road from A to B which the

---

1 The forty NGOs included the Global Alliance for Vaccination and Inoculation, the Global Fund, the Clinton Foundation, Fighting Malaria, Schistosomiasis Control Initiative, the European Malaria Vaccination Initiative, Gain, Stop TB Partnership, Partnerships for Health, and the President's Emergency Plan for Aids Relief.

2 Annual report of the Bill and Melinda Gates Foundation, 2009. See www.gatesfoundation.org/annualreport/2009/Pages/overview.aspx

minister wishes to complete can be financed by any of a group of donors with the necessary funds available. In sectors such as education and health the number of donors can run into the tens if the NGOs and philanthropics are included. Dealing with a large group of uncoordinated donors all milling around in a sector such as health can seriously impact on the development of a coordinated approach to establish an effective health system. While individual programmes aimed at HIV/AIDS, malaria or child immunization are important, it is usually the developing country government's intention that they should be developed within the context of an overall health sector strategy. Since every programme must be audited and evaluated, government officials are often inundated with requests from donors, DAC or otherwise, to facilitate the visits of audit or evaluation teams. Dealing with donors has become a full-time occupation for some government officials in developing countries and in many cases has led to the setting up of specific divisions within the ministry of finance to deal with high-value donors.

Thus, far from being a clear case of supply and demand, the aid business presents a very complicated picture. The problems of coordination have rather belatedly been recognized, and the Paris Conference on Aid Effectiveness and the follow-up conference in Accra adopted some recommendations to improve the situation. However, while these conferences were taking place other market entrants, both bilaterals and nascent NGOs, were standing in the wings waiting to offer their particular solutions to the development problem. The non-DAC donors, and particularly the BRICS with their 'out of the model' offerings, add a further layer to the already complicated picture. Aid is indeed a business in terms of financial flows and the existence of a supply-and-demand profile. However, it is a substantially more complicated business than the automobile, pharmaceutical or oil businesses. Its complexity has been realized, but the solutions adopted to overcome this complexity have thus far proved ineffective.

Developing a country strategy

The basis of all aid agency operations within a developing country is the establishment of a country strategy paper (CSP). This exercise takes place every four or five years depending on the aid funding cycle of the particular aid agency. The CSP represents a snapshot of the situation within country X in the specific year of the establishment of the document. The agency will review the economic and political situation within the country and will examine retrospectively the operations undertaken in the previous cycle period and their relative success.

Meetings will be held with interested stakeholders in the key sectors such as education, health, agriculture and infrastructure. An analysis will be carried out on the situation of democracy and governance. A new progamme for the coming cycle will be developed in cooperation with government. In general, the budget for the coming period will already have been developed by the agency's headquarters so that all that is necessary is to cut the cake into its constituent parts.

Each aid agency carries out its own exercise, but since the Paris and Accra Accords there has been a high level of involvement by all agencies in each other's strategic approaches. Each agency selects its own strategic sectors and develops its approach and intervention mechanisms.

Donors generally set up sector advisory groups (SAGs) which include all donors with an interest in the sector along with government ministries and agencies. An SAG is the repository of all the relevant information on its sector and advises both donors and government on the establishment of the CSP. SAGs, which are chaired by the sector lead donor, meet regularly to exchange information on the sector and to review progress on the aid interventions.

Once the CSP has been drafted and approved by the donor head-quarters and the government of country X, the strategic programme, which will include the specific operations and interventions and their funding, will be signed by the two parties. The die has now been cast and the aid programme between the donor and country X has been established for the next four to five years. A mid-term review will generally take place after two years and an end-of-term review will be conducted in the last year of the programme.

The project approach

From the inception of aid in the 1960s, the individual project has been the standard approach of the aid agencies. Agency A would build a road between towns X and Y while agency B would be working on a road between towns L and M. There was little attempt by either the agencies or the ministry concerned to link individual projects. In some cases individual projects, especially if they involved infrastructure, were not part of a national approach but were done as prestige projects at the president's, or some other senior politician's, behest.

Although there was much talk about sustainability of individual projects or programmes, whether they were infrastructural or not, the main objective of the aid agencies was to find viable projects in order to disburse the budgets which had been allocated to individual countries.

A huge range of projects and programmes have been carried out by aid agencies. These projects cover many facets of virtually every sector of the government. In education, projects have provided textbooks, recruited and maintained teachers, and built classrooms. In health, drugs have been procured, clinics have been built, and hospital staff have been trained and maintained. In infrastructure, roads have been built, public buildings have been renovated, and the capacity of government has been augmented. The range and depth of projects are dependent on the specific agency and the country in which the project is being undertaken.

Upon arrival in an aid agency, all new recruits are introduced to the project cycle in their first training course. They learn about pre-feasibility, feasibility, formulation, et cetera, as well as implementation and the very important evaluation. There is supposed to be a closed loop, as the results of the evaluation are fed into the pre-feasibility of the next project. However, considering that the basic approach remains the same today as it did in the 1960s one is forced to agree with Easterly (2009) when he suggests that there is a learning problem in the aid industry.

Individual projects have several attractions for the aid agency. First, they can be reviewed and their efficacy can be calculated. A wide range of methodologies have been developed (principally by the World Bank and by the academic community) in order to establish whether a particular initiative undertaken by an aid agency was effective. However there are many problems with the traditional methodologies. Most of these problems are associated with data collection, but in addition issues around measurement of the impact of a project have militated against showing whether aid works or not. The relatively new approach of randomized evaluation (RE) looks at the impact of an individual initiative by examining the impact with reference to a group not benefiting from the project. The results of REs mirror those of earlier evaluations in demonstrating that in virtually all cases the programmes did not attain their objectives and did not produce significant benefits to the target group.

The second major attraction of the individual project approach relates to visibility. There is no doubt that from the aid agency's viewpoint the development impact of an individual project is important. Aid has its basis in foreign policy and is therefore a diplomatic tool, which means that the local community should see the project as the contribution by country X to the development of the local community. The local government has a similar concern with visibility. It needs to get elected at the next general election so the aid-agency-funded road is immediately adopted by the government as its contribution to the development of its people. Government ministers also have to handle the issue of ethnicity. Africa is very much a tribal continent, and, despite efforts to create national feeling, elections are still fought on an ethnic basis. Therefore the location of projects and their visibility is a major issue for local politicians.

Finally, there is the fact that despite statements to the contrary, the donor is effectively in control of the project for good or for evil. The tendering may be carried out according to local procedures or the donor's own tendering procedures, and while the donor may not be part of the tender evaluation process it will inevitably have observer status on the tender committee. There is therefore a level of control with the individual project approach which does not exist in other development initiatives. The project approach therefore provides the donors with an additional level of comfort that funds are being properly spent.

Despite its simplicity of operation and the attractions to both the donor and the recipient, the project approach has been proved to be unsuccessful. A review of the literature demonstrates that virtually every independent evaluation has proved that aid interventions have been unsuccessful in attaining their objectives. A major study of development projects by Burnside and Dollar (2004) showed that relatively few projects achieve their desired result and then only if they are implemented in a country which has 'good governance'.

The disadvantages of the project approach appear to far outweigh the advantages. First, there is the question of sustainability. Although sustainability is a prime consideration during the feasibility stages of a project, there is ample evidence to show that in many cases no provision has been made for future operation and maintenance with the consequence that within several years the one-time excellent project is in a state of terminal decay. This sustainability problem led to the proposal that the agency building the roads, schools, clinics or hospitals should commit itself to the long-term sustainability of the project by including sufficient funds in the programme to cover future maintenance and operation. This is an abrogation of the whole concept of development, which *should* ensure that ownership of the development process is in the hands of the country being developed. The final communiqué of every conference and the conclusion of every major report point out the importance of ownership in the aid process. However, if there is no commitment from the local government, or more likely no funding, to keep going the facilities that have been provided by the aid agency, sustainability cannot be guaranteed. The problem of sustainability is not confined to the DAC donors' projects. Brautigam (2011) has shown that virtually all the first-phase (pre-2000) projects carried out by China in Africa were failing and could only be revived during a second phase by means of additional finance and a return to Chinese management.

The visibility issue helps to create the symbiotic relationship between aid agency staff and government officials. Under the input model of development aid, the agency staff are appraised on their ability to spend the allocated budget and create visibility opportunities for the aid agency and the country it represents.

Another issue that must be addressed in relation to the project approach, and indeed to all aid funding, is the question of fungibility, that is the mixing of funds so that the provision of additional funds (for a specific section of road, say) can free up government funding for a prestige project that the donors do not specifically approve of. The provision of donor funding could then be said to have made the prestige project possible. This situation gave rise to the sarcastic comment that in some cases donors thought that they were funding a clinic when in actual fact they were funding a brothel. The fungibility problem is not one that can be easily overcome.

While the project approach does give additional comfort to donors with regards to the correct allocation of funds, there is even with this approach the possibility of corruption. There is a large body of literature on the effects of corruption on projects. On every scale of measurement, especially the Kaufmann-Kraay-Mastruzzi measure (see Danaiya Usher 2010), African countries are the most corrupt in the world and have shown little improvement during the period 1996–2006. Corruption is a rent on each project and can seriously affect the efficacy of the project by reducing the level of inputs. Corruption can be countered in several ways, but most of these are dependent on the existence of effective government institutions within the country. Project auditing sometimes exposes corrupt practices. Where projects are managed by government entities, the role of the Auditor General is vital in pointing out areas where government officials have succeeded in purloining aid funds. The effectiveness of the Auditor General is directly proportional to the independence of the institution and the willingness of the parliament and the director of public prosecutions to follow up the recommendations made by the audit. Another effective method of reducing the level of rent taking at every stage of the project is to publish details of the funding to those who are supposed to benefit directly from the project. Reinikka and Svensson (2004) tracked funds for a local primary schools project in Uganda and found that only 13 per cent of the funds allocated to a specific school arrived. The Ugandan government responded to this study by publishing the funds allocated to each individual school. The level of funding accorded was also posted at each school so that parents (the proxy for the ultimate beneficiary) could examine whether the allocated funds had actually arrived at their school. This initiative had a considerable effect on the ability of administrators to divert funds that had been allocated to specific schools or clinics.

Sector-wide approaches (SWAPs)

Although the classical project approach has survived more or less intact since the 1960s, the aid community has recognized that the disparate projects that have been implemented in many sectors did not create systemic change or transformative change in the management of the sector. The existence of an individual clinic or school in some province or other had little or no effect on the overall performance of the education or the health service sector.

The logical extension of the classical project approach was for the aid agencies to combine their efforts in a more strategic and synergetic manner so as to create systemic or transformational change. This approach was entitled the sector-wide approach (SWAP). The SWAP would combine the funding and efforts of several aid agencies along with the national government to channel aid funding to projects and programmes that would respond to the strategic objectives of the sector. The funding would be held in a so-called 'basket', with each agency making a contribution (not always an equal contribution). The 'basket' fund would be managed by the government and would be dedicated to projects in the sector in question.

The SWAP represents a change from considering a sector as a series of problems that need to be solved one at a time to a more strategic approach to improving a whole sector of activity. For example, one can approach the health sector as a series of diseases that need to be tackled individually or one can concentrate on an overall improvement in health service delivery that is capable of tackling all diseases at the same time. The very successful approaches which have been developed to tackle specific diseases such as tuberculosis, malaria and HIV/AIDS may have had only a marginal effect on the country's health service in terms of improving maternal health or reducing the rate of infant mortality.

SWAPs are therefore a move in the direction of creating transformational change. The objective is not just to benefit one section of the population (as in building one clinic or equipping one school) but to supply a total public good such as health or education.

Issues such as sustainability, visibility and fungability are still important in terms of the SWAP, as is the issue of corruption. The 2009 health sector scandal in Zambia involved 'basket' funds supplied by a group of donors but managed by the Ministry of Health (Danaiya Usher 2010). The level of the fraud was put at $7 million, and a range of government officials were involved.

Programme sector budget support (PSBS)

Programme sector budget support represents the next extension of the SWAP concept. In PSBS the 'basket' does not exist and the funding from the donors is deposited directly into the state treasury, but with the condition that the donor funding is earmarked for spending in one specific sector, for example health, education, roads or agriculture. One of the prerequisites of PSBS is the development of a sector strategy that the donors can buy into. The strategy is normally developed by the government and the donors working together and involves a series of initiatives that must be undertaken in order to maintain donor funding. The sector strategy is normally accompanied by an investment plan that highlights how the donor and state funding will be used in pursuit of the declared strategy.

Once the funding has been disbursed to the state and entered the state treasury there is no qualitative difference between government funds and donor funds. This fact seriously affects the visibility of the donor since no agency can point to any specific initiative as being funded directly by it. Donors actively study how they can gain visibility from budget support activities, but other than announcing to the public the funding given in PSBS there is effectively no way the donor can gain visibility.

PSBS suffers from the other setbacks associated with aid. The fungibility problem is worsened by the existence of PSBS in that during the budget process the ministry of finance will take into account in establishing its allocations the existence of a PSBS programme. More direct budgetary support by donors to the health sector allows the government to deflect funding from health into other, non-developmental activities such as defence.

The move from classical project support to the SWAP and on to PSBS is a move up the complication scale. The project approach requires only the lowest level of complication with government. The essential process is to set up the details of the project, tender for the procurement of goods and services, and follow implementation. A SWAP involves detailed discussion with the government on the future of a sector and the management of the 'basket' fund with government. The SWAP also requires a high level of cooperation between donors who are members of the fund 'basket'. PSBS raises the complication level by involving the donors and the government in establishing a viable sector strategy and a corresponding investment plan. This process will often involve not only a disparate group of donors but also stakeholders in the sector.

The SWAP and PSBS are more appropriate mechanisms for creating transformational change but they require a different approach by the donor agency. A move away from the project approach requires the donor agency to develop negotiation and political skills which are not required in the project approach which uses a more technical skillset. The high level of interaction between donors and government required by a PSBS programme therefore necessitates a different kind of aid agency personnel who are more attuned to the development of strategic approaches.

An important difference between the SWAP and the PSBS approaches is the method of funds disbursement. The funds associated with a SWAP are generally deposited in a 'basket' which is held in trust between the government and the donors. The 'basket' provides the funds required to finance various agreed initiatives and is replenished as required by the negotiated conditions of the SWAP. In PSBS a range of fund disbursements can be considered. The funding is generally disbursed in tranches. The timescale for a PSBS programme will generally be more than three years so the first division of funding will be on an annual basis. The annual disbursement is generally in two tranches – a fixed tranche and a variable tranche. The fixed tranche is paid in accordance with timing established in the PSBS contract. The variable tranche may be made with some elements of conditionality. The conditionality can be the achieving of various benchmarks outlined in the sector strategy. If all the benchmarks are achieved then the equation is simple and the full variable tranche is disbursed. If a range of benchmarks are achieved and some are partially achieved, the donors and government representatives must analyse the level of achievement and a percentage of the variable tranche is agreed for payment. The process of developing the level of achievement of the benchmarks depends not only on the technical skills of the donors but also on their aforementioned negotiation and political skills.

From structural adjustment loans to general budget support

It was apparent by the late 1970s that Africa was falling behind in developmental terms. The euphoria associated with the era of independence had given way to a period in which the negative effects of the colonial neglect of local education on administrative capacity were becoming apparent. Countries such as Ghana which started independent life with an effective economy were gradually submerged by ineffective government and the grandiose prestige projects of their founding fathers. Countries that began life with a less effective economy soon found themselves sinking deeper and deeper into poverty.

It was against this backdrop and the apparent failure of the project approach that the transformational movement was born in order to halt the negative slide in most African economies. The main mechanism developed by the transformational movement was the structural adjustment loan (SAL) which was created by the International Monetary

Fund and the World Bank in 1980. The theory behind the SAL was that it was institutional governance that was dragging Africa down, and that funding was required which would put obligations on the recipient to reform its institutional arrangements. The SAL was therefore contingent on the recipient government agreeing to make significant changes in the way that it managed its economy.

The obligations required by the SAL were concentrated on fiscal policy discipline, tax reform, interest rates, exchange rates, trade liberalization, privatization of state companies or monopolies, deregulation, and the protection of private property. This transformational creed ran counter to many of the policies of the founding fathers of the new African countries who had taken power in their countries on a socialist platform. The new prescriptions became known as the Washington Consensus because Washington was the home of both the World Bank and the IMF and the Consensus represented the hubris of the developed world in setting out how African countries could save themselves and receive substantial loan funding at the same time.

The role of national policy was now seen as primary in ensuring development. Burnside and Dollar (2004) had concluded that the project approach was more successful in countries that had 'good' policies while it had little effect in countries with 'bad' policies. However, the Washington Consensus insisted that the eleven prescriptions developed by Williamson represented the necessary and sufficient conditions to unleash development in Africa.[3] The operation of the SALs over the period 1980–99 shows that this contention was sadly mistaken. Many African countries benefited from SALs. In fact some countries such as Côte d'Ivoire and Kenya benefited from multiple

---

3 The Washington Consensus consisted of the following: (1) fiscal discipline – strict criteria for limiting budget deficits; (2) public expenditure priorities – moving them away from subsidies and administration towards previously neglected fields with high economic returns; (3) tax reform – broadening the tax base and cutting marginal tax rates; (4) financial liberalization – interest rates should ideally be market-determined; (5) exchange rate management – to induce rapid growth in non-traditional exports; (6) trade liberalization; (7) increasing foreign direct investment (FDI) – by reducing barriers; (8) privatization of state enterprises; (9) deregulation – abolition of regulations that impede the entry of new firms or restrict competition (except in the areas of safety, environment and finance); (10) secure intellectual property rights (IPRs) – without excessive costs and available to the informal sector; (11) a reduced role for the state. Williamson first coined the expression 'Washington Consensus' in 1989 in a background paper for a conference convened by the Institute for International Economics.

SALs – an indication that a single SAL was insufficient to ensure the level of structural adjustment which was deemed necessary. In most cases the recipient country did not follow up on its obligations, which was the reason for yet another SAL to bolster the adjustment process.

The contention that there was a series of policies which if followed by developing countries would ensure economic growth was akin to the thesis produced by Peters and Waterman (1988). It is perhaps unfortunate that with time Peters and Waterman's excellent companies have proved to have feet of clay. A similar situation existed in the development field. Policies that have proved successful for one country have not worked when disseminated and many once-successful policies have not stood the test of time. By the start of the twenty-first century, the SALs had been proved not to have worked and were replaced by the Poverty Reduction and Growth Facility (PRGF) in the case of the IMF and Poverty Reduction Support Credits in the case of the World Bank. It is interesting to note that many of the loans that were contracted as SALs were the debts which were forgiven under both the HIPC and the MDRI programmes agreed at the Gleneagles summit.

It is time to move on from this brief historical digression to look at the next great idea in development – general budget support.

> Budget support is aid which is transferred directly into the national budget of the partner country. In practice, donors transfer budget support into the National Treasury account in the partner country's central bank. At that point, the deposited funds become part of the government budget. The partner government then determines which priorities and programmes the funds will be used to finance, within the framework of an ongoing dialogue with donors. Budget support is usually granted over a period of several years with aid being disbursed in several tranches. (European Commission 2008)

The above definition of general budget support is simply an extension of the PSBS which is described above. In this case, however, the funding is not related to a specific area but can be used by government in pursuit of any policy it considers to be a priority.

The core of the budget support arrangement is the performance assessment framework (PAF) which sets out the institutional areas such as public financial management, support for the Auditor General and the judiciary, and sectoral policies that the government should implement during the life of the GBS arrangement.

Like SALs, GBS is not granted to every country. Each country must be assessed on its ability to prudently manage and protect the funds granted. This means that the donor group providing GBS generally establishes a series of core conditions relating to the implementation of an effective system of public financial management and a commitment by government to strenuously pursue the fight against corruption.

The disbursement is usually in the form of a fixed and a variable tranche (as is the case with PSBS), with the variable tranche being disbursed in relation to the achievement of benchmarks on the PAF. Unlike the SALs the funding provided by GBS is a grant and not a loan. The theory is that government should be in control of the development process and should decide the priority actions necessary to reduce poverty. The funding replaces what would have been contributed in terms of project funding.

The claims made in favour of GBS at the start of the new millennium already seem overoptimistic. Some of the countries (such as Senegal) which were seen as ideal candidates have since fallen off the GBS programme while others (such as Zambia) have been under continual pressure to show commitment to the underlying principles. GBS is a transformational programme. It follows in the line of the SALs and is intended to lead to institutional change at the heart of government. The only difference is that the funding is phased, which allows for the achievement of some of the obligations undertaken by the government to be used as a trigger to disburse some or all of the promised funding.

For donors one of the major attractions of GBS is that they become part of the budget-making process. The problems of underspending, which many African countries (particularly the former British colonies) experienced with a budget cycle aimed at budget approval by 1 April and completed commitments by 31 December, became the target of many budget support groups. Since in general the budget cycle is an administrative matter that can be modified by parliament, involvement of the donors in the budget exercise has led to a more rational annual budget cycle with budget approval by parliament before 1 January. This has certainly been the experience in Zambia where the budget is now approved by 1 January and expenditures are made over a period of twelve months and not nine months as in the past.

GBS is highly resource-intensive. At its inception, GBS was considered to be a mechanism for reducing the number of aid professionals in an aid agency. After all, a large amount of funding was being given directly to the government to spend as it wished. It was only necessary to monitor how the budget was established and implemented. The truth of the matter is that GBS requires substantial resources to administer the very high level of contact required by the donor budget support group and the government. There is, therefore, a movement in complexity of donor–government relations as one moves from the project (marginal) approach to the various transformational approaches.

GBS is contentious. Many donors consider it unhealthy to give the governments of countries which have blemishes on their corruption record carte blanche in spending donor funding. There is an insistence that the government of the developing country should demonstrate that they have corruption and graft under control before they can be considered eligible for GBS. This is somewhat akin to donors saying that only countries who have effective financial control institutions should be eligible for funding to develop effective financial control institutions. GBS is a developmental initiative. It is also risky for the donors but it is not irreversible. Should a donor decide that it no longer wishes to use GBS as the preferred mechanism to deliver aid then it can return to the project mode. Some donors have already made this decision, while others have eschewed involvement in GBS initiatives.

Development aid interventions – new wine in old bottles

How development aid works has changed little since the first interventions with the newly independent African nations in the 1960s. The project approach is alive and well and still forms a large part of the aid portfolio of any country. Since the effect (however large or small that might be) of the marginal or project approach is felt by at least some of the population, it can be said that the project approach has been at least moderately successful. A review of the literature by Easterly (2009) leads him to the conclusion that the project approach has had limited success in the education and health sectors and no success whatsoever in the agricultural sector. The lack of success of aid in fostering economic growth in Africa certainly led to the attraction of the transformational model. Yet considering that

transformational initiatives have been in place since 1980 and have
thus far proved ineffective in achieving the growth that was foreseen
by the adoption of the Washington Consensus, the question of 'where
do we go from here' has led to the development of GBS.

If one looks at SALs and GBS with an open mind one can see
that GBS is SALs repackaged. Both are aimed at pushing countries
into the adoption of policies which they have not arrived at by internal deliberations. There is no doubt that enhanced public financial
management is in everybody's interest. In a situation where donor
funds and national funds are interchangeable it is important that both
receive equal protection. Therefore, to the extent that GBS improves
budget execution and that controls are established which monitor the
flow of funds and the results obtained from such funds, then GBS
is accomplishing its aims.

The relations between donors (or, as they are now called, cooperating partners) and the government are difficult. Every nation on
the planet is proud of its sovereignty and it is important that this is
recognized in the relations between the donor community and the
government. The prescriptive approach associated with the SALs
failed because the policy transformation was imposed from outside
and was not a function of an internal process. Top-down policy
transformation will always be problematic for both sides in the aid
business. The government will see the role of the cooperating partners
in proposing transformational change as prescriptive and undermining
the sovereignty of the duly elected government. There will therefore
be a level of resistance. This situation is not new and pre-dates the
independence of Africa's colonies. Adam Smith in his *Theory of Moral
Sentiments* wrote:

> The man of system, on the contrary, is apt to be very wise in his
> own conceit; and is often so enamoured with the supposed beauty
> of his own ideal plan of government, that he cannot suffer the
> smallest deviation from any part of it. He goes on to establish it
> completely and in all its parts, without any regard either to the
> great interests, or to the strong prejudices which may oppose it. He
> seems to imagine that he can arrange the different members of a
> great society with as much ease as the hand arranges the different
> pieces upon a chess-board. He does not consider that the pieces
> upon the chess-board have no other principle of motion besides

that which the hand impresses upon them; but that, in the great chess-board of human society, every single piece has a principle of motion of its own, altogether different from that which the legislature might choose to impress upon it. If those two principles coincide and act in the same direction, the game of human society will go on easily and harmoniously, and is very likely to be happy and successful. If they are opposite or different, the game will go on miserably, and the society must be at all times in the highest degree of disorder.[4]

The hubris of the donor community in assuming that it has the answer to the development problems is substantial, since after forty years of development activities Africa still languishes in poverty.

The aid community has repackaged aid mechanisms in use since the 1960s in an effort to find the Holy Grail of aid – an aid delivery mechanism which is successful in attaining the objective of accelerating economic growth while at the same time reducing poverty and improving access to education and health services. Unfortunately, after forty years and much repackaging it appears that the Holy Grail may not be attained. The academic community has published widely on the effects of this or that initiative and a whole range of evaluation methodologies have been developed within the context of development economics aimed at improving aid delivery. Yet there is no specific initiative that works all the time. Some initiatives work in some circumstances but not in others. At some point the aid community will have to accept that development may not be an exogenous activity. This will be a cause for concern for high-profile advocates of increased funding as the cure for poverty in Africa. Equally it may not exactly please the transformational community as it sees country after country in Africa give greater currency to the Beijing Consensus than to the Washington Consensus.[5]

---

4 Quoted from Easterly (2009).

5 Beijing Consensus is a term that represents an alternative economic development model to the Washington Consensus of market-friendly policies promoted by the IMF, World Bank and US Treasury, often for guiding reform in developing countries. There is no precise definition of the Beijing Consensus, although many have laid out plans, but the term has evolved into one describing alternative plans for economic development in the under-developed world, so named as China is seen as a potential model for such plans.

Despite the negativity surrounding the aid business, a trip around Africa today shows that things have changed for the better in the past forty years. The cities are more modern and boast better buildings than some European capitals. The hospitals are more numerous and cleaner. The staff of the modern (mostly private) hospitals are well paid and happy to stay in their own countries. Private schools are improving the overall quality of education and bringing up the national levels, albeit slowly. There is a range of supermarkets and shopping malls aimed at satisfying the new middle class. In rural areas, poverty is still the order of the day, but as Africa becomes urbanized this situation will undoubtedly improve. In some African countries there is a property boom.

The aid business is in crisis. Yet the entrants to the aid community are increasing day by day. The Paris Declaration and the Accra Agenda are attempts to rationalize a community that is out of control. The mechanisms of aid and the relationships between the suppliers and the demanders are complex. Perhaps they are too complex. The aid space is crowded and is becoming more crowded every day. Dealing with the plethora of entrants into the aid community is an impossible task for a recipient country with limited capacity and resources.

There is evidence to suggest that the 'aid curse' exists and is akin to the 'oil curse'. To quote Diamond (2008):

> In the circumstances of predatory rule in Africa, aid functions like the revenue that gushes from oil exports – it is just another source of external rents that enables rulers to float on a cushion above their societies, controlling the state without having to answer to their own people.

However there is a political point which relates to Diamond's analysis. African governments spend an inordinate amount of time and effort in explaining their policies and actions to the donor community. There is an almost complete rupture of the responsible relationship between governments and the people who have elected them. Governments, possibly because of aid flows but more likely because of arrogance, and the absence of effective political opposition and civil society, totally ignore their accountability to the people (except of course during elections). This use of the donor community as the proxy for the people is not a healthy situation and is certainly undemocratic. However, it is often representatives of the donor community who question governments on their investment decisions.

I will finish with an anecdote. I attended a meeting of the Budget Support Group with the Government of Zambia at the end of November 2010. The government side boasted 24 members led by the Secretary to the Treasury. The donor group was just less weighty at 21 individuals, which included four ambassadors and several heads of aid agencies. The meeting lasted two hours and took no decisions. A total of 90 man-hours (excluding travel) had been wasted without any result. Aid still has a long way to go.

4 | DOMESTIC RESOURCE MOBILIZATION

> The nation should have a tax system that looks like someone designed it on purpose. (William Simon)

Virtually every meeting of finance ministers in Africa includes a call to the various states to improve domestic resource mobilization. For example, the Conference of African Ministers of Economy and Finance held in Cairo on 6–7 June 2009 concluded as the first point on their communiqué: 'Domestic resource mobilisation is the only meaningful way to finance long-term development. Tax income should eventually replace aid as a main source of income.'[1] The International Conference on Finance and Development in its final communique (now called the Monterrey Consensus) also underlined the primary importance of domestic resource implementation.[2]

The idea of domestic resource mobilization (or, if you prefer, taxation) as a replacement for development aid is not new. Nicholas Kaldor in his famous article in *Foreign Affairs* more than fifty years ago stated that 'the importance of public revenue to the underdeveloped countries can hardly be exaggerated if they are to achieve their hopes of accelerated economic progress' (Kaldor 1963). While it is encouraging to realize that the idea of domestic resource mobilization should be directly linked to economic development, one must be realistic in understanding that many of the countries that obtained their freedom in the 1960s did not have the capacity immediately after independence either to develop or to implement tax systems. However, fifty years is a relatively long time and a large donor-funded effort has gone into capacity building in public financial management, so it is not

---

1 Final communiqué of the Conference of African Ministers of Economy and Finance, Cairo 6–7 June 2009. Accessed at www.uneca.org/cfm/2009/docs/MinisterialStatement2009.pdf

2 The Monterrey Consensus states 'An enabling domestic environment is vital for mobilizing domestic resources, increasing productivity, reducing capital flight, encouraging the private sector, and attracting and making effective use of international investment and assistance. Efforts to create such an environment should be supported by the international community.' Accessed at www.un.org/esa/ffd/monterrey/MonterreyConsensus.pdf

inconceivable that many African countries would have already built up a capacity in tax policy development and tax collection.

Kaldor (1963) pointed out that whereas developed countries collected 25–30 per cent of their GDP in taxation, the under-developed countries collected only 8–15 per cent. Things have certainly improved since Kaldor's day and today many African countries collect between 15 and 23 per cent of their GDP as tax revenues.

A concept which is particularly applicable to any discussion on domestic resource mobilization is the question of aid volatility. Aid flows do not have a clear counter-cyclical pattern as would be desirable to help smooth economic shocks but rather depend on funding of specific projects or the donor funding cycle. Bulíř and Hamann (2005) have reviewed the variations between aid commitments and aid disbursement for 76 countries over the period 1975 to 2003. The results of this analysis show that the volatility of aid was a multiple of as much as 20 to 40 times that of domestic fiscal revenue. Also there was little evidence that the volatility of aid had improved in a period when donors were making significant efforts (specifically the Poverty Reduction and Growth Facility of the IMF and the HIPC initiative) to improve the situation. The analysis also revealed that in general aid was delivered in a pro-cyclical fashion, that is, aid flows improve when a country's policies are shown to be effective.

Domestic resource mobilization in Africa presents some unique challenges. Since in most cases the large majority of the people are poor and subsistence farmers, the tax system must be designed in such a way as to ensure that only those with the ability to pay are taxed. There are four kinds of taxes which can be imposed by Governments. Direct taxes include income tax on individuals and corporation tax on companies. Indirect taxes are taxes which can be applied on consumption such as value added tax (VAT) or various kinds of sales taxes. Trade-related taxes are imposed on either imports or exports; excise duties are imposed on tobacco or alcohol. Finally resource taxes are imposed on the extraction of natural resources such as oil, gas and mineral ores.

Africa and trends in domestic resource mobilization

The African Development Bank, using the 50-country African Economic Outlook 2010 survey (African Development Bank 2010), has established the following trends in African taxation:

The trend in taxation has been positive. The average tax revenue as a share of GDP has been increasing since the early 1990s. The average of taxes collected across the continent increased from 22% of GDP in 1990 to 27% in 2007. However, a closer examination of this trend shows that Upper Middle Income Countries (UMIC) benefited most with an average of 35% which is converging on the OECD figure of 38%. The Lower Middle Income Countries (LMIC) have a tax share of about 22% which is the average for their group worldwide while the Lower Income Countries (LIC) have a share of around 15% which is a serious impediment to their development.

Taxes per capita have in general increased in Africa throughout the past two decades. However this average increase hides some important outliers. For example, in countries including Burundi, the Democratic Republic of Congo, Ethiopia and Guinea-Bissau, annual taxes are around $11 per capita. At the other end of the spectrum, taxes in the Seychelles, Libya and Equatorial Guinea reach around $3,600 per capita. These high values are associated with oil producers or, in the case of the Seychelles, high revenues associated with the tourism industry and a very small population.

There are large discrepancies in the tax mix in Africa. Figure 4.1 shows the breakdown of the various taxes for a group of African countries. Most countries use a mix of direct, indirect, trade and resource taxes to mobilize domestic revenue. Since each country is heterogeneous and has its own levels of development, trade penetration and natural resource base, it is perhaps inevitable that each country has sought to optimize its tax take in relation to its overall situation. It is thus easy to see that South Africa, the most developed economy, has the highest direct and indirect taxation with relatively low trade taxes. However, it is surprising to see Zambia and Malawi in the company of the likes of Egypt, Botswana, Kenya and Tunisia in having a sophisticated approach to tax mix.

All the countries in the sample with the exception of Guinea-Bissau have some level of indirect taxation. Mauritius has the highest level of indirect taxation while Equatorial Guinea has the lowest. Despite the efforts to liberalize trade, all countries have a level of trade taxes. However, it is noticeable that the LICs have the greatest dependence on trade-related taxes.

The bottom part of Figure 4.1 includes the major oil producers; they have benefited greatly from the boom in oil revenues and the consequent impact on taxation. Resource taxes predominate within this group to the extent that Equatorial Guinea depends almost exclusively on resource taxes for domestic resource mobilization.

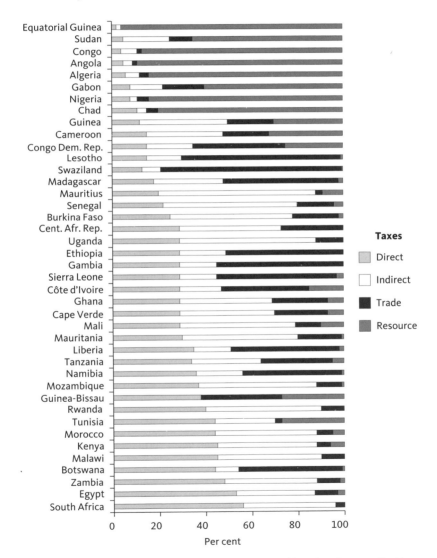

4.1 Tax mix of a group of African countries (*source*: African Development Bank)

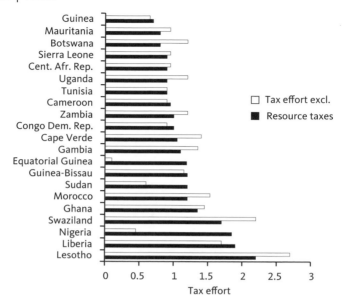

4.2 Tax effort of a group of African countries (*source*: African Development Bank)

Other spectacular resource tax takers are Libya with 66 per cent and Angola with 39 per cent.

Dependence on one or other of the four possible taxes increases the exposure of the country to shocks if that particular tax base collapses. Those countries that have developed a mix of taxes are best positioned to survive a fall in any one particular tax base. A secondary problem is the so-called 'resource curse' which leads to a misallocation of resources in the economy in general. Another element of this 'curse' is displayed in Figure 4.1, which shows the heavy dependence of oil- and gas-producing countries on resource taxes.

Those oil-exporting countries which derive most of their revenues from oil exploitation have little incentive to develop a coherent mix of taxes. Oil taxes are easy to collect while other taxes, particularly indirect taxes, are difficult to collect. There is therefore a tendency on the part of resource-rich countries to concentrate their taxation efforts on resource taxes to the detriment of other tax bases. Similarly aid revenues which flow directly to the treasury may limit the government's interest in imposing taxes on other bases.

The tax effort is an index measure of how well a country is doing in terms of tax collection in relation to what could reasonably be expected given its economic potential. Figure 4.2 shows the tax efforts of a group of African countries. Figures show that some countries collect as little as half what they would reasonably be expected to collect while other countries collect two to three times what they should have collected. The tax effort figures show a discrepancy between the resource-rich countries and the others. In all cases the oil producers have a larger tax effort when the resource is included than when it is excluded. This effect is at its most extreme in the case of Equatorial Guinea but is present in all cases.

The challenges in improving domestic resource mobilization

If we accept the contention that tax mobilization is central to an improvement in development, it is important to understand the impediments and challenges which a country faces in endeavouring to improve its tax policy. Several times each year a team from the IMF visits each developing country and reviews progress on the Poverty Reduction and Growth Facility programme. After each visit the team debriefs the government and then later the diplomatic community. Inevitably there are three prescriptions which are always included in the advice of the IMF team. These are to increase domestic revenue, to increase the tax base and to improve tax administration (to be read as improve tax collection).

Figure 4.3 shows the corporation and value added tax rates for a group of African countries. It shows the situation in 2010 but that situation has been evolutionary and in many cases based on advice from the IMF. The corporation tax rates are very close and converge on the average of 29 per cent which is very much in line with the OECD average corporation tax rate of 35 per cent. This convergence on the average rate of about 30 per cent represents a mature approach by a large group of countries which do not wish to go into competition with each other in order to attract foreign direct investment (FDI) through differentiation of their corporate tax rates. Therefore there is not much scope within the IMF proposals for increasing the revenues from corporate taxes.

Value added tax is a much more complex issue. Trade liberalization (particularly the requirements of the Uruguay Round) has bitten into government revenues by reducing the amount of tax associated with both imports and exports. This revenue must be replaced. In the case of the upper middle income countries (UMICs) and the lower

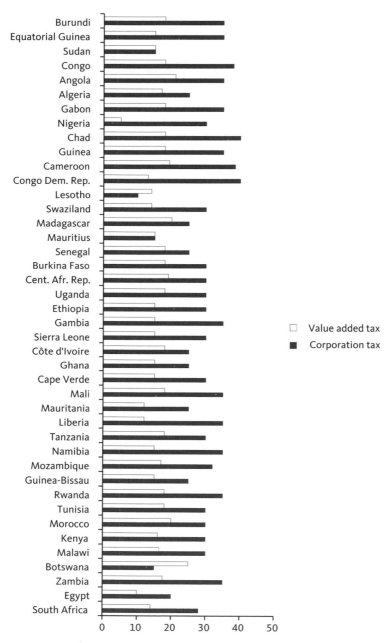

4.3 VAT and corporation tax rates in a group of African countries (per cent) (*source*: World Bank 2011a)

middle income countries (LMICs) the effect is somewhat limited because they already have small levels of trade taxes in their tax mix. The main impact is felt by the lower income countries (LICs). The obvious solution is to replace the import tariff with a consumption tax which leaves the cost of the imported good the same in the eye of the consumer. This is a rather complex operation involving not only setting effective VAT rates but also raising issues of tax collection. It is even more difficult in the LICs who, in general, do not have the fiscal space to totally replace the losses associated with trade liberalization. Baunsgaard and Keen (2005) estimated that the revenue recovery from the suppression of trade taxes in low-income countries is not more than about 30 cents of each lost dollar. The net impact of trade liberalization in the short run is thus a net revenue loss.

In sub-Saharan Africa, the net effect of the downward pressure on trade taxes (from about 6 per cent to 4 per cent of GDP in the period 1980 to 2004) (Keen and Mansour 2010) allied to the more or less flat revenue from income tax has been compensated by increases in indirect taxation (from 2.8 per cent to 5.5 per cent of GDP) and the spectacular rise in resource tax (from just over 1 per cent to 4 per cent of GDP in the 24-year period).

Therefore, there is limited scope for increases in revenue from corporation tax and the losses due to liberalization of trade must be compensated for by increases in or the imposition of indirect taxes such as consumption taxes.

A similar argument can be made in relation to income tax. The tax base for individual income tax is small in most African countries mainly because of the small size of the formal sector of the economy. Some countries have already adopted the PAYE (Pay As You Earn) system but this applies mainly to large employers and the state itself which have the capacity to collect this tax. The burden for small companies in responding to tax collection on behalf of the state can seriously affect compliance. There are therefore only two options to increase revenue. Either the level of income tax can be increased or the number of people in the tax net can be increased.

One method for increasing the revenue from direct taxes is some-how to bring the informal sector into the tax net. This sector is hard to tax, and tax authorities tend to give it a low priority since the return for the cost expended appears to be low. Two important studies carried out on the tax issue in Africa (Keen and Mansour 2010; Bahl and Bird 2008) have concluded that taxes should be levied at low and relatively flat rates across a broad base as they are easier to collect and administer. There are also good public reasons for extending the tax net to the informal sector. If the formal sector sees itself as the main target for revenue generation in terms of income tax and indeed corporation tax, there will be a sense of inequality among those working in the formal sector compared with those working in the informal sector. The case for bringing the informal sector into the tax net is attractive from both revenue and political considerations. However, the cost of such an operation may far outweigh the potential revenue. There are several options open to government, such as vendor or pedlar's licences, but in general the informal sector is tax-averse, especially if it sees no direct benefit to itself from tax. The informal sector does not produce state revenues from VAT because its operations are generally not registered for VAT. This can be an impediment for the informal sector if their inputs come from the formal sector. They must pay VAT to the formal sector which cannot be reclaimed without a VAT registration number. This effect can push a company from the informal sector into the formal sector depending on its level of activity.

The challenge of increasing domestic resource mobilization is a significant one, and although there are some possibilities for increasing resources, particularly from the informal sector, the cost may outweigh the return.

Areas where resource mobilization can be effective

While the taxation of the informal sector raises some difficult technical and political questions, another sector of the economy too has thus far been outside the remit of the tax authorities. The issue of land and property taxes has long been a political hot potato for most developing countries in Africa. Since much of the property in terms of urban housing of significant value is held by the elite, the introduction of property taxes would be considered by them as a direct attack and would be strongly resisted.

Given that most developing countries are urbanizing rapidly (see Chapter 1) there will be an urgent need for urban infrastructure both in terms of habitation and the facilities that are a feature of urban living such as roads, energy and communications. A property tax is the single fairest way to share the burden in the development of urban infrastructure. The elites in developing countries resist property taxes but they are the first to complain about the condition of the roads directly outside their sumptuous villas. The imposition of a properly structured property tax would lead to the development of a cadastral system in order to assess the value of the tax. The system would have the additional advantage of exposing information about property ownership which many would prefer to remain hidden. Such information might be useful in the future if the idea of a wealth tax were ever to become a real issue.

A second unattended area is the question of land tax. Land in Africa has always been a contentious issue (see Kaldor 1963). Even prior to independence, subsistence farming accounted for 50 per cent of the national output but was totally ignored by the tax authorities. Kaldor was a big supporter of land taxes 'not because the land tax yields just revenue but the right kind of revenue; it enlarges the supply of foodstuffs to urban areas, and thus the amount of employment that can be offered outside agriculture without creating inflation. It also promotes agricultural efficiency' (Kaldor 1963). Despite Kaldor's efforts to promote land taxes there is still no effective land taxation in Africa.

Land issues tend to revolve around traditional approaches to land tenure, tribalism and the absence of a proper land registration system. These issues have hampered Africa from reaching its true agricultural potential and consequently have denied the landholder the profit from working his or her land effectively. However, while rural land reform remains an 'unresolved question' (African Development Bank and OECD 2010: 103), the possibility of imposing a land tax is remote.

Transfer pricing – the thief in the night

A recent study by Hollingshead (2010) on the effect of transfer pricing has concluded that the revenue loss to developing countries from trade mispricing amounts to $100 billion per year. This figure is almost the double the $60 billion assessed by Christian Aid (2008). The Hollingshead figure is also double the increased aid agreed by the Gleneagles summit.

Trade mispricing refers to the deliberate over-invoicing of imports and the under-invoicing of exports usually for the purpose of tax evasion. The practice is widespread and is a mechanism by which wealthy individuals can transfer money abroad illegally. Trade mispricing can also include transfer pricing whereby a multinational company with operations in many countries can decide where it wishes to be taxed by arranging pricing between its various national operations to optimize its tax position.

Cobham (2005) estimated losses from three sources of tax leakage: the income earned on assets held offshore by wealthy individuals; profits earned by the corporate sector and then shifted to a lower-tax jurisdiction; and income from 'shadow' economic activity, carried out within the economy but not recognized by the tax authorities. He concluded that developing countries lost a potential revenue of $385 billion per year, made up of $285 billion in the 'shadow' economy, $50 billion in offshore asset holding and $50 billion of corporate profit-shifting.

There is a reasonably close correspondence between the figure developed by Hollingshead and that developed by Cobham. A study by Global Financial Integrity (Kar et al. 2010) estimated that developing countries lost between $858.6 billion and $1.06 trillion in illicit financial outflows. The estimated illicit outflows from Africa account for only a relatively small proportion of the total (perhaps because of the unavailability of data). The list is headed by Nigeria with annual illicit outflows of $12.5 billion. Guinea-Bissau comes last with an annual outflow of $27 million.

The report by Christian Aid (2008) stated that 'In the US, 60 per cent of the corporations with at least $250 million in assets reported no federal tax liability.' Even if it were impossible to close off completely these loopholes the recovery of only a percentage of this leakage would have a significant impact on development resources. However, we must be honest and realize that even the most sophisticated tax systems have been prey to the transfer pricing problem. One UK example was said to involve British American Tobacco: an article in the *Observer* entitled 'Uproar at BATs tiny tax bill' described how BAT had paid only £13 million in tax on profits of £9 billion over five years (Walsh 2005). In 1999, the BBC reported that 'Rupert Murdoch's News Corporation and its subsidiaries paid only A$325m (£128m) in corporate taxes worldwide. That translates to 6% of the A$5.4bn consolidated pre-tax profits for the same period.'[3] News

---

3 http://news.bbc.co.uk/1/hi/special_report/1999/02/99/e-cyclopedia/302366.stm

Corp earned profits of $2.3 billion in Britain from 1987 to 2000 but paid no corporation tax there.[4] This miracle was accomplished by using a three-pronged strategy of: tax relief claimed on debt interest repayments; a reliance on offshore tax havens; and exploiting global differences in accounting standards.

There are, however, some possible approaches to tackling the transfer pricing issue. The principal mechanism is the Arm's Length Principle which has now been adopted by all the OECD countries and which stipulates that all multinationals involved in cross-border trade with a subsidiary should treat their relationship as though the subsidiary was an independent company. This should ensure that the taxable profits of a multinational should stay within the jurisdiction in which they are generated. It is important that countries adopt transfer pricing legislation and double taxation agreements as outlined in the OECD 'Transfer Pricing Guidelines for Multinational Enterprises and Tax Administrations' (OECD 2009).

Tax incentives

Tax incentives grant preferential treatment to specific taxpayer groups, investment expenditures or returns through targeted tax deductions, credits exclusions or exemptions. Incentives are usually used to attract foreign direct investment to a specific country and form part of competitive bidding for foreign direct investment. Tax incentives can take the form of tax holidays, import duty exemptions, investment allowances and accelerated depreciation. Other incentives can be protection from competing imports, inducements to invest in dubious industries or in less well-developed regions, and labour subsidies or taxes which significantly affect the capital–labour share.

Evidence (mainly drawn from surveys of multinational investors) suggests that tax incentives are not the factor that most influences multinationals when they are selecting investment locations. Surveys suggest that other factors such as good infrastructure, political stability, labour availability and costs, and strong laws relating to private property protection are important (World Bank 2002a).

There is evidence that most incentive systems do not work, they attract little FDI, they have costs and are a drain on the country's treasury and make investment procedures more complex (Bergsman

---

4 'Globalisation and Tax', *Economist*, 29 January 2000, p. 5.

1999). Since taxation incentives are developed by public officials or politicians, they are also open to corruption. Surveys have found that government officials rated incentives highly in the decision to attract foreign direct investment while executives of multinational companies did not (World Bank 2002a). Bergsman (1999) considers that one reason for this opinion is that government officials base their view on the daily experience they have had with investors. Investors bargain hard to gain every advantage they can get. This induces the government officials to make concessions that are not strictly necessary to gain the investment.

A major development since the 1980s has been the development promotion agency. These agencies are both national (as in the case of Ireland) and regional (as in the case of the United States, Spain and France). It should be noted that the US does not offer any incentives at the national level to encourage FDI. However, taxation has been developed as a resource collection mechanism and not as a tool to attract FDI.

The majority of FDI in Africa is concentrated on the commodity extraction industries, oil and gas or mining. Bergsman insists that there is no evidence that foreign direct investment would not occur if the incentives were not provided. While the oil and gas industries have standard approaches in terms of government–company relations to resource extraction, the mining sector has no such standardized arrangements. The development of the national oil company and production-sharing agreements along with governments having a strong background in the technical and economic considerations of the oil and gas business has led to a situation where oil and gas taxation is considered to be a mature relationship between government and company.

The fiscal background to resource taxation is well established. The first basic tax is a unit-based royalty which must be paid to the government as a rent for extracting the natural resource. The royalty is generally based on the level of the resource extracted and provides the government with a base taxation irrespective of the profitability of the operation. Royalty is generally based on the ad valoram sales of the commodity and can vary. For example, Botswana levies a royalty of 10 per cent of ad valorem sales on diamonds, 5 per cent on precious minerals and 3 per cent on other minerals (World Bank 2006c). Zambia levies a 2 per cent royalty on copper production.

Aside from royalties (which in many cases are the prime revenue source for the state), mining companies are subject to property tax (where it exists), registration fees, income tax, withholding taxes (amounts deducted at source and used as a credit against a future tax demand), capital gains tax, and in some jurisdictions a windfall profits tax. The latter tax comes into play when the mining company earns excessive profits caused by increases in the price of a commodity or an over-estimation of the investment costs.

The mining industry differs in significant ways from the oil industry. In general, oil exploitation agreements are established on an international basis and are subject to agreement by the national parliament. There is therefore (superficially at least) a high degree of transparency in the case of oil and gas development agreements. The same cannot be said for the mining industry in Africa. In most cases mining agreements were established by government and the individual mining companies in secret, and incentives were granted in terms of tax holidays, concessions on import and export taxes, lower corporate income tax rates, lower withholding taxes and no windfall or additional profits taxes, as well as accelerated depreciation and labour subsidies. While there is no question that such mining agreements are legal, they are certainly not transparent in that they have not passed parliamentary scrutiny and are unavailable to the public at large. All commodity extraction is risky and the markets for such commodities are volatile. Each project requires a great deal of financing, much of which occurs before the first kilo of the commodity is produced. Companies have convinced governments that because of the high initial financing and the risk of market volatility they should receive special treatment in terms of taxation.

The commodity boom which began in 2002 and lasted until the financial crisis of 2008 produced superprofits for the mining industry. However, the effect of these windfall profits was not felt in increases in resource taxes. Box 4.1 shows that for Zambia, whose mining industry was a major beneficiary of the mining boom, revenues from resource taxes are minuscule in comparison to the size of the copper industry. The cyclical nature of mining is well known, and Zambia has seen the ups and the downs of the commodity markets. Many mining contracts were negotiated during the pre-boom years when countries were anxious to attract investment into the mining sector. The concessions made in those negotiated agreements have come

---

Box 4.1 Mining taxation in Zambia

The mining development agreements negotiated with private investors who took over the copper mines after the privatization of Zambia Consolidated Copper Mines in 1998 offered a series of incentives mainly in the form of tax exemptions to mining companies. In 1992, copper prices averaged $2,200 a ton and Zambia earned $200 million in tax revenues. In 2004, copper prices averaged $2,800 a ton and Zambia earned $8 million in tax revenues. By 2006, copper had reached $8,000 a ton and the Zambian President Levy Mwanawasa in his speech at the opening of the Zambian Parliament in January 2008 announced that he would renegotiate the mining agreements with the various companies and that such renegotiation would include an element of windfall profit tax. The reaction of the mining community was perhaps predictable. Some companies threatened legal action to uphold the already signed exploitation agreements, while others started negotiations with a view to toning down what they considered the excessive demands of the Mwanawasa administration.

In 2008, the Zambia Revenue Authority was being advised by the Norwegian government (noted experts in the area of resource taxation) on the renegotiation of the mining agreements and the new tax regime. The new tax system would put Zambia on the same level as Chile and other major copper producers

---

back to haunt countries that saw the benefit of the mining boom pass them by in terms of revenues to the state.

Box 4.1 outlines the example of mining taxation in Zambia and shows the significant revenues which were forgone by the Zambian government through the agreements negotiated from 1998 privatization. This example is typical of single-commodity-based economies.

The additional estimated annual tax revenues of $400 million to $600 million would have totally revolutionized the development of Zambia and would have permitted the country to graduate from aid dependency.

While the loss of revenue is important, a point of equivalent weight

in terms of government revenue. The estimates of increased revenue from the new taxation system were between $450 million and $600 million per year. This level of increase in the national budget would have completely swamped the contributions of the donor community in terms of development aid and would have enabled the Zambian government to fund all the elements of its National Development Plan. The new tax system was passed by Parliament in May 2008. It was perhaps unfortunate that the new tax system was implemented just as the financial crisis hit the world economy. By the end of 2008, President Mwanawasa was dead and had been replaced as President by Rupiah Banda. Copper prices took a dive from $8,000 per ton to just over $2,000, and the mining industry immediately called for the abandonment of the new tax regime. In theory, the tax regime should have been robust enough to cover both boom and bust periods. However, the Zambian government reacted by cancelling the new tax proposals with the stated objective of maintaining investment in the mining industry. By the end of 2010, copper had regained much of the loss and was standing at more than $7,000 per ton. Currently there is talk by the new government of Michael Sata of reintroducing the Mwanawasa tax reform.

Sources: Fraser and Lungu (2008) which provides a historical view of the Zambian copper industry; Christian Aid (2009).

is the issue of transparency. For too long the relationship between government and the extractive industries has in reality been a relationship between the national elite and the extractive industries. The existence of secret agreements between governments and industry only heightens suspicions that governments and the elites that surround them are selling the patrimony of the country for their own benefit.

The Extractive Industries Transparency Initiative (EITI) is an international organization to which a country can adhere with the view to increasing the transparency of operations in the extractive industries. There are two core issues in the EITI. The first is the production of the annual EITI report in which all companies involved in the extractive industry within a given country publish the amount of taxes which have been remitted to the government. On the other side the government publishes within the report the amount of tax they have received from the individual companies. The second strand of the EITI is the multi-stakeholder group (MSG) which is a national group made up of civil society and others interested in the extractive industries who monitor the results of the report.

Tax administration

Tax administration is an important element in ensuring not only that the tax laws are implemented but also that the maximum level of tax is collected from the various forms of taxation. Historically the ministry of finance in most countries was the responsible body for advising on tax matters in the preparation of the budget and also for the collection of taxes. A more modern approach is the establishment of an Autonomous Revenue Authority (ARA); these have grown in number since their establishment in the early 1990s. In sub-Saharan Africa, fourteen countries have established semi-autonomous revenue authorities (Fjeldstad and Moore 2009). An ARA is generally granted some level of autonomy from central government. It usually has its own funding (sourced from government) which is an annual appropriation covered by the national budget and its own human resource planning. Since the educational requirements for staff are in general higher than for the civil service, the ARA is generally exempt from the recruitment rules that are applied to government service. Staff can be hired and dismissed outside of the usual rules, and staff are generally paid at levels which are higher than those of their colleagues in other government departments. An added advantage of the ARA is that it is a centralized authority responsible for all tax collection. While the ARA is a government agency, it has a separate status more akin to a private body, and in some senses the ARA represents a privatization of the tax collection activity. The ARA is generally administered by a management board which may have nominees not only from government but also from other sources such as industry or civil society. However, while the ARA is semi-autonomous there is still the spectre of political interference in that the chief executive officer is generally appointed by the President. In Uganda, President Musaveni and his coterie are believed to intervene directly in the Uganda Revenue Authority (Therkildsen 2004).

While ARAs have many advantages, there are also some disadvantages (see UN [2000] and Box 4.2). The majority of the disadvantages

---

Box 4.2 Disadvantages associated with an Autonomous Revenue Authority

- Improved revenues could be realized without the costs of establishing a new agenc.
- The establishment of a new agency may be promoted by those who stand to benefit.
- Autonomous agencies have proved more costly than the tax agencies they replace. In some cases, the collection costs to tax revenue ratio has increased. The establishment of a new revenue agency invariably leads to increased costs. In Zambia, the costs are believed to have increased from 2 per cent to over 4 per cent of tax revenue, compared to a limit specified in the ZRA Act of 3 per cent and a target of 1.9 per cent. In contrast, in Tanzania, in the first two years the ratio fell significantly, despite a significant increase in annual budget.
- Establishment of executive agencies is not an alternative to civil service reform, and may contribute to fragmentation of the civil service and to problems of inter-agency cooperation.
- A clear regulatory and supervisory framework is needed to ensure that autonomy is not abused.
- There are also risks associated with giving an institution greater autonomy: the Uganda Revenue Authority reportedly abused its autonomy, causing the Minister of Finance to remove the board and some senior staff in an effort to restore performance. This underscores the need for a sound regulatory framework and accountability.
- Autonomy does not guarantee an end to political interference.
- Legal and political factors may continue to constrain human resource policies.
- The creation of the ARA poses a threat to the synchronization of tax collection and tax policy.

Source: United Nations (2000)

relate either to the high rates of pay accorded to the staff of the ARA (much higher than those of the ordinary civil servant in many cases) which can lead to individuals seeking this benefit for themselves by promoting the concept of the ARA, causing friction between government departments, the police and the ARA in the event of prosecutions, or to the question of political interference. It would be naïve in the African context to think that any state body, let alone one which is responsible for the collection of significant amounts of money, is completely free of political influence. Given the power of the presidency in most African states it is inevitable that political interference extends to ARAs. A disadvantage not mentioned in UN (2000) is the high staff turnover. The staff of the ARA are not only well qualified but they also benefit from considerable levels of training, especially from the World Bank and the IMF. The experience they gain is especially respected by the private sector so they are often poached from the ARA.

ARAs have received significant assistance from donor organizations, especially the World Bank and the IMF during the period of the structural loans and more recently by the British government's DfID. Their history shows that they have been created in poor countries suffering from high fiscal stress.

The aim in creating ARAs was to increase domestic revenues from taxation. However, the jury is still out on whether this goal has been achieved. The reason for this lack of clarity has been attributed to the diversity of ARAs and also to the fact that they are a recent phenomenon which is still evolving (Fjeldstad and Moore 2007).

The political characteristics of taxation

While domestic resource mobilization and taxation are important issues from an economic viewpoint, taxation is also important as a political connection between the ruler and the ruled. Perhaps one of the most famous quotations on taxation sums up this important connection: Thomas Jefferson said, 'there can be no taxation without representation'.

Taxation therefore is not an end in itself or a simple arithmetic calculation carried out by functionaries in a ministry of finance. The mechanisms of domestic resource mobilization are a function of the complex relationships between different segments in society. Since each country has its own history and its own particular character of development, each country is bound to have a different approach to raising resources domestically. As Bird (2008) notes, 'taxation is not simply a means of financing government; it is also a very visible component of the social contract underlying the state. Citizens are more likely to comply with tax laws if they accept the state as legitimate and credible.'

Taxation systems in the OECD countries too are very much a function of how those countries have developed and the impact that various forms of government have had on their economies. The history of most African countries is short and many of the elements of the taxation system have been borrowed from the colonial country. Also the issue of taxation as part of the social contract between government and the people has been missed out more or less completely. If one considers taxation to be a long cycle, many African states are only in the preliminary stages of developing it, both in terms of the collection and the redistributive systems which we recognize in the OECD countries today. A major feature of the developed economies is the constant interaction between the government and taxpayers on resource mobilization and, even more important, resource redistribution. In many developing countries the donors, through their financial contributions, have replaced the people as the interlocutor with the government on resource allocation matters. For its part, in many cases the government has been at pains to explain itself to donors rather than to its ultimate constituents – the people who voted them into power.

While most of the 'democracies' in developing countries embody the ideal behind Jefferson's quote, the reality is very far from this ideal. If the people are excluded from discussion of the political and economic implications of the taxation system (as they are in the case of the secret mining agreements) there arises a feeling of inequality: that they as a group are unable to represent their views to government in the same way that the mining companies can.

Taxation is therefore the spine of the social contract between the state and the people, and because of this the institutions of state which oversee this relationship must be developed. To date the donors have concentrated on improving the tax administration. This is a typical area for donor involvement since it is technical and the donors have a long history of tax policy in their own countries. While this technical work is important, it is vital for the future stability of countries that they develop the institutions which bring the rulers and the ruled together to mobilize domestic resources effectively and to agree on how those resources are distributed.

Is resource mobilization a magic bullet?

The simple answer to this question is no. Domestic resource mobilization alone will not assist countries in exiting aid. It is one thing to collect resources but it must also be completed by an equitable resource allocation system. Several countries have received trillions of dollars in resource rents but are still heavily aid dependent. Much of the trillions of dollars has been diverted away from national development and into the pockets of predatory politicians.

Resource mobilization, if properly managed, can be an important mechanism in assisting a country to exit from aid. The level of losses to developing countries from aberrant or ineffective taxation systems is such that resource mobilization must form a major element of an aid exit strategy. The challenges of developing equitable tax systems are not confined to the Third World. It is important that developed countries play their part in closing the loopholes which permit international companies to prey on developing countries. The development of international conventions such as the EITI will inevitably expose the pernicious practices of government officials and companies alike.

The relationship between a government and its people is one of the most important factors in spurring development. The shared vision of a prosperous future can only be attained if trust exists between the rulers and the ruled. Protection of the patrimony and equitable burden sharing allied with effective resource allocation cement the relationship between government and citizens.

5 | TRADE LIBERALIZATION

Trade not aid. (UNCTAD 1986)

While the positive link between trade liberalization and economic growth does not hold in every case (Sharer 1999), it is clear that no country has accomplished sustained economic growth while shutting itself off from international trade. The lessons of history show us that at one point China was the most advanced country in the world until it turned in on itself, and its re-emergence as a world power can be clearly linked to its engagement with the world trade system.

Trade liberalization is usually among the first strategies proposed for spurring economic growth, especially in the case of developing countries. However, experience has shown that a number of significant obstacles must be overcome before a developing country can benefit from a liberalized trade regime. The World Bank has estimated that trade liberalization can generate up to $500 billion in static and dynamic gains by 2015 (World Bank 2003). Another study estimates that the gains from eliminating all barriers to merchandise trade range from US$250 billion to US$680 billion per year. About two thirds of these gains would accrue to industrial countries. But the amount accruing to developing countries would still be more than twice the level of aid they currently receive (IMF Staff 2001). However, in order to achieve this gain, all agricultural export subsidies and domestic support systems would have to be eliminated, and a tariff ceiling of 10 per cent for agricultural products and 5 per cent for manufacturing would have to be established in the OECD countries with corresponding tariff ceilings of 15 per cent and 10 per cent established by developing countries.

Wacziarg and Horn (2004) concluded that:

> Over the period 1950–1998 countries that have liberalized their trade regimes have experienced, on average, increases in their annual growth rates of the order of 1.5% compared to pre-liberalization times. The post-liberalization increase in investment rates was between 1.5 and 2%, confirming past findings that liberalization works to foster growth in part through its effect on physical capital accumulation. Finally, liberalization raised the trade

to GDP ratio on average by roughly 5% after controlling for a time trend, suggesting that episodes of trade policy liberalization did indeed raise the actual level of openness of liberalizers.

The OECD (2011) has found that if G20 economies reduced trade barriers by 50 per cent, they could gain:

- more jobs: 0.3 per cent to 3.3 per cent rise in jobs for lower-skilled workers and 0.9 per cent to 3.9 per cent for higher-skilled workers, depending on the country;
- higher real wages: 1.8 per cent to 8 per cent increase in real wages for lower-skilled workers and 0.8 per cent to 8.1 per cent for higher-skilled workers, depending on the country;
- increased exports: all G20 countries would see a boost in exports if trade barriers were halved. In the long run, many G20 countries could see their exports rise by 20 per cent and in the Eurozone by more than 10 per cent.

A World Bank Research Report demonstrates that poverty in the 'globalizers', that is, countries who have liberalized their trade regimes to integrate into the world economy, has been significantly reduced (World Bank 2002b). The report points out that sub-Saharan African states' failure to integrate their economies with the world economy has led to an increase in poverty levels in most sub-Saharan African countries.

The evidence is therefore fairly conclusive that trade liberalization will have beneficial impacts on both developed and developing countries with the added advantage for developing countries of significantly decreasing poverty levels. However, most of the studies make assumptions (especially relating to export subsidies and domestic subsidies by developed countries) which have thus far proved elusive.

GATT, the WTO and the Doha Development Agenda

The world trade system was established in 1947 when the General Agreement on Tariffs and Trade (GATT) was negotiated and signed in the aftermath of the Second World War. The purpose of the agreement was to develop a rules-based trading system to re-establish trade between countries which had so recently been enemies. The principal proponents of the GATT system were the USA, the UK, Japan and Germany. Since most developing countries were at this point still colonies of the Great Powers, their involvement in the negotiations was covered by the mother country. In other words, developing countries were marginalized from the very start of the world trading system. GATT was successful in re-establishing the trading relationships between the wartime antagonists and led to the economic boom in the developed world during the 1950s.

It was the intention of the initial GATT negotiations to establish alongside the agreement a third institution to handle the trade side of international economic cooperation, joining the two Bretton Woods institutions, the World Bank and the IMF. Over fifty countries participated in negotiations to create an International Trade Organization (ITO) as a specialized agency of the United Nations. This attempt to set up an agency that would span the two worlds of trade and development failed, and the split between these two areas of economic development has persisted since 1949 to the detriment of the developing countries. GATT became the only multilateral instrument governing international trade from 1948 until the World Trade Organization (WTO) was established in 1995.

The wave of colonial independence which took place in the mid-1960s led to a development chapter being added to the GATT, but in reality the developing countries with their minuscule share of world trade at that time continued to be marginalized. GATT itself was a fairly basic trade agreement which established a rules-based system, set out a series of tariff cuts, and set up a dispute system. However, given the situation of world trade in the post-war period, GATT was at least a vehicle to expand trade and speed up the growth in the shattered economies of Europe and Japan.

An attempt was made to reform GATT in the so-called Tokyo Round which lasted from 1973 to 1979 and in which the number of negotiating parties increased to 102. The Tokyo Round recognized that there were limitations in the original GATT agreement, particularly in relation to agriculture, and that the whole trade process was becoming more complicated. The original GATT covered only trade in products and the distortions that could be found in such trade, for example in anti-dumping.[1] Trade in the 1970s was becoming more complicated, with services accounting for a large proportion of trade. The failure of

---

1 Anti-dumping occurs when manufacturers export a product to another country at a price either below the price charged in its home market, or in quantities that cannot be explained through normal market competition.

the Tokyo Round to accomplish reform of the initial GATT and the tortuous nature and length of the negotiations showed the growing importance and complexity of trade.

It was no surprise following the failure of the Tokyo Round that the push for trade liberalization became the core of the World Bank/ IMF programme of structural adjustment (requiring governments as a condition for receiving aid to cut spending, abolish subsidies, deregulate business, privatize previously state-run enterprises, remove price controls et cetera). The Washington Consensus made trade liberalization a central issue, and since growth would depend on developing countries pursuing the tenets of the 'consensus' the Bretton Woods organizations were obliged to support it.

The Uruguay Round was launched in 1986 in Punte de Este with a view to carrying out a major reform of GATT. For this round, 123 countries were in the negotiation and although some concessions were made to developing countries in terms of import tariff reductions on tropical products, the main thrust of the agreement was to obtain for the major trading countries concessions on the trade in services through the General Agreement on Trade in Services (GATS) and the Agreement on Trade Related Intellectual Property Rights (TRIPS). The Uruguay Round continued the trend of marginalization of the developing countries. Since developing countries were (in the main) either commodity producers or agricultural producers, they gained little or nothing from the conclusion of the Uruguay Round in terms of the reduction of agricultural subsidies. The Uruguay Round was signed in 1994 despite the general disagreement of the developing countries.

The developing countries were unhappy with the unbalanced outcome of the Uruguay Round which they felt favoured the developed countries and created difficulties for them in implementing some of the provisions (Finger 2008). The high level of dissatisfaction led directly to the launch in 2001 of the Doha Round, which for good measure has been entitled the Doha Development Agenda (DDA), in order to give some succour to those developing countries that had complained loudest about the results of the Uruguay Round. By this time the World Trade Organization (WTO) had replaced the GATT Secretariat and was located in the former GATT office in Geneva. The Doha Declaration which launched the Doha Round recognized the problems encountered by the developing countries and declared that 'technical cooperation and capacity building are core elements of the development dimension of the lateral trading system' (WTO 2001). This is perhaps the first recognition by the WTO Ministerial of the development dimension of trade negotiations.

There was acknowledgement by the WTO that signing up to multilateral agreements created problems for developing countries. The solution developed by the WTO was the use of Special and Differential Treatment (SDT) through which developing countries could be assisted with the costs associated with WTO membership, capacity building, and defraying the costs of implementing some of the agreement's provisions, while it allowed developed countries to give preferential market access to specific developing countries. This latter approach was widely used by the European Union (EU) in trade dealings with members of the African, Caribbean and Pacific (ACP) countries that had signed the various development agreements with the EU. However, Special and Differential Treatment has always been a thorny issue for those who felt that these individual arrangements transgressed, to their detriment, the reciprocity arrangements built into the WTO agreements. A number of cases, particularly in the area of bananas and sugar, were taken against the EU because of its SDT arrangements with some ACP countries.

The failure of the Doha Development Agenda, and the negotiations which have now been ongoing for a decade or more, demonstrate that the developing countries are no longer willing to be led by the world's largest trading nations. Although developing countries count for only a small share of the world's trade, they have demonstrated their desire for an outcome which will be at least equally advantageous to them in terms of reforming agricultural subsidies. This negotiating stance has countered the developed countries' insistence on including negotiations on trade and investment, trade and public procurement, trade facilitation, and trade and competition.

Figure 5.1 shows the share of world trade for various regions over the period 1948 to 2006, demonstrating in particular the emergence of Asia as a major player on the world trade stage. This increased market share has been at the expense of North America, Central and South America, Africa and to a lesser extent Europe. While the major trading countries have lost some market share, Africa's share of world trade has fallen from more than 7.5 per cent in 1948 to about 3 per cent in 2006. In the same period, Central and South America's share has fallen from 11 per cent to about 3 per cent.

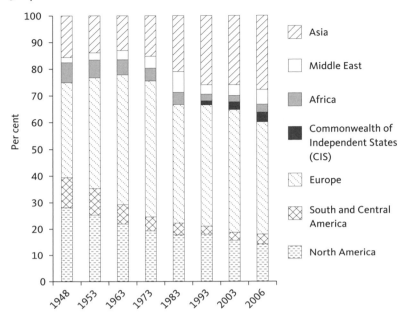

5.1 Share of world trade, 1948–2006 (*source*: IMF database)

Meanwhile Asia's share of trade has doubled from 14 per cent in 1948 to 28 per cent in 2006.

While much of Asia's performance can be attributed to the rise of China, the liberal trade policies of the Asian 'Tigers' have also contributed to this spectacular rise.

Economic Partnership Agreements

Prior to the signing of the first Lomé Convention, the European Community used the Generalized System of Tariff Preferences (GSP) which allowed industrialized countries to grant autonomous trade preferences to all developing countries. This scheme required a waiver from Article 1 of the GATT which prohibits discriminatory arrangements. The European Community was the first to use the GSP in 1971.

The initial agreements signed at Lomé in 1975 between the European Community (now European Union) and the African, Caribbean and Pacific countries (ACP) established a development framework (European Development Fund) but also included a system of non-reciprocal trade preferences set up with the benefit of a GATT waiver.

The waiver, concerned in particular with the Most Favoured Nation (MFN) clause, was supposed to increase ACP competitiveness and promote the diversification of those countries' economies through privileged access for the majority of their products to the European market.

Thus the Lomé Convention established a preferential trade relationship between a specific group of countries and the European Community. However, less developed countries that were not members of the ACP did not have equivalent non-reciprocal market access and were forced to use the GSP system then in force. In February 2001, the European Council adopted Regulation (EC) 416/2001, the so-called EBA Regulation ('Everything but Arms'), granting duty-free access to imports of all products from less developed countries, except arms and ammunitions, without any quantitative restrictions (with the exception of bananas, sugar and rice for a limited period) (European Commission 2007). So, in effect, all countries recognized as less developed countries had in principle complete quota-free duty-free (QFDF) access to the European market. Other issues such as rules of origin on the exported products can obviously affect the decision to grant QFDF in any particular case.

The Cotonou Agreement signed between the EU and ACP in 2000 included a major change in the trading arrangements which had been concluded under Lomé. The new trading arrangement, entitled Economic Partnership Agreements (EPAs), involved the negotiation of separate trading agreements between the EU and six regional groupings (CARICOM, the Pacific, Eastern and Southern Africa, West Africa, Southern Africa and Central Africa). Some of the groups were very diversified and included less developed countries and developed countries as well as some island states. Negotiations on the EPAs began in 2002, but although some interim agreements have been signed the process is still ongoing. The interim EPAs have permitted the WTO to continue the waiver on the Cotonou Trade Agreement which it had granted the EU and which ran out on 31 December 2007. The negotiations on the EPAs have been every bit as tortuous as those on the Doha Development Agenda. The same issues have been stumbling blocks in both negotiations, with some ACP leaders accusing the EU of trying to include the so-called Singapore issues by the back door.[2]

---

2 The Singapore issues are investment, competition policy, government procurement and trade facilitation. See Mutume (2007).

Another contentious issue has been the funds available as part of the development component of the EPAs. While the EU has contended that the additional funding for the EPAs has been included in the 2007–12 Round of the European Development Fund, the ACP countries have sought 'new' funding to allow them to offset the structural costs associated with the new agreements. Nevertheless, hopes are high within the European Union that the EPAs will eventually be signed (European Commission 2010b).

The USA has a corresponding market access programme for less developed countries. The African Growth and Opportunity Act (AGOA) is a US trade act that significantly enhances US market access for (currently) 41 sub-Saharan African (SSA) countries. The Act originally covered the eight-year period from October 2000 to September 2008, but amendments signed into law by US President George W. Bush in July 2004 further extended the AGOA to 2015. At the centre of the AGOA is a series of trade preferences that, coupled with those under the Generalized System of Preferences, allows all marketable goods produced in AGOA-eligible countries to enter the US market duty-free.

The US government provides assistance – most notably through four regional trade hubs – to African governments and businesses that are seeking to make the most of AGOA and to diversify exports to the USA. The US Congress requires the President to determine annually whether sub-Saharan African countries are eligible for AGOA benefits based on progress in meeting certain criteria, including progress towards the establishment of a market-based economy, the rule of law, economic policies to reduce poverty, protection of internationally recognized worker rights, and efforts to combat corruption. In 2009, over 95 per cent of US imports from AGOA-eligible countries entered duty-free, either under AGOA, GSP, or zero-duty Most Favored Nation (MFN) rates. Since its inception, AGOA has helped to increase US two-way trade with sub-Saharan Africa. For example in 2009, US imports from sub-Saharan African under AGOA and the related GSP programme totalled $33.7 billion, more than four times the amount in 2001.

What problems do developing countries face with trade liberalization?

Lack of negotiating capacity The majority of developing countries felt that the Uruguay Round betrayed them and undermined their attempts to join, in an effective manner, the world trading system. The conclusions, especially those relating to the GATS and the TRIPS elements of the agreement, were seen as favouring the developed nations at the expense of the developing countries. This is attributed to the lack of negotiating capacity in the developing countries. Finger (2001) has examined the results of the Uruguay Round and finds that the developing countries' gains were only in the area of traditional market access. In this area, Finger concludes that 'developing countries' tariff reductions covered as large a share of their imports as did those of the developed countries'. Therefore the concessions which developing countries gave in areas such as GATS and TRIPS (areas in which only developed countries make major gains) were not reciprocated in areas such as market access, which for the moment is one of the core interests of the developing countries.

The GATT was located in Geneva and many of the developing countries had no representation there. The ability to follow complex negotiations on a day-by-day basis requires sufficient resources to do so. In general, the trade ministries of developing countries are poorly staffed and more poorly funded. The staff allocated to trade negotiations may be required to follow those negotiations from afar with a view to briefing their minister for the important summit meeting. A major result of the conclusion of the Uruguay Round was the realization by the developing countries that an effort should be made to improve their ability to get on the agenda those issues of major importance to them. A second conclusion was that non-participation in the negotiations was not an option as the countries that did not participate in the Uruguay negotiations found that the outcome damaged them. Page (2003) has examined the negotiating potential of the developing countries over a series of trade negotiations. Although the developing countries were outmanoeuvred in the Uruguay Round, five years later in Seattle their combined action to put on the agenda the issues of most interest to them (export and the domestic subsidies of the developed countries) led to the failure of the meeting. Although the developing countries were not responsible for putting agriculture on the agenda (that can be attributed to the Australian-led Cairns Group which included some Asian and developing countries), they were now in a position, as a bloc, to exert influence on the world trade agenda. This powerful position was reinforced at Doha in 2001 when the developing countries aligned themselves to the position on agriculture taken by the Cairns Group in the earlier Uruguay Round.

One size fits all Developing countries have considerably improved their ability to negotiate, and at the same time have concluded that their main strength is a cohesive approach. The problem with trade negotiations is that the conclusions are generally in the form of regulations which must be implemented. This implies a one-size-fits-all approach to negotiation. Such a negotiating procedure favours participants such as the USA and the European Union which can develop a unified position. The G90 or the G77 can have considerable difficulty in establishing a unified approach to negotiating because of their diverse economic situations. This point was reflected in a speech by Karel De Gucht (2010), who underlined that the approach of the EU would be to 'continue to work with ACP partners to develop tailored trade and development solutions'.

Revenue and employment losses Any general reduction in tariffs, whether import or export, inevitably means a reduction in revenues for the government. Since most developing countries have limited fiscal space, the reduction of revenues from trading can have serious implications. Trading taxes are among the easiest and least costly to collect, so replacing them has a dual effect – loss of revenue and increased tax collection costs if the trading taxes are replaced by a consumption tax as is generally the case. A review of studies carried out on the impact of tariff reductions on employment and fiscal revenues shows that while tariff reductions are likely to reduce trade tax revenue in the short term, increases in country openness to trade can lead to increased total tax revenue (Cirera et al. 2011). This can be interpreted as a negative impact of tariff reductions on government revenue in the short term, while the impact in the medium term is likely to be positive but only if complementary tax policies and increases in customs tax collection efficiency are implemented.

The evidence from the review on employment shows that there is a positive correlation between reductions in tariffs and a reduction in employment. Import tariffs are in place to protect local inefficient industries. Once that protection is removed, these industries are open to external competition. The inevitable result is loss of market share with consequent job shedding. Cirera finds that while there are a large number of studies in this area, the impact of tariff reductions on employment is difficult to measure. The loss of employment can have serious social and economic effects. While developed countries have established systems to finance and to retrench workers, few developing countries have a social safety net for discharged workers. The effects of tariff reductions may be short-lived, but even a brief interruption in employment can have disastrous consequences for workers and their families.

Implementation issues One of the major consequences of the Uruguay Round was that it exposed the very great difficulties encountered by the developing countries in implementing the provisions of the agreement. Uruguay was a major step away from the traditional GATT tariff and market access type of agreement. The final document placed a large burden on developing countries in terms of implementing the provisions, especially in the areas of customs reform, the protection of intellectual property (TRIPS) and sanitary and phytosanitary (SPS) requirements.

Finger (2000) has estimated that conforming with the provisions of the Uruguay Agreement would cost the average developing country $150 million, or the equivalent of one year's development budget. Of the 109 less developed countries, 90 were in violation of the TRIPS, SPS and customs reform provisions. Conforming with the provisions would involve the setting up of state agencies, the construction of buildings to house laboratories, and the recruitment of specialists not readily found on the employment market of less developed countries.

One can only conclude that the provisions of the Doha Round will be equally exigent and will place additional burdens on less developed countries that do not have the means to implement them.

Lack of infrastructure The majority of developing countries lack the basic infrastructure to benefit from improved market access to developed countries. The lack of adequate trunk roads leading to air and port facilities is a serious impediment to those wishing to export indigenous products. The lack of a secondary road system inhibits agriculturalists from getting their produce to the markets. Only 29 per cent of the African road system is paved. The situation is worse for landlocked countries that in many cases have exorbitant costs heaped on them from delays at borders. Inefficient port systems add costs in terms of time to exporters. For example, shipping a car from Japan to Abidjan costs US$1,500, while shipping that same vehicle from Addis Ababa to Abidjan would cost US$5,000 (African Development Bank and Development Centre of the OECD 2010).

African customs administrations are generally inefficient, contributing to barriers to trade within and outside the continent. Customs regulations require excessive documentation, which must be done manually because the process is not automated and information and communication technologies (ICTs) are absent in most customs offices. Furthermore, customs procedures are outdated and lack transparency, predictability and consistency. These inefficiencies result in delays that raise transaction costs. A case in point is southern Africa, where waiting times of up to twenty-four hours to cross a border are the norm. Infrastructure requirements are not limited to roads, rail, ports and airports. The recent pressure on the power systems of many sub-Saharan countries has underlined the lack of future thinking and investment in relation to power requirements. The acceleration of growth in sub-Saharan Africa from minus 1 per cent in the 1990s to between 5 and 6 per cent in the new millennium has created a need for additional power for both industrial and private users. Power projects take five to ten years to come to fruition so the power deficit will grow over the next five years. Communications present another area where significant investment will need to be made. Mobile telephony has been a boon for many developing countries by providing communication at a reasonable cost. In the modern world, business needs access to high-speed communication technologies in order to compete on a global level. The EASSy project presents one possible way forward in terms of infrastructure planning and financing. EASSy is a 10,000km submarine fibre-optic cable system deployed along the east and south coasts of Africa to service the voice, data, video and internet needs of the region. It links South Africa with Sudan via landing points in Mozambique, Madagascar, the Comoros, Tanzania, Kenya, Somalia and Djibouti. The cable incorporates the latest developments in submarine fibre-optic technology, making it economical to connect the eastern and southern coast of Africa into the high-speed global telecommunications network. The system is owned and operated by a group of sixteen African (92 per cent) and international (8 per cent) telecommunications operators and service providers each of whom take an equity subscription. The total cost of the project was $235 million and it is operated by a Special Purpose Vehicle with finance from international lenders as well as the telecommunications operators. This type of cooperative project, benefiting many states at one time, can be used as a model for other innovative infrastructural approaches.

The requirements in terms of financing infrastructure are immense. Foster and Briceño-Garmendia (2010) have concluded that Africa's infrastructure spending needs, at $93 billion a year, are more than double previous estimates by the Commission for Africa.

Despite some encouraging increases in infrastructure finance (official development assistance flows almost doubled, from $4.1 billion in 2004 to $8.1 billion in 2007), there is a huge shortfall in finance for infrastructure. However, the resurgence of economic growth on the continent has led to an upswing in private participation in infrastructural projects. Since the late 1990s, private investment flows to sub-Saharan infrastructure almost tripled, from about $3 billion in 1997 to $9.4 billion in 2006/07 (about 1.5 per cent of regional GDP). In addition, non-OECD countries – notably China and India – began to take a growing interest in financing infrastructure within a framework of South–South cooperation. Their commitments in Africa rose from almost nothing in the early 2000s to about $2.6 billion annually between 2001 and 2006. Yet despite these positive trends, there is still an annual financing gap of $31 billion between Africa's needs and investment. There is little or no possibility of this gap being filled either by development assistance or by government financing. The only other possibility is to involve the private sector in a major way in infrastructural investments which have a revenue model. This is relatively easy in the case of power and communications infrastructure where there are direct revenue flows. It is not so easy in the road sector where tolls would be the only way the private sector could recoup its investment.

Supply side constraints The opening of access to major markets for developing countries is useless if those countries do not have the products or service necessary to serve the markets. For most African countries, rather than tariff barriers the core problem is the lack of capacity to produce a surplus of exportable goods of sufficient quality to meet the stringent standards required by the developed economies. As a result, most African countries have not been able to benefit fully from the duty- and quota-free market access offered by developed countries' preferential initiatives such as the African Growth and Opportunities Act (AGOA) and the Everything but Arms initiative. In 2001, the EBA extended to less developed countries duty-free access in 919 product categories. One year later, imports were recorded in only 80 (Stiglitz and Charlton 2006). In the same way, potential cuts in agricultural subsidies in developed countries may have little real impact if the supply capacity and conformity constraints (particularly in the area of sanitary and phytosanitary provisions) in developing countries remain.

Market size is an additional problem for LDCs. It is difficult for local industry to develop the range of quality products that would be able to compete on the world market without a domestic market on which to test and improve quality. The role of regional integration is important in this respect as it provides a greater potential market for entrepreneurs to test the viability of their products in preferential conditions. The 'resource curse' means that the commodity-exporting countries lack the incentive to diversify their economies.

Reducing the supply-side constraints requires a complex mix of government initiatives aimed at creating an environment in which business flourishes; improving educational standards so that the pool of labour has the required skillsets; improving the energy, transport and ICT services; providing financial services for small and medium-sized enterprises; providing business support services such as management training and market information, and creating linkages to global supply chains.

This prescription has already worked in South East Asia where per capita GDP growth has risen from 4.6 per cent in the 1970s and 1980s to 6.2 per cent in 1991–2001. The export growth performance of South East Asia means that the percentage of citizens living on less than $1 a day has reduced from 55.6 per cent in 1970–80 to 15.6 per cent in 2001 (UNIDO 2007).

Aid for trade

A study by the World Bank has indicated that aid directed towards promoting trade enhances the trade performance of recipient countries (Helble et al. 2009). The study concluded that a 1 per cent increase in aid directed towards trade policy and regulatory reform (equivalent to about US$11.7 million more such aid) could generate an increase in global trade of about US$818 million. This yields a 'rate of return' on every dollar of this type of aid of about US$697 in additional trade. The discussion above suggests that the problems faced by less developed countries in becoming part of the globalized trading network are most likely insurmountable within the context of their national budgets. The very wide range of development initiatives which must be undertaken concurrently would be beyond the less developed countries' capacity. While this fact was not clearly understood in the Uruguay Round, it became quickly apparent in the months and years following the conclusion of the Uruguay Agreement.

The answer to the conundrum of how the LDCs could accomplish the wide range of reforms needed to trade effectively was 'aid for trade' which broadly defined was an initiative by the developed countries to provide financial assistance to developing countries specifically targeted at areas which impeded their effectively benefiting from the globalized trading system. In general, aid for trade comprises the following concrete actions: technical assistance, capacity building, institutional reform, investments in trade-related infrastructure, and programmes aimed at redressing the adjustment costs and the social impact of the implementation of trade liberalization.

'Aid for trade' and the WTO The Hong Kong Ministerial Declaration of the World Trade Organization invited the Director General to create a task force to provide recommendations on how to operationalize aid for trade and how aid for trade might contribute to the development dimension of the Doha Development Agreement (WTO 2005).

The Task Force reported on 27 July 2006. It took note of a wide definition of 'aid for trade' and developed eight pages of recommendations (WTO 2006) in the light of the Paris Declaration on Aid Efficiency. The main recommendations covered the funding of 'aid for trade' initiatives, the mainstreaming of 'aid for trade' by donors and by recipient countries more particularly through the Poverty Reduction Strategy Programme process, and the enhancement of the Integrated Framework (IF; see below) process, in particular the use of the diagnostic tool and the monitoring of 'aid for trade' expenditures and projects. The recommendations covered both the improving of trade negotiations by capacity building and at the same time tackling of the constraints in terms of infrastructure and the supply side.

The Task Force and its report was a step forward in bridging the gap between the development and trade communities which had existed since the failure to establish the International Trade Organization. The report was comprehensive in its approach but perhaps the rather large number of recommendations could have been pared down to what could be established in the short term, medium term and long term. Overcoming the infrastructural constraints would obviously fall into the latter category.

An ILEAP Background Brief (Finger 2006) concluded that the major shortcoming of the Task Force report was that it did little to operationalize its recommendations. ILEAP found fault with the report's language, which overused the words 'effective' and 'strengthened', pointing out that in 32 bulleted recommendations the words 'effective' and 'effectively' appear 21 times while the word 'strengthen' appears 18 times.

The Integrated Framework (IF) The first WTO Ministerial Conference, held in 1996, recognized that the least developed countries faced difficulties integrating into the global economy. This led to the adoption of the WTO Plan of Action for Least-Developed Countries. The following year, the WTO convened a High Level Meeting to discuss the specific needs of the LDCs and to formulate a programme to strengthen their trade capacities, including supply-side and market access capacities. The outcome of this meeting was what became known as the Integrated Framework for Trade-Related Technical Assistance to Least-Developed Countries, or IF. The IF was launched in 1997 by six multilateral institutions: the IMF, the ITC, UNCTAD, the United Nations Development Programme, the World Bank and the World Trade Organization. The remit of the IF was to assist developing countries to assess their needs in terms of trade-related assistance and to bring donors and developing countries together in order to tackle some of the identified needs. Although donors had been funding programmes and projects that were relevant to trade, for example roads, ports and airports, these projects were not undertaken for specifically trade-related objectives. The IF was the first attempt to 'mainstream' trade in the development of the donors' multi-annual or annual strategic programmes.

The primary tool of the IF is the Diagnostic Trade Integration Study (DTIS). These studies examine the situation of a developing country relative to its ability to implement international trading legislation. The study is basically a needs assessment and develops a series of initiatives which can be supported under a technical assistance programme by a donor. The DTIS is a wide-ranging study which looks at many aspects of the social and economic conditions such as macroeconomic developments, trade policy and market access, transport and trade facilitation, product standards, investment climate, trade support institutions, trade and poverty, and sector issues. The process brings together as many stakeholders as possible to formulate a future approach to trade-related problems.

Finger (2008) discusses the problems identified in the DTIS carried out in Lesotho. They include:

• The government does not maintain a centralized inventory of ongoing support programmes;
• The analytical capacity of some donors' local representatives does not include trade issues; and
• Expansion of the local garment industry depends on improved infrastructure – including electricity, telecommunications and water.

Lesotho is a small landlocked country whose infrastructure must necessarily be integrated with that of South Africa. Hence improved trade is complicated by the need for international arrangements.

The IF was renewed in 2000 and renamed the Enhanced Integrated Framework (EIF). The main thrust of the enhanced programme was to ensure that trade was mainstreamed into the Poverty Reduction Strategy Programme process which was now the cornerstone of development assistance.[3] The EIF is currently helping 47 LDCs worldwide, supported by a multi-donor trust fund – the EIF Trust Fund (EIFTF) – with contributions from 22 donors and managed by UNDP. The majority of the 47 countries are in Africa with some in South East Asia and several in the Pacific. The EIF has a two-window approach. Window 1 consists of a diagnostic, the DTIS, led by the World Bank. Funding under Window 1 is generally limited to $300,000. Window 2 is a follow-up programme that addresses some of the capacity-building needs identified in the DTIS Action Matrix. Funding for Window 2 activities is generally limited to $1 million for each country. This funding is considered

---

3 Each developing country benefiting from World Bank and IMF funding is obliged to establish a Poverty Reduction Strategy Programme.

as bridging funding, while the more detailed findings of the DTIS are incorporated into the PRSP.

Joint Integrated Technical Assistance Programme (JITAP) The JITAP initiative which was launched in March 1998 by the World Trade Organization, UNCTAD and the International Trade Centre is a joint programme to help meet the needs expressed by several African countries during the UNCTAD IX conference in Midrand, South Africa in 1986. The three organizations along with donors set up a Common Trust Fund to mobilize donor support. The individual projects were transformed into the JITAP programme and implementation was initiated. Today, thirteen donors contribute to the Common Trust Fund.

JITAP is a sister programme of the Enhanced Integrated Framework but is concentrated on a small number of African countries. The programme assists in building national capacity in the area of understanding the Multilateral Trading System (MTS) and in assisting in the implementation of undertakings related to WTO agreements. The programme also assists exporters.

JITAP consists of a series of capacity-building modules containing a range of implementation actions or programme elements, with each module covering all partner countries. The modules are generally organized by staff of the three major trade organizations. The complete programme is intended to bring national trade officials up to speed on the negotiations of multilateral agreements. The programme aims to set up a national network of trainers and experts in WTO-related issues.

These features are designed to enhance synergies among partner countries, among the Geneva-based organizations, and between the two groups, as well as synergies among programme activities. They are also designed to ensure efficient use of resources, through economies of scale and scope in management and programme implementation; sustainability through networking and other capacity-building features; and replicability of the JITAP programme in other countries, should it be decided to expand the programme. A very important feature is the role of JITAP as a framework for catalysing other trade-related technical assistance, including under the Integrated Framework.

JITAP is funded through a Common Trust Fund (CTF) supported by a number of donor countries. The CTF is composed of two windows: Window one, where funds are contributed by donors to support programme development, generic activities and activities in countries facing shortage of resources; and Window 2, where contributions are earmarked for specific countries. The activities are only implemented when the resources are made available in cash to the three executing organizations. Most partner countries have contributed to the programme activities in the form of counterpart funding.

JITAP currently covers fifteen countries in Africa. An evaluation of the programme in Tanzania highlighted mixed results (Lyimo and Sungula 2008) (at the time of the Tanzanian programme seven other countries were part of the programme). The programme was considered effective in increasing knowledge of the MTS. However, one of the pluses suggested by JITAP, namely the concentration of management in Geneva, was seen by Tanzania as a negative. The lack of counterpart funding from Tanzania meant that many elements of the programme could not be undertaken as funding was limited to the finance available from the Common Facility Fund. Also, and perhaps understandably given the make-up of the managing organizations, the Tanzanians felt the elements of the programme relating to the trade policy process were successful while those elements pertaining to the development of trade were not successfully covered. Towards the end of the Tanzanian JITAP programme the government assigned $300,000 from an old IF programme which succeeded in redressing the negative aspects.

Trade facilitation Facilitating trade is about streamlining and simplifying international trade procedures in order to allow for easier flow of goods and trade at both national and international levels. This means the simplification of requirements and formalities in respect of the release and clearance of goods, including, to the extent possible, collaboration on the development of procedures enabling the submission of import or export data to a single agency; improved working methods and ensuring transparency and efficiency of customs operations; reduction, simplification and standardization of data in the documentation required by customs; application of modern customs techniques, including risk assessment, simplified procedures for entry and release of goods, post-release controls, and company audit methods and provisions that facilitate the importation of goods by simplified or pre-arrival customs procedures. Box 5.1 describes a typical trade facilitation project.

Box 5.1 A trade facilitation project in Tunisia

A typical trade facilitation project is that carried out by the World Bank in Tunisia. Despite initiatives in the 1980s to streamline the flow of information on merchandise trade, trade transactions remained costly and inefficient through the 1990s. Customs clearance requirements, port logistics and procedures, and quality assurance checks strained resources and imposed significant costs on both the government and the private sector.

In the late 1990s, cargo spent an average of eight days in Tunisian ports – and in many cases up to 18 days – due to customs, port, and technical control procedures, compared with a few hours in Singapore and four days in Argentina and Brazil. Similarly, customs clearance required an average of four days in Tunisia – and in many cases up to seven days – while it took just 25 minutes in Singapore, one hour in Morocco, and three hours in Argentina. Moreover, Tunisian customs officials physically inspected 50–80 per cent of imported merchandise, while the corresponding shares were less than 5 per cent in Singapore, 15 per cent in Morocco, and 30 per cent in Argentina.

The reforms were based on the adoption of international standards for trade documentation (a process initiated a few years earlier with support from the European Commission) and significant coordination among various stakeholders. Two documents previously required by the authorities were eliminated, and three (the Certificate for External Trade, submitted

---

Stiglitz and Charlton (2006) list the benefits of improving trade facilitation as: increasing trade in goods and services; promoting competition which can spur productivity gains as well as lower prices; enhancing efficiency in both the public and the private sectors; improving the business environment and thus encouraging FDI and assisting small and medium enterprises to participate in international trade. Since many, or indeed all, of the initiatives necessary to facilitate trade are in the hands of the government it is important that countries take ownership of the trade facilitation process. Donors and multilateral aid agencies can provide technical assistance, but the government

by importers and required by the Central Bank for foreign exchange control, the customs declaration, and technical control documents) were redesigned to reduce duplication and standardize terminology, with the customs declaration aligned with international standards. In addition, two of the four documents required for goods removal were eliminated. The development of electronic formats for trade documents made it easier to share information among stakeholders and process the information contained in the documents.

The project cost $35 million and has been declared an unqualified success. At the end of the project, imported goods were cleared from ports in an average of three days, compared with eight days before the project began. Electronic processing of manifests was accomplished in one or two days. Payment of customs and port duties and storage charges now takes only a few hours, rather than a full day. The time needed to prepare and process customs declarations has dropped to fifteen minutes, down from as long as three days. In 2003 the physical inspection of goods reached the target level of 15 per cent, down from 50–80 per cent in late 1998.

The improvement in the transit times made Tunisian goods more competitive in the world market but also reduced the costs of shipment for Tunisian producers, giving them profit improvements where it counted – on the bottom line.

Source: World Bank (2004)

has all the administrative powers necessary to reform the customs procedures in order to speed up trade. The trade facilitation efforts should be part of government policy and should not need to be part of international trade agreements.

A successful trade facilitation project requires a high level of commitment from the government and a change leader to ensure that the project attains its objectives. Customs clearance and border transit have long been a key area of corruption with officials demanding bribes to facilitate the movement of goods. A lot of vested interests must be overcome in order to make a trade facilitation project successful.

'Aid for trade' financial volumes

The presentation of the recommendations of the Aid for Trade Task Force and its call on donors to redouble their effort in the area of Aid for Trade led a number of multilateral and bilateral donors to make financial commitments. For example, the European Union pledged €2 billion annually to trade-related assistance (TRA) by 2010. The pledge consisted of €1 billion from the European Commission and €1 billion from the 27 member states. Support for TRA from

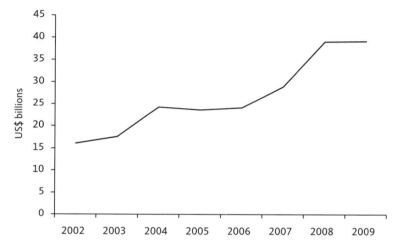

5.2 Total 'aid for trade' volumes (*source*: DAC database)

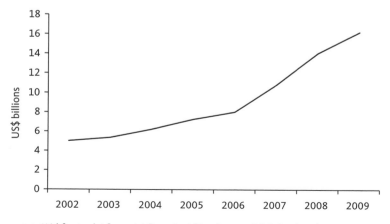

5.3 'Aid for trade' financial flows to Africa (*source*: DAC database)

the EU and its member states totalled €2.15 billion in 2008 – €1.143 billion from member states and €1.007 billion from the EU (European Commission 2010a).

Total trade-related assistance increased from just over $15 billion in 2002 to $40 billion in 2009 (Figure 5.2). The sectors supported included: transport and storage; communications; energy; banking and financial services; business and other services; agriculture, forestry and fishing; industry; mineral resources and mining; trade policies and regulation; and tourism.

Although in Africa finance for the 'aid for trade' programme increased from $4 billion in 2002 to $16 billion in 2009 (Figure 5.3), the continent still only accounts for one third of the 'aid for trade' funding. Considering that Africa is the continent which is furthest behind in gaining access to the globalized market it would be worth asking whether the current financial flows are sufficient to remove all the constraints to trade.

Conclusions

Exiting poverty and aid dependency through exports has been the chimera that has been held out to the developing countries. The $500 billion needed to improve trade, as calculated by the World Bank, is a mirage for most developing countries who are still first and foremost commodity exporters. The proponents of trade liberalization (and there are a lot of them) point to China, India and South East Asia, which have exported themselves up the GDP per capita list. There is a contention that replicating the open-market policies espoused by the Washington Consensus will lead to export nirvana. Those pointing at China ignore the size of its domestic market, the availability of cheap labour in China, the effects of environmental degradation and the currency manipulation which are part and parcel of the Chinese 'miracle'.

Trade liberalization along the lines of the Uruguay Round was not advantageous to the developing countries. They have neither the infrastructure nor the goods to benefit from market access. Agriculture (in which the majority of citizens of developing countries still work) has been the issue of major contention at the Doha negotiations. The resistance of the major agricultural lobbies to creating a level playing field for the agricultural produce of developing countries has denied the latter a valid path to development. Glennie (2008) contends that aid is good business for the developed countries since aid budgets are a minuscule proportion of the gains which developed countries make from market manipulation.

'Trade not aid' is a valid call. But it must be trade that assists in helping developing countries reduce their aid dependency. In the first case that probably means creating a level (or more or less level) playing field in agriculture. A look back at Chapter 1 shows the impediments to foreign direct investment in developing countries. Those very same impediments inhibit the growth of business. Political instability, disrespect for property laws, expropriation and a rancid environment for business all inhibit investment whether by foreigners or locals. So, from a local viewpoint, increased trade will not solve the development problem in the short term, principally because the constituents of increased trade (products, services and the delivery mechanisms) are not in place.

Aid for trade now covers a multitude of sectors. The funding of aid for trade bundles together infrastructure, education, private sector development, agriculture and trade policy development. All of these are elements of a developed society but they take time to implement.

Despite claims to the contrary, trade is not the magic bullet that will reduce aid dependency in the short term. Neither is aid for trade simply a sop to the developing countries. Rules-based trading systems are important but the negotiation of trade agreements should not lead to the inequalities which were characteristic of the Uruguay Round. Developing a business culture takes time and effort. Supply-side constraints cannot be lifted immediately but must be part of the process of development. That is the dilemma for the developing countries.

As long as aid volumes form a significant part of the GDP (more than 10 per cent) there is a disincentive on the part of countries to carry out difficult reforms which are needed. Aid can assist countries in addressing the constraints they face but it should not become an impediment or a crutch to the change process which must take place. The countries of South East Asia have demonstrated that government action aimed at root-and-branch reform can be successful in penetrating established markets. Less developed countries must look at these examples of success and draw lessons which they can implement.

6 | THE BRICS

The Chinese are our friends. (Dambisa Moyo)

China is both a tantalizing opportunity and a terrifying threat. (Moeletsi Mbeki, South African businessman)

BRICS is an acronym formed from the initial letters of Brazil, Russia, India, China and South Africa. The first four are experiencing enormous economic growth and have the potential within the next fifty years to outperform the established G8 countries. South Africa is the powerhouse of Southern Africa and if it can overcome its current economic problems it could join the other four countries in terms of economic muscle. The BRICS are not only important in the development aid context because of their growing economic power, they are important because they add a new element in the aid mix. Their development models – each of them has its own approach – bear no relation to the development model of the traditional donors. That does not necessarily mean that their models are better but it does allow for a comparison of the different approaches. Also such an examination might point the way towards development initiatives that might constitute an aid exit strategy.

It is perhaps incongruous to consider them as a group because while they have some elements in common they have different approaches to their involvement with the countries of the developing world. Therefore, their development models are not consistent with each other since they do not form a coordinated group like the DAC donors.

Despite their differences in economic development, geography, political philosophy and demography, there are some elements of similarity in the approaches of the BRICS to development, listed below.

The BRICS are themselves developing countries and four of them (Brazil, India, China and South Africa) are recipients of development aid. For example, in 2000 Brazil received $305 million in bilateral and multilateral ODA and by 2009 this figure was virtually constant at $364 million. In 2000, China received $2.15 billion in ODA and by 2009 this had fallen to $1.27 billion.[1] India and South Africa were also major recipients of ODA. Therefore they bring a different perspective to the concept of development. They have already been there and done it, and some of them are still doing it. Their development models are unique because they are a product of their dual roles of donor and recipient.

While the aid they receive is reported, because they are not members of the OEDC DAC group of donors they do not report the aid that they give. This makes it very difficult to make a definitive examination of their efforts to assist other developing countries.

The BRICS are not on a moral crusade. They provide aid for political reasons, to protect investment, to gain access to natural resources or out of South–South solidarity. Unlike Western donors they do not mention the end of poverty as their ultimate aim.

BRICS aid is unconditional, or unconditional in the sense of requiring improvements in financial management or governance. There may be economic conditions or political conditions which are not stated in the aid package but to the outside world the aid is unconditional. This lack of conditionality can be advanced as lack of intervention in internal affairs (as in the case of China) or simply as a belief in a development model which is at odds with the Western efforts to turn every developing country into Denmark in term of democracy and financial probity. This leads to the BRICS obtaining a free rider effect from the efforts of the Western donors to improve governance. This free rider effect can be complemented by the fact that the BRICS tend to concentrate their efforts on the productive sector while leaving the support of the social sectors in the hands of the DAC donors. The productive sector needs educated and healthy workers if it is to expand, and this point is recognized by the DAC donors. Therefore the BRICS benefit from improvements in the education and health sectors.

BRICS do not have a strategic approach to development aid. In the BRICS model of development there are no Country Strategy Papers or Poverty Reduction Strategy Papers, there is no consultation process with stakeholders and there is no five years' strategic programme. The model, inasmuch as a model exists, is based on a series of punctual projects or programmes launched after a modicum of discussion

---

1 Figures from the OECD/DAC database.

between the BRICS local embassy and the recipient government. The 'programme' is generally signed off during a high-level visit by the president of the relevant BRICS country. In 2008, a state visit by the Chinese President Hu Jintao to Zambia was the occasion for the signing of a raft of programmes presented as Chinese aid to Zambia. The visit was also the occasion for the signing of a number of economic cooperation agreements which were nominally separate from the aid package. Considered on this level the BRICS approach is more akin to the early days of development assistance where each agency went its own way often to the detriment of the general development effort.

A corollary of the problem of strategic approach is that the BRICS are not part of the aid coordination agreed at Paris and Accra. The BRICS aid is tied to the sourcing of products and services from the BRICS donor. The aid is considered to be 'tied' since it would be the subject of single sourcing. With the concentration on aid efficiency, this practice has generally fallen into disrepute since value for money can only be maintained if aid is untied and goods and services can be obtained on the open market. All the traditional donors have to varying degrees untied either all or some of their aid. However, the BRICS have eschewed this move and continue to tie their aid.

Project or programme evaluation is totally absent from the BRICS development model. In no case is any BRICS-supported project examined for its utility. Without the evaluation phase to act as feedback, there is no information which can be used in the development of future initiatives.

There is the issue that one developing country assisting another developing country might take over some of the latter's markets. While this problem hardly exists for the traditional donors which have moved to a service and knowledge economy, the situation of the BRICS is very different. There is a great deal of evidence of African markets being overwhelmed by cheap Chinese products. While the existence of such products at a relatively cheap price brings goods within the economic capacity of many Africans, it also has the effect of suppressing a local market capable of producing such goods.

The BRICS are an important and growing element in the development assistance scene. They not only bring finance in a time of financial stringency for the traditional donors but they also bring new approaches and non-traditional models. They seem actively to oppose the prevailing logic of the traditional donors, and perhaps there is some benefit in that. It would be stupid of the donor community not to examine critically its long-cherished practices but it would also be unwise of the emerging donors to throw out the development baby with the bathwater.

The Chinese model

Robert Mugabe has his look-East policy, and many other Africans view the Chinese as their friends and suggest their model of development as a replacement for the failed aid policies of the traditional donors. Brautigam (2011) writes a defence of Chinese policy in Africa – the Chinese are certainly flavour of the month. The question is, are the Chinese the natural replacement for the traditional donors? Is their development model superior to the traditional model and will it work where the DAC model has failed?

China by growing at a rate of 10 per cent is set to become the largest economy in the world by 2016, five to ten years in advance of most projections.[2] This fact will obviously have importance for all the countries dealing with China and in particular the developing countries. Historically China has had political relations with the majority of developing countries not only in the Asia region but also in Africa. Many of the African liberation movements in the 1960s were funded by the Chinese state, and a competition with Russia in influencing nascent African states took place in the 1960s and 1970s. At this point China went into a self-imposed retrenchment as the Cultural Revolution tore the country apart. The reform movement and the return to a quasi-market approach in the mid-1980s opened China towards the world economy, leading to the extraordinary Chinese economic renaissance of the twenty-first century.

The Chinese development model is centred on the Beijing Consensus, a political theory 180 degrees at odds with the Washington Consensus. The term 'Beijing Consensus' was coined by Joshua Cooper Ramo and he described it as follows (Costa Vaz and Inoue 2007):

China's new development approach is driven by a desire to have

---

2 'The Age of America ends in 2016: IMF predicts the year China's economy will surpass US', *Daily Mail*, 26 April 2010. www.dailymail.co.uk/news/article-1380486/ The-Age-America-ends-2016-IMF-predicts-year-Chinas-economy-surpass-US. html#ixzz1PFRbxwhK. 'Brazil joins the scramble for Africa's natural resources', *The Telegraph*, 9 February 2010.

equitable, peaceful high-quality growth; critically speaking, it turns traditional ideas like privatisation and free trade on their heads. It is flexible enough that it is barely classifiable as a doctrine. It does not believe in uniform solutions for every situation. It is defined by a ruthless willingness to innovate and experiment, by a lively defense of national borders and interests, and by the increasingly thoughtful accumulation of tools of asymmetric power projection. It is pragmatic and ideological at the same time, a reflection of an ancient Chinese philosophical outlook that makes little distinction between theory and practice. Though it is decidedly post-Deng Xiaoping in structure, the Beijing Consensus still holds tightly to his pragmatic idea that the best path for modernisation is one of 'groping for stones to cross the river,' instead of trying to make one big, shock-therapy leap. Most important, it is both the product of and defined by a society that is changing so fast that few people, even those inside China, can keep up with it.

China's foreign policy is based on the five Principles of Peaceful Coexistence enunciated during China's meeting with India in 1954,[3] and the subsequent Bandung Conference.

The developing countries are thus confronted with two opposing views of development: the traditional approach with its concentration on democracy, human rights, good governance and financial probity, and a conflicting view which concentrates solely on economic activity as a driving force for development. The Chinese model has undoubted attractions for a large number of African leaders. There is no mention of democratic elections or terms of office, no discussions on corruption and financial mismanagement. There is no need for a major aid structure other than the local Chinese embassy. There is no need to consider value for money since projects funded by China will be open only to Chinese companies. No time is wasted on aid efficiency and aid coordination. In short, the traditional aid model has been stripped of all its trappings.

There are two other aspects of Chinese 'aid' that should be noted. Chinese aid efforts have been concentrated on resource-rich developing countries. Unlike DAC traditional aid, China does not spread

---

3 The principles are: mutual respect for others' territorial integrity and sovereignty; mutual non-aggression; mutual non-interference in each other's internal affairs; equality and mutual benefit, and peaceful coexistence.

its largesse to all countries. This lack has been noted and is being addressed in part by including non-resource-rich countries in the overseas visit programme. Second, Chinese aid is generally accompanied by an increase in the Chinese diaspora. Many of the workers who come to build a road stay on to become small merchants. In time their families joins them and they become permanent residents of their new country.

It is clear that China is not a member of the DAC and has no interest whatever in becoming a part of the traditional aid architecture. In fact China, for some very good reasons, does not consider itself to be an aid donor. The DAC definition of ODA includes the fact that aid should have a grant element of 25 per cent. Chinese assistance does not fit this definition since there is generally no specific grant element.

China's approach to Africa's development has been established within the context of the Forum of Chinese Africa Cooperation (FOCAC). The first ministerial conference of FOCAC was held in Beijing during 10–12 October 2000. During 15–16 December 2003, the second ministerial conference of FOCAC was held in Addis Ababa, Ethiopia. The first summit and third ministerial conference was held on 3–5 November 2006 when thirty-four African presidents attended. In his opening speech President Hu Jintao declared eight commitments from the Chinese government, among which were to double its 2006 assistance to Africa by 2009; provide US$3 billion of preferential loans and US$2 billion of preferential buyer's credits to Africa in the next three years; set up a China–Africa development fund and establish economic zones.[4] The conclusion of the summit was the establishment of the Beijing Action Plan (2006–09) which would be made up of the elements of the Hu Jintao speech.

It is difficult to give a clear picture of China's development assistance to African countries. Although the Ministry of Foreign Affairs is the lead development organization, more than twenty-two ministries are involved in development activities; many Chinese regions and even cities have their own development assistance programmes, and companies whether state or private have been known to launch their own initiatives. This plethora of actors makes establishment of the full

---

4 Forum on Chinese African Cooperation, www.focac.org/eng/tptb/t404200.htm

picture difficult since there is no collating body for statistics on funding and projects. It is therefore virtually impossible to disentangle what would be development assistance in the OECD/DAC definition and what would be merely financial flows. Chinese development assistance can take different forms: grants extended for social projects (health, education, housing) in the form of material assistance, technical assistance and personnel training; interest-free loans given notably for infrastructure projects; concessional loans provided by China EXIM Bank; and debt relief.

Kragelund (2008) finds that Chinese aid flows to Africa in 2005 substantially exceeded the $731 million reported by official sources, and may have reached $8.1 billion. Wang (2007) estimates that China's ODA to sub-Saharan Africa averaged between $1.0 billion and $1.5 billion per year in 2004–05. Other estimates include that of Alden (2007), who puts Chinese aid at US$4 billion in 2007; Brautigam estimates it to be US$1.6 billion (Brautigam 2011) for the same year, while Lancaster (2007) puts it between US$1.5 billion and US$2 billion.

China's engagement in Africa, however defined, has not had any impact on the efforts of some African countries to diversify their economies (Berthelemy 2011). There is a possibility that Economic Zones (EZ) set up as a result of the second FOCAC Summit might help some countries to diversify, but since loans are only available to Chinese companies in the EZs this means that diversification will be in the hands of the Chinese. What is needed is a spur to African entrepreneurship. Economic diversification is vitally important in the countries with high trade volumes with China because they are the countries with a high dependence on one commodity. A more positive approach would be for the EZs to promote indigenous goods and not be a simple repository for Chinese companies to produce their products abroad. The Chinese trade mechanisms may have a positive effect on economic diversification. However, the experience of EBA shows that it had a very limited effect on economic diversification in LDCs. The impediments to economic diversification are the lack of entrepreneurship, a business environment which militates against start-ups, an unskilled workforce and a lack of finance. Anything that Chinese involvement in the economy of the LDCs can do to ameliorate these factors will promote economic diversification.

According to the IMF, China currently sits on the highest level of dollar-denominated currency reserves in the world at US$2.422

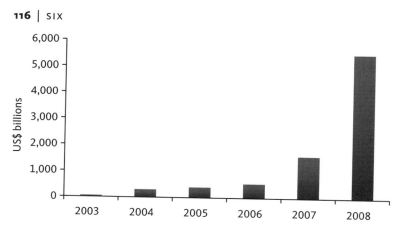

6.1 Chinese FDI to Africa (*source*: UNCTAD 2011, World Investment Report 2010, Geneva)

trillion. This is almost twice the reserves of the next country, Japan; the first European country, Germany, only appears at number 11 with reserves of $181 billion, less than 10 per cent of the Chinese figure. The corresponding figure for the USA is $130 billion. Since the majority of Chinese FDI is made by state or semi-state companies the availability of such a high level of reserves puts China in an unassailable position as the world's potential leader in outward FDI.

Davies (2009) has calculated that China's FDI, which averaged only US$453 million a year in 1982–89, and US$2.3 billion in 1990–99, rose to US$5.5 billion in 2004, US$12.3 billion in 2005, US$17.6 billion in 2006 and US$24.8 billion in 2007. Preliminary figures for 2008 show a rise to US$40.7 billion. If financial FDI (not counted before 2006) is included, the 2008 total was US$52.2 billion, nearly double the US$26.5 billion in 2007.

Figure 6.1 shows the dramatic increase in Chinese FDI in Africa over the period 2003–08. Chinese FDI increased by a factor of 11 in five years to stand at $5.5 trillion in 2008. Despite this impressive increase, Africa in 2008 accounted for only 4.5 per cent of total Chinese FDI.

China has a great potential to assist the development of the LDCs in Africa. Major investments are being undertaken in the resource exploitation sector, in infrastructure, health and training. Nevertheless, despite the many positive points discussed above, Chinese engagement with Africa has some negative aspects. The *New York Times* reported 'Zambia Uneasily Balances Chinese Investment and Workers' Resentment'.[5] *The Economist* headlined 'Try to pull together: Africans are asking whether China is making their lunch or eating it'.[6]

Much of the criticism of China in terms of development can be laid at China's own door. Its insistence on the Five Principles has led it to develop close relations with Sudan, Zimbabwe and Equatorial Guinea – three pariah regimes already deserted by Western companies. China took over the oil concession developed by Chevron in Sudan and continues to support the regime economically, politically and with arms supplies. Chinese companies have been viewed as predators with indigenous companies being 'eaten by the dragon'.[7] China is buying stakes in existing oil companies as a means of guaranteeing future supply. Negotiations have been running for several years to permit China to buy one sixth of Nigeria's oil reserves for $50 billion; in addition, significant infrastructure loans backed by natural resources have been given to Angola and the Democratic Republic of Congo (Zhao 2011).

One of the central questions of Chinese 'aid' is whether China is part of the solution or part of the problem. Building infrastructure and setting up Chinese-operated value-added companies in economic zones is development with a small *d* rather than the transformational development which is the aim of the traditional aid model. Chinese investment has the potential to accelerate African development. However, simply investing in African resource projects has not reduced aid dependency in resource-rich countries. Building prestige projects such as stadia and imposing presidential palaces will lead to economic possibilities for Chinese firms but may have a limited effect on the national causes of poverty.

The Indian model

India's booming economy, its appetite for overseas investment and its desire to export Indian technology and know-how have led it to seek economic opportunities in Africa and other developing countries. The Indian model of development assistance is closer to the Chinese model than to the traditional DAC model. India's development cooperation

---

5 *New York Times*, 20 November 2010.
6 *Economist*, 20 April 2011.
7 *Economist*, 11 November 2010.

has been governed by the so-called Panchsheel Principles which have been the guiding principles of India's foreign policy since the 1950s. These five principles are exactly the same as the Chinese Five Principles of Coexistence; both Chinese and Indian relations with developing countries have a similar point of departure. (These principles were later extended and developed into the ten Bandung Principles following the Asian–African Conference in Bandung on 18–24 April 1955.)[8] India's development policy is shaped by its own experience as a recipient of development assistance and its specific role in the Non-Aligned Movement (NAM). This experience of development is considered by the Indian government to be its competitive advantage when exporting technical knowledge to other developing countries.

Initially, Indian development cooperation was strongly ideological and political. After India's reform towards economic liberalization, privatization and globalization, however, the country's foreign policy also became increasingly influenced by geo-economic considerations. In order to continue its expanding growth path, India has concentrated its economic activities on developing its regional market through regional integration initiatives and economic relations with numerous African countries.

India has a historical connection with many developing countries through the Indian diaspora. This is particularly true for the countries of Eastern and Southern Africa, where the Indian population forms an important part of the business community. Perhaps because of this historical connection, India has been especially active on the African continent.

---

8 The ten principles which the conference accepted on 24 April 1955 are as follows: respect for fundamental human rights and for the purposes and principles of the United Nations Charter; respect for the sovereignty and territorial integrity of all nations; recognition of the equality of all races and of the equality of all nations large and small; abstention from intervention or interference in the internal affairs of another country; respect for the right of each nation to defend itself, singly or collectively, in conformity with the UN charter; abstention from the use of arrangements of collective defence to serve the particular interests of any of the big powers and abstention by any country from exerting pressure on other countries; refraining from acts or threats of aggression or the use of force against the territorial integrity or political independence of any country; settlement of all international disputes by peaceful means, such as negotiation, conciliation, arbitration or judicial settlement as well as other peaceful means of the parties' own choices, in conformity with the UN Charter; promotion of mutual interest and cooperation; respect for justice and international obligations.

India is not a member of the DAC and its aid does not conform to the DAC definition of ODA. India's primary mechanisms for providing development cooperation are the provision of financial support and technical assistance. Financial assistance is provided as grants, as concessional lines of credit by Export–Import Bank of India (Exim Bank), as assistance through joint ventures and as debt forgiveness (German Development Institute 2009). Indian international development cooperation is uncoordinated and has been implemented through various ministries, institutions and programmes. The Ministry of External Affairs (MEA) is the principal actor in the delivery of international assistance.[9] Grants are administered by the MEA, and loans are administered by Exim Bank and the Ministry of Finance.

Indian Technical and Economic Cooperation (ITEC) was launched on 15 September 1964 at the very inception of India's overseas aid initiative. The ITEC is a core activity of the development programme as it is responsible for the dissemination of Indian technology and know-how to developing countries. The ITEC programme, fully funded by the Government of India, has evolved and grown over the years. Under ITEC and its corollary SCAAP (Special Commonwealth African Assistance Programme), 158 countries in Asia, East Europe (including the former USSR), Central Asia, Africa, Latin America, the Caribbean as well as Pacific and Small Island countries are invited to share in the Indian developmental experience in various fields.[10] ITEC has trained thousands of developing-country officials, and its training courses utilize the expertise of a large number of Indian institutes and training establishments. ITEC also provides technical assistance linked to projects, mainly in agriculture: 80 per cent of its R500 million (US$11 million) annual budget is for such projects and technical assistance, with the remainder going to military cooperation, study tours in India for developing-country delegations, and disaster relief (German Development Institute 2009).

The Exim Bank Annual Report for 2010 states:

---

9 The Indian Ministry of External Affairs (MEA) is the principal agency responsible for development assistance and coordinates technical cooperation which is the main focus of Indian aid. It is directly responsible for assistance to Bhutan, Nepal and Afghanistan, and advises other ministries, notably the Ministry of Finance, on assistance to other countries.

10 ITEC website, http://itec.mea.gov.in/

During the year under report, the Bank extended 22 new Lines of Credit (LOCs) aggregating US$753.31 million to 18 countries, which would result in additionality of exports of projects, goods and services from India. In line with the Bank's special emphasis on extension of LOCs as an effective market entry mechanism, the Bank now has in place 136 LOCs covering 94 countries in Africa, Asia, CIS, Europe, Latin America and Caribbean, with credit commitments amounting to US$ 4.5 billion. (Exim Bank 2010)

India International Development Cooperation Agency (IIDCA)

In his speech presenting India's 2007–08 budget, India's finance minister announced the setting up of an India International Development Cooperation Agency (IIDCA), which would be an umbrella organization bringing together the ministries and organizations involved in development aid. The idea was to create an organization along the line of USAID. However, no action on this initiative was forthcoming, the delay in acting on the proposal being attributed to the 'long-drawn-out' process of inter-ministerial consultation. The MEA finally gave up on the IIDCA initiative in April 2010 because of objections to the grounds behind the decision (DEVEX 2010).

As India has no nodal agency for international development cooperation, only rough estimates exist about the magnitude of India's development aid. For example, an examination of the Ministry of Finance data for the budgetary year ending March 2006 gives a figure of between $524 million and $1 billion for overall development assistance. These very different figures would correspond to 0.0007 per cent of GNI for the former and 0.0013 per cent for the latter.[11] The lower figure of $524 million would represent a doubling of Indian aid compared to the budgetary year 2001/02.

However, figures calculated by the German Development Institute (2009) indicate a global figure for development aid of $416.48 million for the budgetary year 2005/06. The corresponding figures for 2006/07 and 2007/08 are $219.34 million and $378 million. The 2007/08 figure included assistance to Afghanistan of $96.44 million. These figures would suggest that there is no specific trend in volumes of Indian development aid. This makes comparison of national figures or even figures within national budgets extremely difficult.

---

11 Ministry of Finance, Revised Union Budget 2006–07, http://indiabudget.nic.in/ub2006-07/ubmain.htm

Bhutan is by far the number-one target for Indian aid, accounting for approximately 50 per cent of all aid over the period 2005–2008. Other countries in the region are among the main beneficiaries, with Africa accounting for between 1 per cent and 3 per cent.

India allocated approximately $547 million to aid-related activities in 2008. It is now the fifth-largest donor to Afghanistan (with commitments of over $1 billion since 2001) and is increasingly seeking out new recipients – India's aid to Africa has grown at a compound annual growth rate of 22 per cent over the past ten years. India's aid programmes are increasingly including countries outside its immediate neighbourhood of Afghanistan, Bhutan and Nepal (Ramachandran 2010).

Exim Bank has a large portfolio of lines of credit with developing countries. All the lines of credit (which have the status of sovereign loans) are tied to the supply of Indian goods or services and as such are commercial arrangements and not development aid. India promised to double the existing levels of credit to Africa and allocate US$5.4 billion in lines of credit in the next five years. These credits would be utilized for agricultural production, development of infrastructure and energy sectors, small and medium enterprises, irrigation, food processing, information technology and pharmaceuticals. As of 30 June 2008, Exim Bank had US$1.9 billion worth of lines of credit open for Africa (German Development Institute 2009).

India is a signatory of the Paris Declaration on Aid Effectiveness although it plays no part in the establishment of national efforts at aid efficiency. The latest manifestation of India's increased and intensified cooperation with African countries was the India–Africa Forum Summit in 2008 during which the duty-free tariff scheme was announced. The meeting concluded with the unveiling of the Delhi Declaration and the Africa–India Framework for Cooperation. The aid-to-Africa budget of the MEA would be increased to more than $500 million, with human resources development and capacity building as the main focal areas. In addition, it was decided to increase the slots in ITEC's long-term scholarship programmes from 1,100 to 1,600 every year. A follow-up summit was organized in 2011: the commitments from the Indian side included a $5 billion line of credit for three years for development projects and $300 million for an Ethiopia–Djibouti railway line. They must be understood in the context of a key phrase, repeatedly used at the summit: 'capacity building'. This has been New Delhi's thrust since the first summit in 2008 when it offered $5.4 billion for regional integration through infrastructure development. In terms of trade, it is not in the same league as Beijing. China–Africa trade in 2010 was $126.9 billion while India–Africa trade was barely $40 billion. However, India has focused its trade efforts on leveraging its experience in state building and economic growth.[12]

India's cooperation with Africa has in general been of a commercial nature. Because of India's own experience as a developing country, its non-interventionist and sovereignty-respecting policy approaches, and its orientation towards mutual benefit and equality, African governments feel rather comfortable when dealing with India. India and African countries are also benefiting from the diaspora-related advantages by identifying the interests of both partners involved. This positive perception of India and the existence of a large diaspora have led to Indian FDIs to Africa reaching US$105 billion.

While there is no doubt that India has gained from the access to natural resources and from the new markets for its own goods, there have been some beneficial aspects for Africa in gaining access to Indian technology and training. Cooperation is intensifying with the results of the two India–Africa summits producing promises of increased investment and increased trading opportunities.

In the long term it is important that India's development cooperation does not concentrate solely on investments in oil and gas and other natural resources. If it does, India will be viewed as a mini-China. Investments by the Indian diaspora, especially in Eastern and Southern Africa, range far beyond natural resources.

As India develops and its own poverty issues recede there may be the possibility that it could be part of an aid exit strategy for some developing countries. However, at present India is a minor player in the development game. As Channa (2009) has concluded, India cannot compete either with the traditional donors in terms of volume of grant aid or with the soft power being employed by other emerging donors such as China. Rather, India should recognize that its aid and investment strategy has permitted it to develop its industrial capacity and that perhaps that and not altruism is the reason for the existence of an aid programme.

12 'A Strong Beginning', *Times of India*, 26 May 2011.

The Brazilian model

Brazil sees its involvement in development assistance not simply in terms of South–South cooperation but also as an extension of its competition with India and China for soft power.[13] Brazil is now the sixth-largest investor of all developing countries.

The development agenda of Brazil is managed by the Agencia Brasileira de Cooperaçao (ABC) which is housed within the foreign ministry as an autonomous unit. Brazil maintains cooperation agreements with 53 bilateral partners; these agreements cover technical assistance within the context of binding international agreements. In terms of the breakdown of aid, in 2003, 38 per cent of aid was made available to South American countries, particularly Paraguay, 34 per cent went to lusophone Africa, and the Central American region received only 6 per cent.[14]

The funding provided for Brazil's technical assistance has been rising steadily from BRL19 million in 2006 to BRL52 million in 2010.[15] While this represents the official external aid from the ABC's budget, Brazil's contribution to developing countries is somewhat larger. The fact that Brazil is a non-DAC donor and does not submit annual aid figures means that commentators must make estimates of the overall aid figures. *The Economist* magazine has calculated Brazil's overall contribution in 2010 as follows: $30 million from the ABC budget, $440 million from other technical cooperation, $30 million for humanitarian aid, $25 million contribution to the UNDP, $300 million to the World Food Programme, $10 million to Gaza, and $350 million to Haiti, giving a total of $1.2 billion.[16] To this can be added $3.3 billion in loans to LDCs during the period 2008–10. New loans in 2010 amounted to $1.5 billion. The $3.3 billion in commercial loans were provided by the state development bank BNDES. The figures calculated by *The Economist* confirm an earlier estimate that for each $1 spent by ABC approximately $15 is spent by other Brazilian institutions (Costa Vaz and Inoue 2007).

Initially the projects undertaken by ABC were punctual in nature

---

13 'Brazil's Lula Pays Tribute to Africa's Historic Role', BBC News Africa, 4 July 2010, www.bbc.co.uk/news/10500100

14 'Speak Softly and Carry a Blank Cheque', *Economist*, 15 July 2010. www.economist/node/16592455.

15 See note 13.

16 See note 14.

but of late the projects have taken on a more strategic nature. The Cotton 4 project, launched in 2006, is a partnership between Brazil, Mali, Burkina Faso, Benin and Chad aimed at developing the region's cotton value chain.[17]

The normal mechanism for Brazilian involvement is technical assistance. Diplomatic contacts generally generate a request for technical assistance which is fed through the Foreign Ministry (MRE) to the ABC which then organizes technical meetings leading to the preparation of a complementary adjustment document and finally to a project document.

Brazil is gradually adopting a more collaborative approach to development assistance through triangular or trilateral cooperation. This new approach could mark a willingness on the part of the Brazilian government to become a traditional donor but it is more likely that the massive increase in the financial volume of Brazilian aid has placed unbearable pressure on the established institutions. For example, Brazil has launched triangular cooperation projects with Japan International Cooperation Agency (JICA) in the education and agriculture sectors and with the Canadian International Development Agency (CIDA) in immunization projects in Haiti.

Cabral and Weinstock have examined Brazil's development efforts and have highlighted some of Brazil's shortcomings as an international aid donor. These include: the ABC's cadre of technical staff is insufficient; there is an insufficient degree of coordination and exchange of experience at various levels; monitoring and evaluation of development effectiveness and impact remain a major gap in Brazilian technical cooperation; documentation and dissemination of experience and best practice still seems to be very limited; Brazil's presence in international debates on development cooperation has to date been relatively modest; and there is still no domestic constituency for international development and development aid (Cabral and Weinstock 2010).

Brazil lacks the 'principle' approach of China and India but has the same considerations with regard to seeking out commercial opportunities for its companies in the developing world. Its impact as a donor is very limited but its willingness to cooperate with traditional donors to gain knowledge of the aid business sets it apart from the other BRICS.

17 Ministerio das Relacoes Exteriores, 'Programma de apoio ao desenvolvimentodo setor Cottonicola nos paises do cotton-4', www.abc.gov.br/projetos/cooperacaoPrestadaAfricaCotton4.asp

The Russian model

Russia's economy began to surge again at the end of the twentieth century and its foreign policy became one of reasserting Russia's role in the world. This inevitably led to Russia looking at the developing world. This move was driven not by political concerns alone. Russia also has commercial interests in Africa and Latin America.

Evidence of the new approach to Africa can be seen in the visit of President Medvedev who spent a week in Africa in June 2009 visiting Egypt, Nigeria, Angola and Namibia. A business delegation of four hundred Russian businessmen accompanied the President but the visit was more about political relations than commercial ones. This opening towards the developing world can be seen in the move away from the West and an increased solidarity with the less developed countries.[18] The *Wall Street Journal* reported the visit as a revival of the old Soviet Africa strategy. While this new engagement with Africa can have positive effects in the form of increased FDI and jobs, there is also the possibility that elites will reap the greatest benefits with little accruing to the national treasuries.[19]

Russia's involvement in development aid has so far been fairly insignificant. A Russian strategy paper from 2007 set a target for foreign aid of between $400 million and $500 million and talked about the setting up of a specialized agency to deal with foreign aid. Russia is therefore well behind the other BRICS in establishing its foreign aid architecture. In 2010 Russia spent £470 million on foreign aid, the least of all the G8 countries.[20] Most of this aid was concentrated in the areas of food security and health. Agriculture training and technology in African countries accounted for $98.2 million and more than 60 per cent of Russian aid for global food security was channelled through multilateral organizations. In 2007, Russia committed to the UN aid spending target of 0.7 per cent of gross national income (GNI), but set no specific timeframe for meeting the target. If it had met the 0.7 per cent target in 2009, Russia would have been the world's sixth-largest aid donor, with a budget of $9.27 billion. Like the other BRICS, Russian politicians have the problem of selling foreign aid to a domestic population who think that the money would be better spent combating poverty at home.

---

18 'Russia's plans for Africa', *Guardian*, 26 June 2009.
19 'Russia's New Scramble for Africa', *Wall Street Journal*, 2 July 2009.
20 'The Rebirth Of Russian Foreign Aid', *Guardian*, 25 May 2011.

Russia's foreign direct investment in Africa is in the range of $12 billion (African Development Bank 2011b). Most of the investments are in the natural resources area, the largest being a joint venture between Gazprom and Sonetrach of Algeria to exploit Algerian natural gas with an estimated investment of $4.7 billion. Russian investment funds are also becoming interested in Africa. Capital Renaissance, a Moscow-based investment firm, in 2007 launched an Africa Fund with an initial capitalization of $1 billion to invest in sub-Saharan African businesses.

It is evident that Russia does not possess a definitive model for development aid. There is neither a philosophy nor a structure to promote development aid as a feature of either foreign or commercial policy. Russia is therefore not a player in the development aid business and cannot be considered as part of any country's aid exit strategy.

The South African model

South Africa is Africa's biggest economy, with a gross domestic product (GDP) of approximately US$524 billion in 2010 (CIA n.d.). This represented a modest increase of 3 per cent over the 2009 figure. South Africa is classified as a medium-income country according to the United Nations Development Programme Human Development Index (HDI). The country holds a unique position not just in the Southern African Development Community (SADC) but across the entire African continent and internationally, where it often represents Africa. It is Africa's strategic economic and military powerhouse and is politically stable. It thus has the capability to both foster and lead South–South cooperation in Africa.

Until 2000, South Africa's development efforts were managed institutionally through the Development Assistance Programme, which was situated in a Chief Directorate in the Department of Foreign Affairs. However, the programme was replaced in 2001 by the current African Renaissance and International Co-operation Fund for the purpose of enhancing international cooperation with and on the African continent and to confirm the Republic of South Africa's commitment to Africa.[21]

The structure of the African Renaissance and International Co-

---

21 Department of Foreign Affairs of South Africa, www.dfa.gov.za/foreign/
Multilateral/profiles/arfund.htm

operation Fund (ARF) enables the South African government to identify and fund, in a proactive way: cooperation between South Africa and other countries, particularly African countries; the promotion of democracy and good governance; the prevention and resolution of conflict; socio-economic development and integration; humanitarian assistance, and human resource development.

Although the ARF is the official body involved in South Africa's external assistance programme, the organization accounts for only a minimal amount of South African development assistance – 3.8 per cent in 2002 and 3.3 per cent in 2004 (Braude et al. 2007). The fund has grown from under US$7 million in 2003 to almost US$40 million in 2008/09. Based on reports from the Department of Foreign Affairs total development assistance from South Africa was estimated at US$61 million for 2006/07. The African National Congress Policy Conference in 2007 confirmed that the focus of such assistance continued to be regional. It is estimated that around 70 per cent of South African aid is channelled to countries in the SADC. In 2010, South Africa contributed almost $2 million to UN agencies, $3.6 million to the African Development Bank and $5.5 million to the World Bank/IDA.

The South Africa development aid procedure is among the heaviest, requiring the involvement of the President and the national treasury. In many cases, South Africa uses memoranda of understanding (MOU) to establish development partnerships with other African countries. The lack of a coordinated approach has led to the situation where various government departments have conducted most of the assistance undertaken since 2000. At least half of all South African government departments are engaged in projects on the continent. However, since there is no coordinating mechanism, government departments and agencies do not always inform the Ministry of Finance, which makes the overall aid situation difficult to assess.

A portion of South Africa's aid figures are currently reported in national budget documents by the Ministry of Foreign Affairs (MFA).[22] Expenditure on international cooperation increased nominally from $64.3 million in 2006 to $110.7 million in 2010, and is expected to reach $134.7 million in 2011. However, these figures do not include

---

22 Estimates of Public Expenditure 2009, Foreign Affairs, National Treasury of South Africa, accessed at www.treasury .gov.za

aid from other departments, such as the Department of Education or the Department of Defence, which are estimated to account for 55 per cent and 36 per cent respectively of total aid spending. In 2006, International Development Research Centre estimates of total development assistance from all South African departments ranged from $363 million to $475 million, approximately six to seven times the volumes reported by the National Treasury. Although it accounts for a small percentage of the country's total aid, ARF funds have been growing in recent years, from $22.7 million in 2006 to an estimated $81.3 million in 2011.

South Africa has committed to increasing development assistance levels to between 0.2 per cent and 0.5 per cent of GNI, though no target date has been set. Its aid is directed almost entirely towards

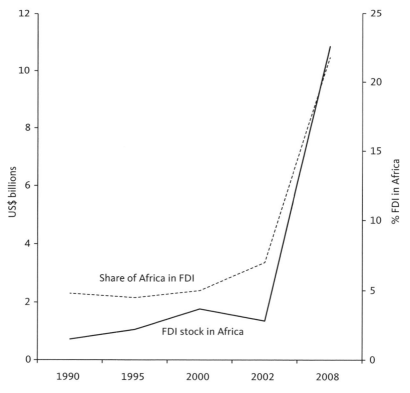

6.2 South Africa's outward FDI stock (*source*: UNCTAD World Investment Report, Geneva 2010)

other African nations, and is largely focused on governance, conflict prevention and peacekeeping. South Africa's largest troop contribution in 2009 – 1,173 – was to the United Nations Organization Stabilization Mission in the Democratic Republic of the Congo (MONUC).

South Africa has been investing heavily in Africa. Figure 6.2 shows the outward FDI stock which increased rapidly during the first decade of the twenty-first century.

There was a more than tenfold increase in the FDI stock to Africa between 2002 (US$716 million) and 2008 (US$10,843 million). The corresponding percentage of South African outward FDI to Africa accounted for 21.8 per cent of all outward FDI in 2008.

Despite the positive movements in both external assistance and outward FDI, South Africa's assistance efforts lack cohesion and a strategic approach to the continent. There have been several complaints that the African Renaissance and International Co-operation Fund's random spending should be more strategically focused (Games 2010). These complaints led to the government's decision in early 2011 to create a development assistance agency to be called the South African Development Partnership Agency (Ramachandran 2011). It is to be hoped that this initiative will not suffer the same fate as the still-born Indian initiative.

South Africa can play an important role by stimulating the economies of a large group of countries in Eastern and Southern Africa. At present South Africa is extending its economic prowess to other countries via its exports. In the future it will have to help its neighbours to diversify their own economies and not look at them as simply a market for South African goods.

A BRICS collaborative model

A feature of the desire to collaborate of some of the BRICS was the establishment of a major cooperative venture within the context of the India–Brazil–South Africa Dialogue Forum (IBSA) in June 2003. IBSA is a coordinating mechanism of the three emerging countries whose aim is to pool their funding and development expertise in order to advance their views on the development process and to carry out cooperative projects in partnership with less developed countries.

The establishment of IBSA was formalized by the Brasilia Declaration. The signatories' status as middle-income countries facing development challenges themselves, their common need to address social inequalities within their borders, and the existence of consolidated industrial areas in the three countries are additional elements that bring convergence among the members of the Forum. IBSA concluded its first round of Heads of State and Government summits in 2008.

While the cooperation has taken concrete form in terms of projects, IBSA has no structure. Although the cooperation is beneficial in terms of providing development finance and expertise, there is no stated process for the establishment of a viable project pipeline. Projects to date have been scattered and minimal. For example, in Haiti a solid waste collection project in the community of Carrefour-Feuilles, one of the high-social-risk areas of Port au Prince, was carried out. This project helped in diminishing infectious diseases and flood risks, generated jobs and income, and raised awareness on environmental problems. A second project in Guinea-Bissau helped to introduce new seeds and build additional agricultural capacity which allowed a second annual harvest of rice in the communities involved. In Cape Verde the refurbishment of two local, isolated health units was supported by IBSA.

The work of monitoring and coordinating the IBSA activities is the responsibility of senior officials of the foreign ministries, known as Focal Points. Given the political nature of the IBSA, these individuals may not be development specialists. Therefore there are significant gaps in the project chain with light vetting of project proposals and inadequate monitoring or evaluation of results.

In 2009, a workshop on HIV policies was held in Burundi, starting a new initiative yet to be concluded. New projects include the construction of a sports complex in Ramallah, a direct consequence of the coordination of positions among the three countries in matters relating to the Israeli–Palestinian conflict.[23]

Despite the high level of political coordination, the setting up of sixteen sectoral groups and the establishment of a $3 million IBSA Fund (each country has contributed $1 million) aimed at supporting viable and replicable projects, IBSA is essentially a political vehicle which permits three emerging economies to present themselves in a cooperative manner on the world stage. This does not mean that it

---

23 'The Governments of India, Brazil and South Africa (IBSA), through UNDP Inaugurate the First Project in the Middle East – a Sports Centre in Ramallah'. Accessed at http://204.200.211.31/Update_November_2011/IBSA%20in%20PAPP.pdf

serves no purpose. The Paris Declaration on Aid Efficiency and the Accra Agenda have underlined the importance of donors acting in cooperation in order to maximize aid funds. While IBSA represents a very limited approach to cooperation it is a step in the right direction for countries that up to now have gone their own way in terms of development.

The BRICS and an aid exit strategy

While many Africans are looking to the BRICS in their efforts to reduce aid dependency, involvement with the BRICS can be a double-edged sword. The situation is clear with regard to China, where 'aid' means the provision of infrastructure aimed at assisting the export of commodities and increased trade can mean greater exports of commodities and increased imports which can stunt local production. South Africa presents a similar threat to many countries of sub-Saharan Africa, where experienced South African companies are already establishing a South African hegemony in areas such as mining and retail carrying essentially South African-produced goods.

The Chinese and Indian models with their overtures of South–South solidarity and their own experience of rapid development are attractive to developing country elites from both a political and an economic viewpoint. None of the BRICS would claim that they are in the business of transformational change. Therefore, the conflict between the Washington and Beijing Consensuses is not simply philosophical but also cultural. The Washington Consensus has a typical Western approach to democracy and financial management. The Beijing Consensus is moving more in terms of crossing the river stone by stone. The poor would say that they cannot wait for the Beijing Consensus because it might arrive too late.

Naim (2007) has categorized Chinese (and by association BRICS) assistance as 'rogue aid', that is, aid that distorts aid initiatives. It is true that despite efforts by the European Union and China to coordinate their efforts on some level, developing-country governments are now adept at playing off the traditional donors against some of the emerging donors. If an infrastructural or a prestige project is refused by a traditional donor, the Chinese ambassador is on speed dial.

7 | REGIONAL INTEGRATION

Competition has been shown to be useful up to a certain point and no further, but cooperation, which is the thing we must strive for today, begins where competition leaves off. (Franklin D. Roosevelt)

Regional integration organization or regional economic communities?

By the year 2000 almost every region of the world had somewhere within it a regional integration organization (RIO). While the mushrooming of regional integration organizations can be attributed to the success of the European Union project (Draper 2010), it is perhaps naïve to think that this example alone is the driving force behind such a strong movement for economic, and in some cases political, integration. Undoubtedly, though, many of the members of the various geographical organizations were influenced in applying for membership by the anticipated advantages they would gain. As Faíña Medín et al. (2010) concluded, 'Governments become members of international organizations in order to derive benefits from the membership of intergovernmental clubs in which there is a logical trade off between independency and participation. However, such engagement generates utility losses due to constraints derived from the membership of the club.' Being a member of an international 'club' is obviously attractive: there are currently 14 recognized regional integration organizations involving developing countries in the world, 8 in Africa, 4 in Latin America and 2 in Asia. There are at least another half-dozen regional organizations which exist as virtual or more or less virtual organizations and which have aspirations to establish a regional integration agenda despite the plethora of existing regional integration agendas. For example, the African Union began by recognizing eight regional organizations as the building blocks of a united Africa but has recently added the East African Community (EAC) which already includes states that are members of other regional organizations. However, the African Union is currently resisting the addition

TABLE 7.1 Details of regional integration organizations

	GNP (PPP) 2007 (US$ billion)	Population 2009 (million)	Number of members	Inter-regional trade (US$ billion)
Sub-Saharan Africa				
ECOWAS	252	390	16	–[1]
WEAMU	139	108	8	–
ECCAS	263	149	10	–
CEMAC	109	135	6	1.8
COMESA	360	400		15
SADC	903	101	15	–
EAC	149	132	5	1.6
SACU	576	57	5	20,515
Latin America and Caribbean				
CACM	318	51	7	–
Andean Community	903	101	10	–
CARICOM	91	16	15	–
MERCOSUR	2,895	267	4	–
Asia and Pacific				
ASEAN	601	3,084	10	376
SAARC	4,383	1,600	8	–

Source: CIA Factbook and websites of the various organizations (*note*: 1 figures not available)

of the Intergovernmental Authority on Development (IGAD) which also includes members of other regional organizations. It therefore seems from the convoluted and overlapping membership of many clubs that being a member of two clubs (or even three) is infinitely preferable to being a member of one. Table 7.1 lists the main regional integration organizations.

Although most of the regional integration organizations started their lives as economic partnerships or trade organizations, Box 7.1 shows the depth that regional integration has reached. However, the achievement of such a wide range of objectives can be a major challenge for a poorly funded and capacity-constrained RIO.

Given the wide range of activities to be undertaken by a RIO which inevitably puts a stress on the resources available, the attraction of belonging to more than one is difficult to understand. Figure 7.1 shows the overlapping situation currently existing in Eastern and Southern Africa. A similar, but simpler, diagram could show the overlapping arrangements in West Africa and South America. Because of the many intersecting arrangements this complicated diagram is known as the 'spaghetti bowl'.

Each of the RIOs has had its own history and reasons for its evolution. The Southern Africa Customs Union (SACU), which was

---

Box 7.1 Functions of a regional organization

- the strengthening of trade integration in the region;
- the creation of an appropriate enabling environment for private sector development;
- the development of infrastructure programmes in support of economic growth and regional integration;
- the development of strong public sector institutions and good governance;
- the reduction of social exclusion and the development of an inclusive civil society;
- contribution to peace and security in the region;
- the building of regional environmental programmes;
- the strengthening of the region's interaction with other regions of the world.

Source: Van Langenhove and De Lombaerde (2007)

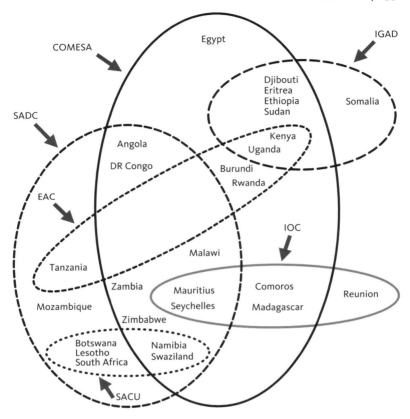

COMESA: Common Market for Eastern and Southern Africa
EAC: East African Cooperation
ICAD: Intergovernmental Authority on Development
IOC: Indian Ocean Commission
SACU: Southern African Customs Union
SADC: Southern African Development Community

7.1 The East Africa RIO spaghetti bowl

founded in 1889, is the oldest regional organization in Africa. It owes its genesis to the Customs Union Convention between the British colony of Cape of Good Hope and the Orange Free State Boer Republic. A new agreement, signed on 29 June 1910, was extended to the Union of South Africa and the British High Commission Territories (HCTs), that is, Basutoland (current Lesotho), Bechuanaland

Box 7.2 Evolution of PTA/COMESA

The Common Market for Eastern and Southern Africa (COMESA) traces its genesis to the mid-1960s in the context of the buoyant and optimistic mood that characterized the post-independence period in most of Africa. The mood then was one of pan-African solidarity and collective self-reliance born of a shared destiny. In 1965, the United Nations Economic Commission for Africa (ECA) convened a ministerial meeting of the then newly independent states of Eastern and Southern Africa to consider proposals for the establishment of a mechanism for the promotion of subregional economic integration. The meeting, which was held in Lusaka, Zambia, recommended the creation of an Economic Community of Eastern and Central African states.

An Interim Council of Ministers, assisted by an Interim Economic Committee of officials, was subsequently set up to negotiate the treaty and initiate programmes of economic cooperation, pending the completion of negotiations on the treaty.

In 1978, as a first step to creating an economic community, the ministers of trade, finance and planning adopted the Lusaka Declaration of Intent and Commitment to the Establishment of a Preferential Trade Area for Eastern and Southern Africa (PTA) and created an Inter-governmental Negotiating Team on the Treaty for the establishment of the PTA.

On 21 December 1981 the treaty establishing the PTA was signed by the heads of state. The treaty came into force on 30 September 1982.

The PTA was established to take advantage of a larger market size, to share the region's common heritage and destiny and to allow greater social and economic cooperation, the ultimate objective being to create an economic community. The treaty establishing COMESA was signed on 5 November 1993 in Kampala, Uganda.

From 1960 up until the mid-1990s, the economic growth of the COMESA region averaged 3.2 per cent a year, a figure marginally above the level of the region's population growth. By 1993, this region of about 280 million people (excluding Egypt), which had more than doubled its population since independence, had a total GDP of around US$90 billion, and included fifteen of the twenty-three states classified as Least Developed Countries (LDCs) by the United Nations.

Source: COMESA website

(Botswana), and Swaziland. South West Africa (Namibia) was a *de facto* member, since it was administered as part of South Africa before it became a *de jure* member. The primary goal was to promote economic development through regional coordination of trade. A more modern path of evolution is presented in Box 7.2.

The RIOs are continually working to extend the range of services they offer current members. The ability of the RIO to supply a range of services represents its competitive advantage. The membership will only remain if it continues to offer advantages associated with membership. This competition on the level of services is possibly the reason why the RIOs have continued to expand the number of areas in which they are active. For example, COMESA has recently become involved in regional food security and regional environmental issues.

Why join an RIO?

The logic behind the desire to join a larger grouping of countries can be attributed to several factors. The colonial history of Africa, South East Asia and Latin America has created states based on lines drawn on a map as the colonial powers retreated. In many cases the colonial retreat created a series of relatively small countries which were potentially non-viable. The process is more apparent in Africa than in South East Asia and Latin America. The effects of fragmentation, as this process is called (Collier and Venables 2008), have forced countries to band together to form viable units as they develop their own countries.

Regional integration and employment Africa has not yet developed magnets of employment and if it were to do so, fragmentation would prevent it from realizing the benefits. Where magnets of employment exist in Africa there is a strong level of migration towards those magnets. For example, emigrants from Benin, Ghana and Niger head to Nigeria which is their local employment magnet. South Africa is a popular destination for emigrants from Mozambique, Swaziland, Lesotho, Botswana and Zimbabwe. Evidently, the prospect of a better work environment plays a significant role in attracting these emigrants. Côte d'Ivoire, even during civil unrest, has drawn a large proportion of its workforce from Burkina Faso, principally because of the better economic opportunities it offers due to its coastal position and its rainfall. In East Africa, Sudan is the most common destination for emigrants from Chad, Eritrea and Ethiopia, while Kenya is a popular destination for emigrants from Uganda and Tanzania; the latter destination is most favoured by emigrants from Democratic Republic of Congo, Zambia and Burundi despite the fact that the difference in per capita GDP is negligible or in some cases even negative. A corollary of migration is the rise of xenophobia in the economic magnet countries. Employment is an issue in all sub-Saharan Africa (including South Africa), and an influx of poorly qualified immigrants can set off ethnic violence as has recently been the case in South Africa where attacks were made on Zimbabwean immigrants. While in their manifestos all the RIOs propose the free movement of labour, the existence of economic disparities between members of the club can cause competition for employment between nationals and immigrants and consequently xenophobia.

Regional integration as a shock absorber Virtually all African countries are commodity exporters. Oil dominates Africa's exports and if the continent were united 65 per cent of its exports would be oil. The bulk of the remaining exports are mineral products, which are subject to the commodity cycle of boom and bust. Shocks relating to extraordinary price movements are asymmetrical in that price reductions adversely affect production while price rises have a less significant effect. The majority of African countries do not export oil, and for them being a member of an economic club can reduce the effect of adverse shocks through the existence of an internal market.

Regional integration and the creation of economies of scale Manufacturing and services benefit from economies of scale. Except for a few specific cases, African countries have small markets which are in many cases too small to engender the level of competition necessary to develop products and services which are competitive on a regional or global scale. The relatively small scale of the economies not only inhibits industrial development and innovation but can also lead to the creation of monopolies with consequent predatory pricing. All these effects can act as a disincentive to invest. Small markets are also prone to what is known as 'hold-up' which in effect means that an investor who has sunk costs in his investment may be subject to a monopolistic purchaser of his product. That purchaser can exert price pressure on the investor thereby reducing the profit to be gained from investing. Hold-up is a serious risk for investors and is a major deterrent to investment.

Regional integration as a producer of clusters Another major impediment to economic growth caused by fragmentation is the lack of productive clusters of industrial activity, which have proved effective whether located in Silicon Valley or in Shanghai. Africa's cities are only now reaching the size where clusters can be developed. The Chinese development model for Africa includes the economic export zones which have been set up in several countries, most notably Zambia. These zones are targeted at Chinese firms but the model, if successful, could lead to individual countries setting up industrial zones where companies could benefit from each other's efforts. If African countries were to launch such an initiative, they would be following the successful example of Asia.

It is easy to see that membership of a regional integration club can be an advantage in countering the effects of small markets and economic shocks. Belonging to a RIO like COMESA or ECOWAS with a population of 400 million potential customers can open many doors for an entrepreneurial firm. The growth of inter-RIO trade has been impressive but is still considerably less than that of Asia. Inter-COMESA trade accounts for less than 10 per cent of overall COMESA trade. For ASEAN the figure is 24 per cent while for the European Union it is approximately 70 per cent. The establishment of effective common markets is certainly one reason why the EU and ASEAN have significantly increased trade between members. While African RIOs have given lip service to the creation of common markets, implementation at the national level remains a major obstacle.

Regional integration as a producer of public goods All developing countries suffer from a deficit in terms of infrastructure (in particular

---

Box 7.3 The North–South Corridor project

The North–South Corridor for Eastern and Southern Africa is an innovative infrastructure project which is being developed by three RIOs, COMESA, EAC and SADC. The project was launched during a major conference held in Lusaka in April 2009 where donors and development institutions pledged $1.2 billion to finance the NSC Aid for Trade Programme project.

The North–South Corridor links the Copperbelt region of southern DR Congo and northern Zambia to the port of Dar es Salaam in Tanzania and the ports of Southern Africa. The corridor, with its spurs, services eight countries: Tanzania, DR Congo, Zambia, Malawi, Botswana, Zimbabwe, Mozambique and South Africa. Since elements of the corridor pass through each country it was important that the overall project was in the hands of the relevant RIOs. The project is complex and involves interconnection between different modes of transport (specifically road and rail) as well as a programme to improve container handling at the ports.

While the building of new links or the rehabilitation of

---

trunk roads, rail connections and ports) and a major deficit in power generation. It is difficult for a landlocked country to invest in a port in a neighbouring country in order to gain access to the sea and global markets. There are some examples of countries developing 'dry ports' close to the border of a neighbour with access to the sea. The Zambian government is currently examining the possibility of a 'dry port' in Chipata close to the Mozambique border which could be used as a path to the sea. Transport costs in Africa are already among the highest in the world and act as a disincentive to invest as well as impeding goods from getting to market. There are major gaps in the continental trunk road system. Both the North–South Corridor, which links the port of Durban in South Africa with Dar es Salaam in Tanzania, and the Northern Corridor, which links Mombasa with Kigali, have several links missing. These gaps can only be closed by concerted regional initiatives. The launching of the North–South

existing links is an important initiative to be undertaken in the programme, of equal importance are the software segments of the programme. There is no point in improving infrastructure if the customs regulations and the trade facilitation aspects of the programme are ignored. Information and communication technology will be an important factor in speeding commercial transport and in reducing costs. The project has been prioritized under NEPAD.

The project is not only innovative in bringing together the three RIOs: the financial requirements, which are substantial, will be provided by a mixture of donor, bank and commercial financing. Among the funding institutions will be the EU–Africa Infrastructure Fund; funds from the regional development banks (with DBSA being the main funder); and funds from the African Development Bank, the World Bank, and the Emerging Africa Infrastructure Fund (commercial lending).

The first project under the North–South Corridor will be the link between Lusaka and Chipata in Zambia, funded by the European Union, the European Investment Bank and the African Development Bank.

Corridor project was a joint initiative of COMESA, SADC and EAC and is an example of where a regional approach can have positive effects (see Box 7.3).

The efforts of the RIOs in the area of common public goods such as transportation links, common power pools and common communications technologies are perhaps the most important areas of their activity. The EASSy programme, a 10,000km submarine fibre-optic cable system deployed along the east and south coasts of Africa to service the voice, data, video and internet needs of the region, is typical of the type of cooperative project which can benefit participating countries. EASSy links South Africa with Sudan via landing points in Mozambique, Madagascar, the Comoros, Tanzania, Kenya, Somalia and Djibouti, demonstrating the potential for regional action in the area of common public goods. Other examples are the East African Power Pool and the South African Power Pool which share power between their members. Considering the very considerable deficit in power in the Southern African region, a project is currently proposed to connect the two pools.

The RIOs have experienced organic growth. The example of COMESA is fairly typical of the other RIOs. COMESA began life as a Preferential Trade Arrangement linking twenty countries in Africa in a trading bloc. Since then it has developed a bank, the PTA Bank, launched a development fund, the COMESA Fund, established a Common External Tariff (CET) which is equivalent to its sister organization EAC and launched a common market. At the moment it does not contemplate a monetary union along the lines of that proposed by EAC but it has launched a clearing house to assist exporters who are working in the different currencies of the region.

Regional integration and food security Food security has been a constant issue in Africa. Food security will be enhanced as long as the basis of regional cooperation is the increase in intra-regional trade which itself should foster economic growth and increase the employment prospects and the income-earning capacities of the poor. The incorporation of agriculture into regional trade agreements will harmonize agricultural policies through the development of policies at the supranational and regional levels and by coordinating individual national policies. The issues which will need to be addressed in this process include the level of the common external tariff, rules on domestic subsidies to farmers, the priority to be given to tackling different kinds of market-fragmenting barriers, and the need for financial mechanisms to address any adverse inter-country distributional effects of supporting farm prices within the union. The European Union in 2009 released €1 billion to assist developing countries to improve food security to counteract the effects of rising food prices.

The EU Commission (2000) has also addressed the role of regionalism in food security in its concept paper on food security:

Many of the critical elements of poverty reduction strategies and the promotion of food security have regional dimensions, including, among others:

- macro-economic reforms and the promotion of sustainable growth;
- reducing barriers to trade, as a way of promoting integration of countries into the wider economy;

- assuring the availability of secure food supplies, and managing shocks through increased regional trade;
- strengthening good governance through the promotion of political integration at the regional level;
- improved management of shared regional natural resources;
- capturing economies of scale by creating regional capacity for research and human resource development.

The key links between regionalism and food security emphasized in the EU paper are (a) the way membership of the regional grouping helps to 'lock in' and sustain macroeconomic policy reforms as well as promoting political cooperation in the region, (b) trade and market integration, and (c) regional cooperation through joint institutions in areas where there are clear spillovers or economies of scale.

Regional integration and central decision making A corollary of the above point is that decisions made at the regional level can sometimes mitigate the effects of patronage which exist at the national level. It has been one of the experiences of the European Union process that national politicians can deflect criticism of their policies by pointing the finger at Brussels. The taking of communal decisions can remove the possibility of policy decisions being made on an individual basis.

Central decision making is at the core of the regional integration process. Integrating trade policies, establishing free trade areas and often moving to the setting up of a customs union require member countries to enact legislation implementing regional decisions at the national level. National legislation aimed at improving market access can often be hampered by lobbies which may lose some monopolistic power through the opening up of national markets. Despite commitments to regional integration, governments are often deflected from regional initiatives by the dictates of national interest.

The RIO as a negotiating platform While trade is no longer considered to be the single major element of the integration process, it is an important factor in establishing the credentials of the RIO. The experience of the Uruguay Round convinced the least developed countries and the developed countries of the wisdom of joint action. Therefore, while the focus of the RIOs has been on developing inter-regional trade, there is also a major benefit to negotiating trade agreements as a group. The EPA process started by the EU and the ACP countries through the Cotonou agreement is intended to develop trade relations between the EU and the various regions of the ACP in the context of specific regional groupings. For example, in the Eastern and Southern African region, EAC, COMESA and SADC have been active as the regional partners of the EU in the EPA negotiation process. It has always been the contention of the EU that EPA was more about regional integration than a simple trade agreement between itself and ACP regional groupings. This aspect has been well understood by the RIOs which see that the establishment of rules-based trade at regional level and the consequent improvement in trade facilitation will inevitably lead to economic growth in the various regions.

Does the RIO need a leader? One of the characteristics of RIOs is that they generally have a hegemon, a linchpin country which holds the whole group together. In West Africa the linchpin of all the groups is Nigeria, in Southern Africa the linchpin of SACU and SADC is South Africa, in MERCOSUR it is Brazil and Argentina and in the East African Community it is Kenya. Without an economically strong hegemon that can act as a leader the RIO may exist but will have little or no effect. In general the secretariats of the RIOs are weak since they are maintained by the members and are subject to political pressure from them. The economically strong member with significant trade links to the other members can use its muscle to enforce adherence to communal decisions.

While the hegemon can play a positive role in influencing the direction of the RIO, there is also the negative effect that it will draw to itself the lion's share of the region's FDI because of its industrial weight. This is particularly true in Africa, where FDI is attracted to South Africa, Kenya and Nigeria, and in South America where FDI is concentrated on the two MERCOSUR giants, Brazil and Argentina.

Can the RIO help with poverty 'traps'? Four 'traps' have been identified in which the countries in the bottom billion are enmeshed: the conflict trap; the natural resources trap; the trap of being landlocked with bad neighbours, and the bad governance trap (Collier 2007). This suggests that a large element of under-development can be attributed to factors outside the control of the state in question. Regional integration and the key role of the hegemon can be part of the answer to at least three of the traps: security, assistance to landlocked countries and convergence to good governance.

The RIO can have a significant effect on security. The role of Kenya (the hegemon in the EAC and IGAD groups) as a local peacemaker is already well established. Kenya was instrumental in pushing the Southern Sudan Peace Agreement which was negotiated in the Kenyan town of Naivasha and which was signed in Nairobi in January 2005. It is debatable whether this process would have succeeded without the intervention of the Kenyan government. In a similar vein Kenya has been instrumental in trying to solve the Somali question. The negotiations which set up the Somali Transitional Government took place in Kenya during 2004–05 and succeeded in establishing a level of political agreement which unfortunately was insufficient to solve the problem. Kenya is also at the heart of the efforts against the scourge of Somali piracy. This type of response is not totally altruistic. Research has established that there is an economic effect for a country contiguous to a conflict. Solution of the Southern Sudan question and the possibility of installing a workable government in Somalia were very much in Kenya's economic interest.

The RIO also assists landlocked countries that have bad neighbours. Since the initial purpose of the RIO is free trade, the development of trade facilitation measures links countries together. The establishment of one-stop border posts can also be a mechanism to dispel the bad neighbour trap. In 2010, COMESA inaugurated the Chirundu one-stop border post (OSBP) as a pilot initiative.[1] Plans are already being made to replicate this innovation between other countries in the region. The decision to make Chirundu the pilot OSBP was taken not by Zambia and Zimbabwe but at the May 2005 COMESA Council of Ministers meeting in Kigali, Rwanda. The regional integration dimension has been vitally important in establishing this important trade facilitation measure in the COMESA region. The OSBP was funded by donors in what could be considered the quintessential aid-for-trade programme.

It is apparent that landlocked countries suffer in trade terms from a lack of access to the sea. Regional free trade agreements (FTAs) which promote cross-border trade between landlocked and coastal

---

1 The border at Chirundu is the main entry point for commercial traffic entering Zambia from South Africa and other commercial ports to the south, or proceeding through to Central and Eastern Africa to the north.

Box 7.4 The RIO and inter-regional justice

The Treaty on the Economic Community of West African States was revised in July 1993 to replace the non-existent tribunal originally envisioned with a Community Court of Justice. The Revised Treaty entered into force in 1995, and the judges of the Community Court of Justice were appointed in January 2001. The original court had a narrow field of access in that only the member states acting either collectively or individually were permitted to initiate a contentious case in the court. The effect of this limited standing in the court was that until 2003, the court was idle.

The court is composed of seven judges appointed by the authority of heads of state and government from a list of up to two persons nominated by each member state. It received its first case in 2004. The first landmark case (Olajide Afolabi v. Federal Republic of Nigeria) exposed the access problem and began a discussion, headed by the Judges themselves, on the need to amend the protocol to allow for legal and natural persons to have standing before the court. In January 2005, ECOWAS adopted the Additional Protocol to permit persons to bring

---

countries, offer the former the possibility of external trade. COMESA, which is the largest trading bloc on the African continent, is still experiencing difficulties in persuading some of its member states to move to the next level of integration by joining the FTA. This is despite the heads of state declaring their approval of the FTA process at annual COMESA summits. While most countries are members of the FTA, countries such as Uganda have not yet subscribed to it. This is a somewhat bizarre position since COMESA is Uganda's leading destination market for its goods. Ugandan products continue to be less competitive due to its inability to join the free trade area.[2]

The RIOs have become increasingly aware of their responsibilities in responding to the bad governance trap. By connecting various countries the RIOs have a convergence effect in sectors other than trade. Some RIOs, most notably the African ones, have established

---

2 'COMESA FTA Deal in Final Stages', *East African Business Week*, 25 February 2011.

suits against member states. Beyond this monumental change, the Council took the opportunity to revise the jurisdiction of the court to include review of violations of human rights in all member states. The Additional Protocol also gave national courts of member states the right to seize the ECOWAS Court for a ruling on the interpretation of Community law. Previously, the language in the Protocol was unclear as to whether a member state court could only seize the Community Court of a matter through the auspices of the national government.

Since the adoption of the Additional Protocol, the court has received several cases from individuals and the institutions of ECOWAS itself. Notably, the court has been seized by Nigerian politicians complaining of violations of their human rights in the determination of election outcomes. The court's handling of these cases has been controversial in Nigeria, as some in the Nigerian legal community believed that the court should have rejected them immediately, without issuing interim orders.

Source: ECWAS website accessed at www.aict-ctia.org/courts_subreg/ecowas/ecowas_home.html

courts (in the case of COMESA) or tribunals (in the case of SADC). However, the most comprehensive is the Community Court of Justice set up by ECOWAS (see Box 7.4).

The RIO courts can exert a push for good governance especially if the court has the ability to hear cases brought by individuals concerning human rights. On the negative side it is important that member states abide by the judgments made by the regionally established courts. In one case, which received wide public and political attention, the SADC court ruled in 2008 that Zimbabwean farmers should be allowed to return to their farms unhindered. This ruling in effect declared the Government of Zimbabwe's policy of land reform illegal. The Government of Zimbabwe refused to accept the ruling of the court and Zimbabwe's High Court rejected the regional court ruling by refusing to enforce it.[3] This was not totally unexpected. However

---

3 BBC News, Zimbabwe court rejects SADC ruling to end farm seizures, accessed at http://news.bbc.co.uk/2/hi/8483644.stm

the response of the other SADC member states, in not insisting that Zimbabwe enforce the judgment, nullified the validity of the court and puts the whole concept of a regional court in doubt. Along with a court there has to be political will to force the adherence by RIO members to the rules of the club.

The African RIOs have been effective in setting up structures which can encourage member states to improve their governance. Another area where they have been effective has been in expelling members which have been the subject of an illegal seizure of power. The African Union (AU) and SADC suspended Madagascar from their groups after Andry Rajoelina, a former mayor of Antananarivo, the capital, seized power in a bloodless coup in March 2009. SADC hinted darkly at military intervention to return the ousted president, Marc Ravalomanana, to power.[4] Unfortunately, within six months Madagascar was back in the fold, with Mr Rajoelina still in power and elections promised within twelve months. At the time of writing, the elections still had not taken place, giving succour to those who believe that coups can still pay. Politically inspired back-tracking, whether it is in the context of the rulings of the court or decisions to suspend membership, only undermines the concept of regional solidarity. The AU does not like coups and suspended Guinea and Mauritania after coups in 2008.

ECOWAS has an exemplary record in supporting the concept of democracy among its members. Guinea and Niger, two resource-rich but coup-prone countries, recently provided big tests. In the first case ECOWAS rose to the challenge. Guinea's junta finally handed over power to a transitional government after a concerted squeeze by ECOWAS, other African countries and the West. ECOWAS took the lead by holding talks with the soldiers and pro-democracy groups. It had also suspended Guinea from the club and had put sanctions on the regime of Captain Moussa Dadis Camara, who seized power in 2008 after the death of General Lansana Conté, a dictator who had run the country for twenty-four years.[5]

This shows the very positive impact that an effective RIO can have on helping their members avoid the governance trap.

---

4 'Coups can still pay: A diplomatic compromise keeps a coup-maker happily in power', *Economist*, 15 October 2009.

5 'Quietly impressive: As others falter, one regional club has notched up some successes', *Economist*, 25 May 2010.

The RIO and security Africa has been the continent of internal conflict before and after independence. Conflict and lack of security have been identified as among the greatest impediments to development and to efforts aimed at increasing FDI. Africa, South East Asia and Latin America have all had their liberation struggles, and more than their fair share of coups and have been the area where many of the proxy wars of the Cold War were played out. The main result of all these conflicts has been low economic growth, the continuation of poverty and the inability to benefit from globalization. While the Cold War powers were happy to play out their games in the Third World because it was assumed that developing countries were not geo-strategically important, the situation has changed radically in the twenty-first century.

Failed states (such as Somalia) have become security threats either in terms of international terrorism or as regional menaces and havens for illegal activities like piracy. Developing countries are now viewed as geo-strategically important especially in the context of the 'war on terror' launched by the George W. Bush administration. Failed or semi-failed states, even states governed by a dictator, pose a threat to world peace. The US, China and the EU are of one mind that the reduction (if not the overall removal) of conflict is an important strategic objective.

The United Nations has played an important role in international peacekeeping. There were a series of interventions by the UN in Africa during the 1990s, principally in Angola, Rwanda, Somalia and Liberia. It is generally agreed that most of these missions were unsuccessful. This is particularly true of the missions in Somalia and Rwanda. Outbreaks of conflict in Côte d'Ivoire, Democratic Republic of Congo and Liberia have brought the UN back into the picture as a major player on the African security scene. Sometimes the effectiveness of that return has been criticized.[6] However, despite the lack of success the response to UN involvement in peacekeeping has been positive. For example in Congo, Southern Sudan and Liberia – the UN's three biggest operations – the military intervention is ensuring that the peace agreements are being respected. But in countries such as Côte d'Ivoire, the military intervention, which has

---

6 'Is this the world's least effective UN peacekeeping force?', *Economist*, 2 December 2004.

been backed by both Nigeria and ECOWAS, has not succeeded in staunching the conflict.[7]

Since the misadventures in Rwanda and Somalia, there has been a call for Africa to do more to solve its own internal conflicts. Because of their regional remit, the RIOs have become the cornerstones of what has been termed the African Peace and Security Architecture (APSA) which constitutes the framework for crisis management on the African continent. The African Standby Force (ASF) is the operational arm of this framework and it was the African Union's ambition to make the force operational in 2010. The ASF is composed of the Regional Standby Forces which are being developed across the continent in order to provide Africa with a capability to deal with crises. Africa and the European Union have adopted a joint strategy comprising several action points in order to meet the objectives. Thus far procedures have been developed, forces identified, exercises mounted and evaluation is currently under way (African Union, n.d.).

Two of the standby forces were set up by RIOs. The first, EAST-BRIG, was established by IGAD (not a recognized RIO since it does not have a specific integration agenda) by a draft protocol signed by thirteen countries (IGAD 2004).[8] The second, the SADCBRIG, was launched in 2007 in Lusaka – as part of the SADC Summit.[9] In 2003, the African Chiefs of Defence and Security set goals for the African Standby Force (ASF) to be in place by 2010. However, even before the planned 2010 deployment date a study concluded that the resources currently being expended on the ASF might be better spent on improving the capability of the individual armies in the Eastern and Southern African Region (Burgess 2010).

Integrating the RIOs The spaghetti bowl of African regional organizations needs to be reformed. In East and Southern Africa there are four RIOs with overlapping membership. One, SACU, already has an operating customs union and the other three have launched their versions of a customs union. Most should be in place by 2015 if the

7 'Call the blue helmets: Can the UN cope with increasing demands for its soldiers?', *Economist*, 4 July 2007.

8 Comoros, Djibouti, Eritrea, Ethiopia, Kenya, Madagascar, Mauritius, Rwanda, Seychelles, Somalia, Sudan, Tanzania, Uganda.

9 Zambia: speech of President Mwanawasa: Launch of the SADC Brigade (17/08/2007) accessed at www.polity.org.za/article/zambia-mwanawasa-launch-of-the-sadc-brigade-17082007-2007-08-17

declarations signed up to at summits are implemented. However, the WTO rules insist that member countries can be a member of only one customs union. If the RIOs are successful in implementing their own customs unions and if countries wish to maintain their WTO membership then they will have to choose which RIO they wish to belong to. The African Union has not been helpful in this process since for political reasons it had designated seven RIOs as the building blocks of African unity. This meant there was no place for EAC which immediately protested and was admitted into the group. This ran against the need to rationalize the RIO situation.

There are two theories, the 'integrate now' and the evolutionary approach. 'Integrate now' is not a valid option, given the diversity of the membership, so RIOs have gone for the evolutionary approach. The first step in this process is the so-called Tripartite which is an integration of the activities of EAC, COMESA and SADC. This process was launched at the Tripartite Summit which was held in Kampala in 2008. Points 10 and 11 of the Final Declaration outline the vision of the leaders:

> The Tripartite Summit agreed on a programme of harmonisation of trading arrangements amongst the three RECs, free movement of business persons, joint implementation of inter-regional infrastructure programmes as well as institutional arrangements on the basis of which the three RECs would foster cooperation.
>
> The Tripartite Summit underscored the fact that the tripartite arrangement is a crucial building block towards achieving the African Economic Community as outlined by the Treaty of Abuja.[10]

In 2010 the Tripartite Secretariat published the revised legal texts aimed at setting up a Tripartite Free Trade Area.[11] The texts were discussed at the Tripartite Summit held on 21 June 2011. In its Final Communiqué, the summit

> Launched negotiations for the establishment of an integrated market of 26 countries with a combined population of nearly 600

---

10 Final Communiqué of the COMESA-EAC-SADC Tripartite Summit of Heads of State and Government, Towards a Single Market, accessed at www.tralac.org/cause_data/images/1694/FinalCommuniqueKampala_20081022.pdf

11 The texts of the Revised Agreements can be downloaded at www.tralac.org/cgibin/giga.cgi?cmd=cause_dir_news_item&cause_id=1694&news_id=97849&cat_id=all

million people and a total Gross Domestic Product (GDP) approximately US$1.0 trillion.

Noted that the region makes up half of the African Union (AU) in terms of membership and just over 58% in terms of contribution to GDP and 57% of the total population of the African Union. The establishment of a Tripartite Free Trade Area will bolster intra-regional trade by creating a wider market, increase investment flows, enhance competitiveness and develop cross-regional infrastructure.[12]

The integration of these three large RIOs would be a major step forward in rationalizing the situation of the RIOs in Africa. The process appears to be evolutionary and other RIOs can be added to the process through the auspices of the AU. A similar process will be necessary in other regions in order to comply with WTO rules.

Conclusion

The colonial history of much of the developing world and the independence movements of the 1960s have created a series of countries that have had difficulty in establishing themselves in the post-colonial period. This process continues into the twenty-first century with Southern Sudan seceding from Sudan. Somalia is a failed state, and there are rebel movements in Chad, Mali, Mauritania and the delta region of Nigeria. The turmoil in the Congo is currently under control while the situation in Côte d'Ivoire continues to smoulder. In Africa, conflict and poverty have been synonymous with each other. Looking at this situation now it is perhaps easy to forget that in the twentieth century Europe ripped itself apart not once but twice. The breakup of Yugoslavia has shown us that even in the 1990s Europe could be the site of internecine conflict.

The existence of the European Union created a vehicle for bringing the countries of Europe together in a common approach to democracy, trade and economic growth. The European project has been more than fifty years in the making and has not yet reached its end point. The current financial upheaval surrounding the common currency shows how difficult the process of political and economic integration can be.

---

12 Communiqué of the second COMESA-EAC-SADC Tripartite Summit, Sandton Convention Centre Johannesburg, South Africa, accessed at www.eac. int/trade/index.php?option=com_content&view=article&id=129:comesa-eac-sadc-tripartite&catid=40:press

The pan-African movement is not new. It can trace its origins to Nkrumah, Nyerere and Banda. The Organization of African States was the first attempt to draw the very disparate countries of Africa together. The task of its successor, the African Union, is daunting. Africa is an enormous continent made up of radically different people from north to south and east to west. There are a wide range of different religions and indigenous resources. The regional integration agenda is ambitious but sometimes the ambition outweighs the reality. Declarations at summits are grandiose but making the political expression fact is often beyond the capacity of the RIO and its membership.

RIOs have the ability to address many of the constraints to economic growth. Their role in trade facilitation, negotiating trade agreements, creating economies of scale and fostering peace and democracy at regional level makes them an indispensable factor in developing the future. But all is not sweetness and light. Some elements of the RIO militate against their effectiveness. Membership is too open. Most clubs have no conditions of membership other than the ability to pay the membership fee. The RIOs in the developing world permit membership without any conditions in terms of democracy or governance. This can be contrasted with the EU which requires new members to undergo a relatively long negotiation period and adhere to more than 30,000 pages of *acquis communitaire*, much of which requires acts of parliament to enforce. RIOs are clubs and like any club the people in charge set the rules. Once the rules are set there should be a mechanism to command adherence. Countries like Zimbabwe regularly flout the rules of the club of which it is a member but there is never an admonishment. Solidarity is important but not at the expense of democracy and good governance.

The RIOs are not without their critics and their decisions (particularly their political decisions) sometimes leave them in exposed positions. Support for pariah regimes is a case in point. There is an element of regime boosting and shadow regionalism on the part of some members of the RIOs. There are even those who contend that the RIOs are hotbeds of corruption (Söderbaum 2010). A club is only as good as its rules and the adherence of its member to them. Tightening the rules of entry to include elements of commitments to democracy and good governance would allay many of the criticisms of political chicanery.

RIOs are important actors in promoting security, trade and regional initiatives. They certainly have the potential to be part of an aid exit strategy but their weaknesses outweigh their strengths in assisting their members to reduce their aid dependency. A high-capacity RIO with strong political backing and the power of a regional court backed up by real sanctions would certainly place the RIO in a strong position to be an integral part of an aid exit strategy. Unfortunately very few RIOs tick all the relevant boxes in this regard.

Sustainable access to microfinance helps alleviate poverty by generating income, creating jobs, allowing children to go to school, enabling families to obtain health care, and empowering people to make the choices that best serve their needs. (Kofi Annan, speech to mark the International Day of Microfinance, 2004)

The genesis of microfinance

The exclusion of the poor, and sometimes the not so poor, from financial services in developing countries has been a consideration for governments for quite some time. From the 1950s, subsidized credit programmes run by state-owned or private agricultural development banks made loans to agricultural communities. Given the make-up of these loans, generally backed by a government guarantee, several problems were encountered. The principal problem was the poor repayment rates which were mainly attributed to farmers concluding that since the loans were guaranteed by government, they were in fact a government subsidy. A second major problem was that some of the loans made their way into the hands of larger farmers.

In the 1970s, Muhammad Yunus, a Bangladeshi banker and economist recently returned from the US to his homeland and at that point Head of the Rural Economics Programme at the University of Chittagong, started looking for a more practical way to help the poor. He saw that many of the poor had no access to funds in order to engage in entrepreneurial activities. He decided that he would make a loan, from his own pocket, and he made his first transaction in 1976, lending US$27 to a group of forty-two villagers who needed to buy raw materials for the bamboo stools they made and sold.

The fact that he gave the loan to a large group turned out to be a bonus in terms of repayment since nobody wanted to let down his friends. The whole group felt a collective responsibility for the loan. Whenever one individual was unable to make a repayment, the others in the group would make up the shortfall. This seemed to be a mechanism to counteract the repayment problems that had plagued the normal agriculture-based loans. The small loan of $27 launched the start of the microfinance era and the beginning of what became the Grameen Bank, the first recognized microfinance institution (MFI).

The success of the microfinance project in the village of Jobra encouraged the Bangladesh Central Bank and some of the nationalized commercial banks to support the roll-out of the scheme to the Tangail region. With success in Tangail, the project was extended to several other districts in the country. In October 1983, the Grameen Bank Project was transformed into an independent bank by government legislation. Today Grameen Bank is owned by the rural poor whom it serves. Borrowers of the bank own 90 per cent of its shares, while the remaining 10 per cent is owned by the government.

The focus of the loans made by Grameen were initially women. It has been well known in development circles that projects which concentrate on women have a much higher chance of success than those centred on men. This is perhaps because women are more concerned with issues of education and health than their spouses. A second element of the Grameen process was the use of the solidarity group. The group usually consisted of twenty or more women who took the loan as a group and were then obliged to pay back as a group. This solidarity aspect was central to ensuring high levels of repayment. Another aspect of the microloans was that they were granted without collateral.

The microfinance industry today

The small, $27, loan which Professor Yunus gave in 1976 has spawned a global industry with currently more than 1,800 MFIs offering financial services to the poor. There have been many changes in the basic model developed by the Grameen Bank. The solidarity model is no longer in vogue, having fallen into disrepute. While the model was appropriate for the lender in terms of repayment of the loan, there were unintended social consequences. Women unable to pay were shunned by other members of the group and there were instances of suicide (see Dichter 2007 and Arvind et al. 2011). Another problem with the initial model was that group leaders tended to benefit more from loans than individual members. The Grameen Bank and many of the first-generation MFIs were not-for-profit organizations. The most important change to the original model has been the introduction of the for-profit MFIs.

In Phase I of the microfinance approach, funding was provided by government, donors or NGOs generally as a grant to the microfinance organization. Microfinance was therefore positioned as a development aid initiative, with the recipients only obliged by the solidarity rule to repay their loan. In Phase II microfinance, the MFIs have become more like private financial organizations with their continuity subject to them turning a profit. In Phase II microfinance, sustainability of the operation is as important as the mission to provide financial services to the poor.[1]

Microfinance became such a hot topic in the development world that the UN declared 2004 as the International Year of Microfinance. By 2004, of course, microfinance had already passed from being a donor- and NGO-driven process to being a for-profit enterprise. Some commentators (particularly Bateman) see second-generation microfinance as an extension of the neoliberal approach of the World Bank and the IMF to development. The development community, for their sins, saw microfinance as a win-win development tool. The poor would have access to finance and that finance would be supplied by a bona fide financial institution which would be self-sustaining.

The clearing house for information on microfinance and MFIs is the Microfinance Information Exchange (MIX) which compiles annual data. In 2011, MIX listed 1,390 microfinance organizations on its database; they consisted of banks, credit unions, classical micro-financers (usually NGOs with funded programmes) and Phase II for-profit microfinancers. The concept has spread to every continent including Europe, where a number of MFIs are operating.

Forbes magazine compiles a list of the top 50 MFIs each year. The institutions are sorted by scale which is a measure of their gross loan portfolio, efficiency which considers the operating expenses and the cost per borrower, risk which looks at the quality of their portfolios and return which is measured as a combination of return on equity and return on assets. The top MFI on the overall scale is ASA from Bangladesh, Microcredit Foundation of India is the most efficient, Consumer Credit Union 'Economic Partnership' has the lowest risk portfolio and Banco Compartamos has the highest return (Forbes 2007).

The story of Compartamos is not unique: there are many more

---

1 For a description of the two phases of microfinance see Bateman (2010).

Box 8.1 A case study of Compartamos

Compartamos operated from its inception in 1990 until 2000 as a not-for-profit, non-governmental organization (NGO). During this period, it received US$4.3 million in grants or near-grant soft loans from international development agencies and private Mexican sources. The NGO made tiny loans to poor and lower-income women, mainly in rural areas.

By 2000, the Compartamos NGO was reaching 60,000 borrowers. To tap commercial funds for even faster growth, the NGO and other investors set up a regulated finance company, organized as a Phase II for-profit corporation. Around that time, USAID granted $2 million to ACCION who extended technical services, bought stock in the new company and lent $1 million as subordinated debt.

At this stage Compartamos received over $30 million in loans from public development agencies and $15 million from private socially oriented investors. These loans were generally at market interest rates or above.

Beginning in 2002, Compartamos was able to issue roughly $70 million in bonds on the Mexican securities exchange. Most of these bonds were partially guaranteed by the International Finance Corporation (IFC). In addition, the company raised about $65 million by borrowing from Mexican banks and commercial lenders. In June 2006, the finance company received a full banking licence. The company was serving 616,000 borrowers by the end of 2006 and expects to continue its rapid growth.

The shareholders of Compartamos at the time of the Initial Public Offering (IPO) were: Compartamos AC (the NGO): 39.2 per cent, funded mainly from the CGAP and USAID/ACCION grants; ACCION Gateway fund: 18.1 per cent; IFC: 10.6 per cent; directors and managers: 23.7 per cent; other private Mexican investors: 8.5 per cent.

ACCION's Gateway Fund also bought $1 million worth of shares in the finance company. Compartamos repaid the subordinated loan ahead of schedule when less expensive funding sources became available.

The original price these investors paid for their shares in

1998–2000 totalled roughly $6 million. By the end of 2006, the book value of these shares had risen to $126 million, because of very high profits. The book value of return on shareholders' equity has averaged over 53 per cent a year since commercialization in 2000, and over 80 per cent of this profit has been retained within the company to fund growth in the number and size of its loans, rather than being paid out in dividends to shareholders.

The profits reflect the high interest rates Compartamos charges on its loans. Compartamos's interest yield on average loan portfolio was about 86 per cent for 2005. (Very high interest rates are common among both for-profit and not-for-profit providers in the low-end Mexican loan market.)

On 20 April 2007, IPO shareholders sold about 30 per cent of their shares to new investors. Existing investors received about $450 million for 30 per cent of their shares, which represents more than 12 times the book value of those shares. This implies a market valuation of the company at over $1.5 billion, and an internal rate of return on the selling shareholders' original investment (about $6 million) of roughly 100 per cent a year compounded over eight years.

Most of the sale proceeds went to public-purpose institutions – IFC and the ACCION and Compartamos not-for-profit NGOs. A third of the proceeds, about $150 million, went into the pockets of private shareholders. The unsold shares that remain in the hands of these private shareholders are worth about $300 million.

Source: Compartamos website

---

like it.[2] It is unfortunate that providing financial services for the poor should be such a boon to those who invested in it. However, does the fact that the shareholders of the privatized MFIs have made a killing demean the work that was done by the MFIs? Banks have been providing financial services to their communities for more than

---

2 See Elisabeth Malkin, 'Microfinance's success sets off a debate in Mexico', *New York Times*, 5 April 2008.

a hundred years and making a handsome profit for their shareholders in the process.

Aside from the MFIs (non-profit and for-profit) there are a number

---

Box 8.2 Alternative mechanisms for financing the poor

- Financial cooperatives (including credit unions): This category embraces a wide range of member-owned savings and loan institutions. Financial cooperatives tend to be relatively small, since membership is usually based on some common bond, such as employment at a company or residence in a village. Healthy ones focus more on savings than on credit.
- Low-capital rural and/or local banks: Several countries offer a special licence for small, locally owned, non-cooperative financial intermediaries (e.g. Philippine Rural Banks and Indonesian BPRs). Some of these institutions are owned by individuals, others by a combination of local and regional governments. These banks usually remain small-scale in comparison with other regulated financial intermediaries in a given country.
- State development and agricultural banks: In order to reach sectors that commercial banks serve insufficiently, many governments have established state-owned, often large, banks to promote agriculture or other perceived development priorities. Many of these banks focus more on credit than on savings, making them particularly susceptible to political interference. Governments have often been willing to subsidize continuing losses in these institutions.
- Postal savings banks: Many countries take advantage of their wide-spread postal infrastructure where it exists to provide financial services. These services are usually limited to savings and payments/transfers. Account and transaction sizes tend to be quite small.
- Non-postal savings banks: This category includes both private and public institutions, of which the latter are often very large. Some of these savings banks have loan portfolios, but most of their loan assets are in large investment loans rather than small retail loans.

of other solutions for the poor in accessing financial services. These alternatives are provided in Box 8.2. It is important to get away from preconceived ideas that finance for the poor should always be provided at a loss which will then be covered by a donor agency or the government. The 'bottom billion' require financial services also and they constitute a market segment. It is important to remember that the large number of poor people now accessing loans through MFIs would have been excluded otherwise or would have been required to look to the informal sector, namely moneylenders to satisfy their requirements. The supply of microfinance could not exist without a demand.

There is, however, one worrying aspect. The large number of MFIs might create a microfinance bubble. MFIs have moved to taking on consumer lending which, as the worldwide financial crisis has demonstrated, is a riskier business than enterprise loans. Also the large number of MFIs in some countries have led to intense competition for clients. This competition has a positive aspect in driving interest rates down, but there is a corresponding risk that pushing loans will cause clients to take on debt they cannot service. For example, in India, average household debt to microfinance lenders rose from $27 in 2004 to $135 in 2009. Despite this large rise, repayment rates remain above 95 per cent.

Who are the clients of microfinance?

The poor are not a homogenous group and neither are they composed entirely of people with entrepreneurial flair. The initial concept behind microfinance – of providing finance to poor people who would then invest the loan in a productive activity the returns from which would then be used to repay the loan – is not always the case. The poor have needs other than investment in productive enterprises. They need food on a daily basis, they need education for their children, and they need money to pay for health care. They also need money to absorb shocks due either to crop failure (the majority of the 'bottom billion' are agricultural labourers) or to environmental disasters. The concept that the loan recipient rushes off to buy a goat, chicken or goods to sell in the market is just unrealistic. One of the ideas that must be scrapped at once is that microfinance is there to turn poor people into entrepreneurs. This is blatantly not true.

It is equally unwise to think that it is only poor people in developing countries who are excluded from mainstream financial services. In the USA, the world's largest economy, 51 per cent of the respondents to a survey indicated that they did not have an account at a bank (CSFI 2008). This in US terms would amount to 40 million households or 106 million individuals. The World Bank (2008b) has estimated that in some countries fewer than 10 per cent of people have access to formal financial services. In Cambodia only 20 per cent of the population have access to financial services; the corresponding figure for Ghana is 16 per cent while in Tanzania it is only 5 per cent.

The average clients of an MFI operate in a mini-economy where production, consumption, trade and exchange, saving, borrowing and income occur in very small amounts (Matin et al. 2002). They are mainly women, and not necessarily the women who conform to the 1980s image of the female entrepreneur. Their involvement with the MFI is probably associated with their need to balance the household budget and to hedge against unforeseen needs. They generally live in a world of food insecurity and the risk of environmental disaster. If they live in Africa, they possibly live tens if not hundreds of kilometres from the nearest source of financial assistance from either the formal or the informal financial sector. In times of need they may first turn to family and friends to tide them over during a difficult period. If they have family working in the capital city, they will impose on them to provide finance, and if relatives are working abroad they will expect remittances. If all avenues fail, they may turn to the local moneylender (if one exists in their village or a town nearby) who will charge them usurious interest rates.

There is a vital difference between the microfinance client in Asia or Latin America and the client in Africa. The latter continent is vast, taking up a geographical area which would encompass the USA, Western Europe, China, Argentina and India. Reaching the chronically poor in Africa with any kind of service, whether it is education, health or financial services, is a major challenge. Geography and, in particular, population density play an important role in what services can be supplied at a reasonable cost. Since the poor must absorb, through the interest rate, the costs associated with servicing them this militates strongly against microfinance services in low-density areas. Given the transaction costs involved in setting up and managing a loan, it is likely that MFIs are concentrating their efforts on the urban poor or the rural poor close to urban centres.

Interest rates on microcredit are high, typically 50 to 100 per cent. This presupposes that the borrower can obtain returns higher than the imposed MFI interest rate if the loan is to be repaid and the borrower's situation is to be improved. If the borrower cannot generate a return on the loan higher than the MFI rate of interest, the loan will make the borrower poorer (Boudreaux and Cowen 2008). The latter situation means that the microfinance actually becomes a microdebt (Dichter 2007; Arvind et al. 2011). This would seem to contradict the whole concept of microfinance. How then can one rationalize the high levels of borrowing demonstrated by most MFIs? It is apparent that there is either a debt 'bubble' growing in the microfinance sector or the loans are being made to a class of the poor (an upper class of the poor) who are already engaged in an entrepreneurial activity. The main object of the initial concept of microfinance – the chronic poor – are again the subject of exclusion from financial services. However, this exclusion is probably in their own best interests since it may help them avoid the debt trap. A study of take-up rates for microfinance has concluded that 'the fact that participation in microfinance is not universal shows that microfinance is not a panacea, and is not for everyone' (Karlan et al. 2010).

While take-up rates in Asia are reasonably high (estimates show that the take-up in Bangladesh and Indonesia was more than 40 per cent), in sub-Saharan Africa only 20 per cent of adults use formal or semi-formal financial services. It appears that while there may be some constraints on the supply side there are also issues relating to the demand side. The main reason given for not taking up MFI services is the desire 'not to get into debt'. It is therefore evident that the poor are aware of the debt trap.

One of the myths of development is that the poor do not or cannot save (Matin et al. 2002). In effect the contrary is true despite the fact that the amounts which the poor are able to save are small. In the absence of deposit accounts, poor people are obliged to keep savings in insecure places and thereby run the risk of losing them through either theft or disaster. Potential savers will sometimes be inclined instead to purchase a tangible asset, such as a cow, a goat or even additional land. The trouble with such assets, however, is that prices of assets may fluctuate and some of the savings may be lost as a result.

There is a strong desire among the poor for a secure and stable home for their savings and for savings-related financial products. The existence of a pot of savings lodged in security removes some of the anxieties associated with the existence of the poor. Several studies have indicated that ownership of assets has more beneficial effects than income levels – including wealth, health, and education. There is evidence that savings are the product in highest demand when peace breaks out after conflict.

However, the concentration of the MFIs on lending (or supply) has led to a situation where the actual demand of the poor for savings security has largely gone unmet. Saving has often been described as the 'forgotten half' of microfinance. MFIs encounter several barriers to offering savings services, not least the substantial operational costs involved in managing a large number of small savings transactions to which depositors want easy access. Government regulation is much more onerous for financial organizations taking deposits, in order to ensure depositors' money is kept safe. And initiatives are limited by the costs and other challenges of reaching customers. In Malawi, for example, Opportunity International (the largest local MFI) has a fleet of five armoured trucks to take banking services to rural poor.[3]

As a result of these challenges, CARE International has piloted a new concept in saving for the poor. The Village Saving and Loan Association (VSL) model promoted by CARE is an accumulating savings and credit association that is time-bound, with a periodic action audit at which point all the funds are paid out. The CARE concept responds to the increasing popularity of community-managed services. Rather than expose customers to credit risks, they intermediate small local pools of capital to satisfy the cash management needs of individual households. The savings created can then be used to offer small loans, providing communities that previously were financially excluded with a first step from using more risky informal savings mechanisms to more formal financial services. The model was launched by CARE International in Niger in 1991, and is now being used by almost 1 million participants in Africa, Latin America and Asia. An assessment of a VSL set up by CARE in Tanzania concluded that 'the financial performance of the groups has been strong, both in lending and producing returns to members' savings at a mean rate of 53 per

---

3 Opportunity International is building a network of scalable, sustainable and accessible banks throughout the developing world. Since 2001, Opportunity International has built thirteen regulated microfinance institutions including nine banks.

cent in the last cycle'. This suggests that despite weak training, local people have been able to implement the approach very effectively. The action audit at a date agreed in advance creates a vital means of transparency and accountability at the end of the cycle that is very different to the usual self-help group methodologies.

Meanwhile, some microcredit institutions, including Bank Rakyat Indonesia (BRI), have conducted market research on the demand for savings, which has enabled them to build savings products which are appropriate for the poor. An examination of BRI's local banking portfolio shows that BRI has increased its number of micro outlets from 4,229 in 2006 to 4,649 in March 2011. As of March 2010, BRI had assets of Ind. Rp.307 billion (US$34 million) with a savings portfolio of Ind. Rp.243 billion (US$27 million). Loans and receivables amounted to Ind. Rp.209 billion (US$23 million).[4] In 2006, BRI had a total of 31 million depositors and 3.45 million clients who had taken loans. This demonstrates that there is a healthy appetite among the poor for savings products which are appropriate to their situation. It also means that banks like BRI can operate their loan portfolio from their deposit base. These conclusions regarding demand have been verified by Rutherford (2002).[5]

Does microfinance empower women?

One of the much-touted advantages of microfinance was that it empowered not only the chronically poor but also women. Studies examining the effects of microfinance have proved exceptionally difficult to mount. The normal mechanism of evaluation of the impact on a village or group availing itself of microfinance services against a control group who are not exposed to microfinance has been proved wanting. The main argument against such evaluations is that it is impossible to judge what the impact on the target village might be if the microfinance effort had been put into some other developmental activity, improved sanitation for example.

---

4 BRI website accessed at www.bri.co.id/

5 Rutherford (2002): 'Our conversations with poor households suggest that their needs for financial services are not dissimilar to those for other groups, and may in some respects be even more intense. Like the rest of us, (first) they need to find safe places where money can be stored, especially while it builds up into a lump sum, or into a repayment on a borrowed lump sum, and (second) they need quick access to overdraft facilities or other forms of small-scale household credit.'

The existence of solidarity groups in the first phase of microfinance put considerable pressure on women. They were made responsible for the repayment of the loan, they were obliged to attend the weekly meeting of the group and they were the ones who had to bear the social stigma if they were unable to pay their part of the loan repayment. And unfortunately they were the ones who committed suicide when they were ostracized. For example, a study established that, in the case of the Grameen Bank I, bank workers were putting intense pressure on women borrowers in order to accomplish high recovery rates (Rahman 1999). A study in Uganda concluded that 'NGO programmes did not translate into meaningful economic empowerment of the beneficiaries' (Muhumuza 2005).

Another study on the effect of microcredit on empowerment found that participation in a microcredit programme 'had limited potential for improving the condition for empowerment since participation has little impact in altering gender-based access to resources within the household and outside' (Mahmoud 2003). However, contrary views do exist. One study has concluded that in some cases 'microfinance has the potential to have a powerful impact on women's empowerment. Although microfinance is not always empowering for all women, most women do experience some degree of empowerment as a result' (Cheston and Kuhn 2001).

It would appear that the jury is out on whether microcredit empowers women or not. What is not in dispute is that it places a sometimes unbearable burden on women as the primary recipients of the loan. Anyone who has worked in the developing world knows that the position of women is one of the major impediments to development. It would be more than naïve to expect microfinance to put more than a minor dent in the traditional social fabric which has been developed over the millennia.

Regulating the MFI

MFIs have grown up as fairly free-form organizations. Many, such as the Grameen Bank, have been established by a single individual, while others have been established by NGOs. The MIX count of 1,400 MFIs of different sorts operating throughout the developing countries points to the difficulties associated with regulating what are in effect financial institutions.

Regulation of the banking system generally requires that financial institutions should be subject to prudential regulation and supervision for two main reasons: first to protect depositors, particularly small depositors, from loss of their savings if the financial institution becomes insolvent, and second to ensure the financial system as a whole does not become unstable through loss of confidence as a result of major financial institutions becoming insolvent.

The 'protection of deposits' reason suggests that MFIs should generally be subject to prudential regulation and supervision if they accept savings. While there are cases of extremely large MFIs, in general the operations of the MFI are at the micro level and consequently they are not likely to threaten the stability of the financial systems in which they operate. This fact highlights why many MFIs have shied away from savings mobilization: savings facilities provide a valuable service to clients, and can be important in reducing poverty, but offering this facility opens up the MFI to the regulatory process. Mobilizing savings places an onerous responsibility on an institution to ensure that the savings of clients are not at risk.

It is perhaps not surprising that the first MFI was established in Bangladesh given the total lack of regulation in that country. Regulations governing the operations of the MFI in Bangladesh date only from 2006, when the government of Bangladesh established the Microcredit Regulatory Authority (MRA) with a view to creating an enabling environment for NGO MFIs to work, promote and foster sustainable development of microfinance institutions in Bangladesh. Accordingly the MRA is authorized to monitor and supervise the microcredit sector under a full-fledged regulatory framework. Experiences of the Authority indicate that there are other important issues which need to be addressed with caution, among them issues of service charges, sustainability of the sector, overlapping borrowers, establishing effective supervisory tools to monitor, new issues like foreign investment and securitization etc. All these problems place huge responsibilities on the shoulders of the MRA (Rashid 2010).

Most countries have processes for registration of NGOs, cooperatives, and other institutions engaged in microfinance which do not usually involve central banks. However, there are cases where central banks become involved in the registration or licensing of certain categories of MFIs. By far the most prominent example is Nepal, where the central bank is the main regulatory and monitoring body

Box 8.3 Regulation of MFIs in Tanzania

Regulation of the microfinance industry took place in Tanzania under the umbrella of the 1991 financial reforms embodied in the Banking and Financial Institutions Act aimed at creating an effective and efficient financial system. Also in 1991 the government enacted the Cooperative Societies Act which provided the basis for the development of Savings and Credit Cooperative Societies. The regulations are set out by the Ministry of Finance's National Microfinance Policy of May 2000.

The Policy covered the provision of financial services to households, smallholder farms, and small and micro enterprises in both rural and urban areas. It covers a range of financial services, including savings, credit, payments, and other services. The vision for the policy was achievement of widespread access to microfinance throughout the country incorporating the best practices combining commercial financial principles with a variety of ways to adapt service delivery techniques to the circumstances of low-income clients.

The core of the policy is the following:

- The price of services should be set by the microfinance organizations themselves.
- MFIs need to produce relevant financial and operational information.
- Financial information should show subsidies explicitly.
- Institutions should have sound governing structures suitable to their institutional types.
- A supervisory authority would oversee the protection of the depositors and the financial system.
- Only MFIs accepting deposits would be subject to regulation and supervision.
- Risk assessments would be based on portfolio risk rather than on legal security for each loan.
- The Supervisory Authority would decide on licensing requirements for MFIs.
- Government and political parties cannot be providers of microfinance services.

- The Ministry of Finance has overall responsibility for the development of the financial sector.
- The Bank of Tanzania would ensure the regulatory and supervisory framework consistent with financial prudence.
- The Bank of Tanzania would be responsible for collating and disseminating information on the microfinance sector.

Source: United Republic of Tanzania, Ministry of Finance, National Microfinance Policy, May 2000

for the licensed nonbank MFIs, consisting of NGOs and cooperatives (Asian Development Bank 2000).

The Asian Development Bank (ADB) has concluded that in the Asia/Pacific region the central banks in general do not have the capacity (aside from their obligations in terms of bank and currency regulation) to regulate a plethora of small MFIs. In line with the general conditions for prudential oversight the general rule is that only MFIs which are deposit takers should be regulated, and among those that do not take deposits only those large enough to impact on the stability of the system. In order to overcome some of the problems associated with prudential oversight the ADB has suggested that MFIs accepting savings simply as a condition for loans should not be regulated. One of the suggestions is that it may be possible to set a 'threshold' below which savings mobilization is unregulated or, alternatively, any savings might have to be deposited with a licensed financial institution. Given the capacity constraints which exist within the central banks, it does not appear practical to regulate the full range of nonbank MFIs; however, in the interests of the clients any institution accepting deposits from the public should be regulated and supervised. Other areas which have been considered for regulation are the capping of interest rates and limits on the number of clients who can be accepted.

Box 8.3 describes the situation with regard to the regulation of MFIs in Tanzania. The considerations of the government of Tanzania are fairly general. For example the recommendation of the National Bank for Agricultural and Rural Development Task Force to the Government of India included:

- Self-regulation of all MFIs under organizations created for the purpose.
- Registration of all MFIs with a regulatory authority.
- External regulation and supervision of MFIs mobilizing savings in excess of a threshold.
- Imposition of reserve requirements, calibrated to the volume of savings held.
- Savings to be mobilized only in the context of the loan contract, not *from nonmembers*. (NABARD Task Force 1999)

Ethiopia is among the countries that have established specific regulatory and supervisory frameworks for microfinance businesses. Licensing and supervision of microfinance institutions proclamation number 40/1996, which was repealed and replaced by proclamation no. 626/2009 and consequent directives issued by the National Bank of Ethiopia, has helped to set general principles, rules and standards that have to be complied with by MFIs. The government and the National Bank of Ethiopia have made efforts to improve gradually the regulatory framework by liberalizing the interest rate, increasing the lending size and loan term, allowing MFIs to extend loans with lending methodology at their own discretion, introducing capital adequacy, liquidity and provisioning requirements. The National Bank of Ethiopia is also currently carrying out Business Process Re-engineering that will enable it to improve its current overall performance (Kassa 2010).

Each government will, of course, develop its own legal provisions for the MFIs in accordance with the particular situation of the country in question. There has been a call from the industry itself and from some in the NGO community for self-regulation in the microfinance area. Precisely the absence of regulation in microfinance has enabled MFIs to develop innovative methods (Berenbach and Churchill 1997).

Depending on self-regulation in any financial sector is a risky business. Despite the mostly small scale of operations of most MFIs, the MIX figures for number of MFIs varies from year to year, which means that some MFIs are disappearing or possibly coalescing. MFIs which are taking deposits must be prudently regulated in the normal fashion if the depositors are to be protected. Financial innovation is important but not at the expense of the depositors, who are in general the poor.

Microfinance and mobile banking

One of the major problems (and costs) of microfinance has been accessing customers and managing accounts. The vastness of a continent such as Africa is a severe impediment to customer capture and maintenance. New mobile phone banking technology has already been proved in Kenya and is now spreading throughout Africa, permitting customers to save and withdraw funds via mobile banking, or m-banking. As of today, microfinance and m-banking inhabit different worlds. The MFI world is concentrated on the provision of credit with some MFIs also providing a savings service. M-banking is concentrated on transfers and payments.

However, many MFIs see the potential for synergy between their concept and new mobile technology. This is already happening. In Pakistan, Tameer Microfinance Bank with 120,000 customers and $17 million in deposits launched an m-banking service called 'easypaisa' that within six months processed more than 1 million transactions. This system was conceived through a partnership with Telenor, the second-largest mobile phone operator in Pakistan. For Telenor this was not simply a straightforward business decision but a response from the company to a requirement by the regulator for the operator to develop an m-banking service in cooperation with a bank. One year after the launch of the new service Telenor took a 51 per cent shareholding in Tameer (Kumar et al. 2010).

While this level of cooperation will probably be the exception rather than the rule, the case does demonstrate the potential synergy between the two business models.

Conclusion

The genesis of microfinance was the desire to assist the poor to access enough finance for them to establish microenterprises which would produce additional funds to help them rise steadily out of poverty. The initial concept employed funding mainly from NGOs and government, which subsidized the interest rate and stood as guarantor should the microfinance institution fail. Clients were generally in solidarity circles which assisted with the achievement of high repayment rates.

That early model has been consigned to the dustbin of history and has been replaced with the for-profit model that we have today. The current business model could be described as simply providing financial services to the 'bottom billion' or the 'base of the pyramid' as it is sometimes called. The developmental approach of the initial concept has been slewed off and the poor are simply considered as a market segment to be serviced by a specific entity, an MFI.

The latest outpourings on the subject of microfinance have been highly critical of both the initial concept and its evolutionary relation (see Bateman 2010). The poor need access to financial services but the question is whether the high-interest model of the MFI is the most suitable vehicle to provide these services. There is now considerable evidence that two effects are in progress. The first is that microfinance risks becoming micro-debt that the non-entrepreneurial segment of the poor will have to bear. There are few businesses that can produce rates of return which are higher than the current interest rates demanded by the MFIs. And of course, not every poor person can invest in the few businesses that do have higher returns than interest. The developmental model is therefore dead and buried. The second effect is the 'bubble effect'. The financial crisis of 2008 has amply demonstrated the negative effect of providing funds to individuals who have no possibility of repaying those funds. Many governments in the developed world have reaped a whirlwind as their banking systems have almost collapsed under the weight of bad loans and exposure to the various sub-prime markets. The microfinance industry must have taken note of the similarities between their business model and the virtual collapse of the world financial system.

There is evidence that many poor people are playing a game which has been played in the developed world for some time in the area of credit cards. Some poor people are customers of more than one MFI, using loans from one to pay off the debt to others in a vicious cycle which can only spiral downwards. While the figures posted for the profitability of the MFIs are impressive, the business model is such that infinite care is required by the regulatory authorities to ensure that the system stays afloat. However, the ADB says that central banks are already overstretched by their tasks in relation to banking regulation and the maintenance of the financial system (Asian Development Bank 2000). The mushrooming of MFIs in the developing world can be seen as a scramble to service a segment of the market ignored by the mainstream banks. The long-term validity of this industry has still not been demonstrated.

Morduch (2000) hits the nail on the head when he talks about the 'microfinance schism', that is, the difference between the rhetoric and the actuality on the ground, the schism between the socially conceived ideal and the pro-profit fact.

Microfinance arrived on the scene as the answer to the problems of development and poverty. Pierre Omydiar, the founder of eBay, has launched with $100 million of seed capital a microfinance company with Tufts University. Omydiar is no neophyte where business is concerned, and he has estimated that the market for microfinance runs to $60 billion.[6] This is the effect that the magic bullet of micro-finance has on people. It is the quintessential piece of development alchemy – a loan that turns poor people into entrepreneurs and lifts them out of poverty. Although there is a large body of literature on microfinance, there is currently no proof that it can be a panacea for the poor and a candidate as an element of an aid exit strategy. The answer to the 'bubble' issue of microfinance may be some years down the road but come it surely will.

---

6 For Omydiar's remarks see Goldberg (2009).

9 | REMITTANCES

Migrants underwrite development through their remittances.
(Ban Ki-Moon, speech to the UN General Assembly, 19 May 2011)

There is mounting evidence from recent studies suggesting that migrants, particularly from Africa, are a reservoir of great potential that can be used to transform the development prospects of many countries and assist in the fight against poverty, hunger, diseases and human suffering. A report from the International Fund for Agricultural Development (IFAD 2009) notes that some 30 million African workers outside their countries send home approximately $40 billion a year in remittances.

Nations throughout Africa receive a significant share of their foreign exchange from remittances, a share which is stable and predictable (Ratha et al. 2008). In general developing countries suffer from a skill deficit. The loss of skilled citizens, in particular skilled health professionals, can have a negative effect on national development but if this outflow can be accompanied by a regular return of professionals who have upgraded their skills then the overall effect of migration can be positive. Possibilities for transfers of skills acquired over the years by returning migrants could also create a significant externality to the skill-starved economies of most countries in Africa.

Most important, the change in demographic structure in both origin and destination countries in the decades ahead is expected to generate huge labour market imbalances at a global level that could create substantial impetus for migration. It is unlikely that Africa will be able to provide jobs for the 1.1 billion workers who will be available by 2040 (McKinsey Global Institute 2010). The projections indicate that the global jobs deficit could reach 440 million by the next decade (Somavia 2011). Migrant-sending countries will have a labour surplus particularly among the young and less educated, who will be hard pressed to emigrate especially since they will be wishing to emigrate into a market with already high youth unemployment. Creating employment in the respective regions will be a serious policy challenge in the years ahead.

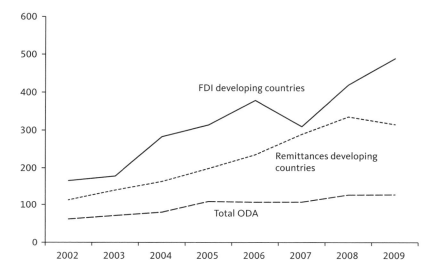

9.1 Overseas development aid, foreign direct investment and remittances for developing countries, 2002–09 (US$ billions) (*sources*: UNCTAD, OECD/DAC, World Bank)

Global remittances in 2009 topped $300 billion per year, three times more than OECD development aid and 80 per cent of all foreign direct investment (FDI) to developing countries (UNCTAD 2008). Figure 9.1 shows the evolution of remittances, aid and FDI in Africa.

Remittances like FDI rose steadily after the year 2000 and would probably have continued to do so in 2009 if it had not been for the financial crisis. It is clear therefore that remittances from migrants rank as highly as FDI as a principal source of external finance for most developing countries. The actual level of remittances, including unrecorded flows through formal and informal channels, could be substantially larger, and even greater than FDI.

The top ten recipients of remittances in 2010 were, in order: India, China, Mexico, the Philippines, Bangladesh, Nigeria, Pakistan, Lebanon, Vietnam and Egypt. All ten have a large diaspora, particularly the four highest. Poland and Romania dropped off the list from 2008. Their inclusion at that time can be attributed to their accession to the European Union which increased their mobility within the EU. However, the financial crisis in Europe has hit both countries hard in terms of remittances. Of equal interest are the countries whose remittances are a major part of their GDP. In 2007, remittances to Lesotho accounted for 29 per cent of GDP while for Tajikstan the figure was 45 per cent.

Officially recorded remittance flows to developing countries recovered quickly after the global financial crisis to reach $325 billion in 2010. But they have not kept pace with rising prices in recipient countries. Remittance flows are expected to grow at lower but more sustainable rates of 7–8 per cent annually during 2011–13 to reach $404 billion by 2013 (Mohapatra et al. 2011).

Remittances and poverty alleviation

Evidence from a World Bank study in 2006 on remittances and migration suggests that remittances can

- reduce poverty, even where they appear to have little impact on measured inequality;
- help smooth household consumption by responding positively to adverse shocks (for example, crop failure, job loss, or a health crisis);
- ease working capital constraints on farms and small-scale entrepreneurs;
- lead to increased household expenditures in areas considered to be important for development, particularly education, entrepreneurship, and health (World Bank 2006c).

Even without the depth of the study referenced above, it is clear that if one puts money directly into the pockets of the poor, all of the above points should hold. Remittances are not development programmes, they represent the choices which the recipient will make when the cash arrives in his or her hand. Therefore a major portion of the remittances will go on consumption, whether of food or other goods, some will go on education and health, and some might even find its way into entrepreneurial activity or the purchase of land or machinery. In general, the choice of what to do with the money is in the hands of the recipient except for those cases where the sender states a preference for the use of the money. Preferences generally arise in the case of education or entrepreneurial activities including agriculture.

At the head of the list of countries receiving remittances were India and China. Both countries have large poor populations and it is fair to assume that some (but not all) remittances find their way to the chronically poor or even those just above the poverty line. However, given the fact that migration from countries like India and China takes place not only from the poorest class but also from what could be called the middle class, a large proportion of remittances miss out the poor.

The same effect militates against sub-Saharan Africa. From the 2009 total remittance figure of $315.6 billion only $20.7 billion, or 6.5 per cent of the total, was remitted to sub-Saharan Africa. This highlights the fact that migration from extremely poor countries to the major developing countries is extremely difficult for the poorest classes. The majority of the migrants from sub-Saharan Africa find their way to South Africa which is the economic powerhouse of the region and within travelling distance by land for migrants from the surrounding countries. Indian and Chinese migrants, with the advantage of their extensive diaspora especially to OECD countries, have greater possibilities to develop remittance flows.

A secondary problem for sub-Saharan Africa is that many migrants are skilled individuals who have the funds and the job prospects to gain entry to developed countries. This has been particularly true of health professionals, who have been deserting sub-Saharan Africa for employment and experience in the developed world. These migrants are a source of remittances but since they come from the middle classes only a small proportion of the remittances reaches the very poor.

One study found that international migration and remittances have a strong, statistically significant impact on reducing poverty in developing countries.[1] This study shows that a 10 per cent increase in the share of international migrants in a country's population will lead to a 2.1 per cent decline in the share of people living on less than $1 a day. A similar increase of 10 per cent in per capita official international remittances will lead on average to a 3.5 per cent decline in the share of people living in poverty. The study concludes that these 'results provide strong, robust evidence of the poverty-reducing impact of both international migration and remittances in the developing world'.

Remittances and economic development

Intuitively one would think that remittances would assist economic development. Remittances are spent in the economy whether on

1 For a discussion on this point see Adams and Page (2005).

consumption of goods and services or on improving the business activities of the recipient. Conversely an IMF study found that 'altruistically motivated remittances intend to compensate their recipients for bad economic outcomes, but also create incentives which lead to moral hazard problems. The moral hazard problem created by remittances can be severe enough to reduce economic activity. Our empirical estimations reveal considerable evidence both that remittances tend to be compensatory in nature and that they have negative effects on economic growth' (Chami et al. 2003).

This result is certainly counter-intuitive and is challenged by a World Bank study which finds the empirical evidence on the growth effects of remittances to be mixed (Ratha et al. 2008). This anomaly can be explained by the difficulty of disentangling remittances' countercyclical response to growth, which suggests that the causality runs from growth to remittances when in fact the correlation between the two variables is negative. Remittances tend to respond to adverse household shocks. There is an appreciable rise in remittances directly after an environmental calamity such as a flood or a famine. Remittances are also high in the case of a failed state such as Somalia.

Although this is not the place to discuss the efficacy of development aid, there is a body of evidence which indicates that aid is more efficient in countries with good governance (Burnside and Dollar 2004). The same appears to be true of the effect of remittances on economic growth. Remittances are more effective in a good policy environment with well-developed financial systems and sound institutions. Remittances may also enhance financial systems which in turn will stimulate growth.[2]

A study of remittances in Asia and the Pacific countries concluded that remittances seem to have a positive but marginal impact on economic growth through the improvement of domestic investment and human capital (Jongwanich 2007). Also, remittances have a significant direct impact on poverty reduction through increasing income, smoothing consumption and easing the capital constraints of the poor.

Remittances can also improve a country's creditworthiness and thereby enhance its access to international capital markets. The World Bank study cited above points out that the calculation of a country's credit ratings by major international rating agencies also depends on

---

2 For a more detailed discussion see Aggarwal et al. (2006).

its magnitude of remittance flows (World Bank 2006c). The higher the magnitude of remittance flows the better the credit rating rank the country could reach. This is another way to increase both physical and human capital investment, thereby enhancing economic growth.

It has also been suggested that sub-Saharan countries can potentially raise bond financing by using securitization of future flows such as remittances through the use of a special-purpose vehicle whereby the future receivables are deposited directly in an offshore account managed by a trustee (Ratha et al. 2008). The debt could then be serviced from this account, and excess collections could be forwarded to the borrowing entity in the developing country. This would be an innovative approach to reducing the level of interest which the developing country would be required to pay under normal circumstances.

While there is no doubt that remittances cannot be classed as traditional growth engines like exports and foreign direct investment in promoting long-term economic growth and a country's prosperity, remittances can have an effect at the micro level by providing capital savings which can be used for productive investments and by permitting the use of innovative financial instruments where security is required.

Large inflows of remittances can cause the real exchange rate to appreciate ('Dutch disease'), which can impair growth. In this way remittances can act similarly to a resource windfall or a large volume of ODA. Large inflows of foreign currency (usually US dollars) create a demand for local currency from the banking system which in turn leads to appreciation of the local currency, making local products more expensive on international markets while at the same time making imports cheaper.

Despite UN Secretary General Ban Ki-Moon's assertion that remittances underwrite development, there is little evidence, especially in the poorest parts of sub-Saharan Africa, that remittances have spurred development. Those poor people in Africa who are lucky enough to receive remittances will use them for the same reasons that they would use microfinance, for consumption and to hedge against an uncertain future.

Remittances and inequality

As mentioned above, the patterns of migration, with the better-off having greater potential to emigrate to a developed country due to their superior skillset or even the ability to pay the cost of travel, means that they have a disproportionately greater ability to generate remittances for their already well-off family. This form of remittance can widen national disparities.

It is apparent that if remittances represent a large share of total income of any group (either the poor or the middle class), they may potentially have a large impact on inequality. However, in the very unlikely event that they are perfectly equally distributed, they cannot influence inequality even if their magnitude is large. If remittances are large and unequally distributed, they may either increase or decrease inequality, depending upon which households receive them. If remittances are unequally distributed and flow disproportionately towards households at the top of the income distribution, their contribution to inequality will be positive. However, if they are unequally distributed but target poor households, remittances may have the effect of reducing inequality. A major study of remittances in Mexico bore out this intuitive hypothesis. International remittances (usually from the US to Mexico) tended to be larger than national remittances (intra Mexico) and also tended to flow to the better off, thereby increasing inequality. Because of this, international remittances have an unequalizing effect on rural incomes (Taylor et al. 2005).

A UN study on the effect of remittances in the Philippines concluded that

> as monetary resources are injected into local economies, prices in general tend to rise. While small-scale farmers of migrant families struggle to compete with larger-scale producers and imported products, families that do not receive remittances from abroad struggle to keep up. On the one hand, the high prices of the inputs (such as fertilizers and pesticides) necessary to guarantee agricultural subsistence often prevent many of these farmers from accessing them. On the other hand, they are also unable to compete with migrant families once these have made technical investments in their farming practices. Add to this the lack of financial power that non-migrant families have for purchasing store-bought food products and the results seem to point to increased levels of inequality within remittance-receiving communities, as well as increased risk of food insecurity in those households that do not receive remittances. (UNINSTRAW 2008)

This inequality effect will in theory be greater in areas like sub-Saharan Africa where a great deal of the migration is interregional.

Remittances and food security

Between 2006 and 2008, international food prices doubled. The effects of the price surge were felt globally, although the hardest hit were low-income, food-deficit countries with low stocks. Many of these countries were located in sub-Saharan Africa. During this period of high prices, about 100 million poor rural and urban people were pushed into the ranks of the world's hungry. International food prices have declined since mid-2008, but they are still substantially higher than prior to the price increases, and they are likely to remain at 2010 levels or higher for the next decade. The developed countries have been the first to respond to the crisis by increasing production. However, it will be important for future food supplies that the agricultural potential of the least developed countries is developed. Current estimates suggest that feeding a global population of just over 9 billion in 2050 will require a 70 per cent increase in global food production. Without significant investment in agriculture (and for the least developed countries that means smallholder agriculture), food security will remain a dominant issue for all developing countries. There is therefore an urgent need to find mechanisms which will assist smallholders to improve production and thereby create access to increased food supply for all.

Even if only a small percentage of the poor receive them, remittances will increase the funds flow to the rural poor. Depending on spending patterns, this should lead to increased funds for investment in improved agricultural production. The overall management of the agricultural sector is in the hands of the government, and it is their remit to adopt policies and concrete measures – to be funded by the national budget – which will enhance agricultural production and improve the food security situation of their people. Remittances will never supplant this important role of government and cannot be used to pay for vital services such as agricultural extension services. Neither will remittances increase the number and capacity of veterinary surgeons. However, a flow of additional funds to rural communities could, if managed properly, contribute in whatever small way to an improvement in food security. This hypothesis has not been tested to any great extent. Studies on remittances have concentrated on their effects on poverty and on economic growth. Babatunde and Martinetti (2010) examined the impacts of remittances on food security and nutrition, using micro-level household survey data from Nigeria. They concluded that, compared to non-receiving households, remittance-receiving households are better off in terms of mean total income, assets, calorie supply, micronutrients supply, as well as child nutritional status. Econometric analyses confirmed that remittance income contributes to improved calorie supply at the household level, an aspect which has not been analysed previously. Likewise, household income net of remittances increases calorie supply in a significant way, but the effect is twice larger than the effect of remittance income. Remittance income has no impact on diet quality, micronutrients supply and child nutritional status, thus limiting the extent to which nutrition programmes will benefit from remittances increase. In contrast, household income net of remittances has a significant effect on these indicators. Many studies have questioned whether remittance income is spent on food consumption; the preceding analyses suggest that remittances are important for food consumption, but it appears they are not spent on quality foods and micronutrients apart from that which is used for buying starchy staple foods.

Although the empirical literature is scant, what is there does appear to uphold what one might conclude intuitively. If poor rural households receive additional discretionary funds, it is likely that at least some of that funding will go into improving the food security situation of the household and by extension of the village. This effect may not be significant in national terms but may have a limited local impact.

Remittances and gender

Nearly 50 per cent of the world's migrants are female. Women migrants include professionals in all fields, doctors and nurses, women caring for the aged in the developed world, as well as maids and domestic workers. Many have gained status from their employment either internationally or nationally. And many are among the largest remitters of money to their families. There is therefore a growing recognition that gender plays an important role in the remittance process, particularly in the area of targeting the use of remittances in the migrant's country of origin. Despite the equal share of female migrants, there has until recently been limited research dedicated to understanding how gender affects the remittance process. An overview of the theoretical and empirical issues that emerge within the literature on the effects of gender on international migration and remittances points out the lack of sufficient data to enable clear conclusions to be drawn on this issue and makes suggestion for areas of future research in the subject (Pfeiffer et al. 2007).

To explore how the remittance behaviour of women and men differs and what the impact of these differences may be, one strand of literature mainly examines the behaviour of migrants in sending areas. A key question is whether gender influences the share of income that is remitted to the origin family. A sample of Thai women migrants concluded that they have a higher propensity to remit funds to their households than men. Additionally the women who did remit funds sent a higher proportion of their available funds than did men (Osaki 1999). In addition, researchers have also examined whether female migrants channel a larger fraction of their transfers into health, nutrition and educational investments for the origin family, and whether they are more likely to maintain social ties with their origin families, which tends to be associated with future remittance flows. It is unfortunate that even in developed countries female employees (whether migrants or locals) suffer from discrimination in rates of pay. This fact puts additional pressure on female migrants in terms of how much they can remit in comparison to men.

Migration and remittances have had a number of positive impacts on gender equality in the Philippines. First, migration has the potential to economically empower many women by increasing and diversifying the employment opportunities available to them. Some women are able to transition from unpaid subsistence agricultural work to gainful employment and thus to become breadwinners in their own right. Likewise, the investment of remittances in migrant children's studies has increased levels of educational attainment among the daughters of migrants, opening up new opportunities for future generations of women.

Women's household decision-making power has also increased due to their leading role in international emigration. As both remitters and remittance recipients, women in these Filipino communities of origin have acquired land and financial capital, which, in turn, has led to changes in their power and status in their households and communities of origin.

Another strand of literature focuses on the impact of gender on remittances using data based on the recipients based in the origin country. A survey of rural households in the Dominican Sierra found that

> insurance is the main purpose to remit for female migrants to the United States. Only when a male is the sole migrant in his household does he feel compelled to remit as an insurer when his parents are subject to health shocks. Investment toward inheritance is, by contrast, gender neutral. However, only migrants to the United States are in a position to (or feel compelled to) invest toward this purpose. Common property problems reduce this incentive to remit as the number of heirs in the migrant's household increases. (De la Brière et al. 2000)

The authors find that the relative importance of these two motives to remit is affected by destination (international versus internal migration), gender, and household composition. Female migrants to the US mainly fulfil the insurance function. Remittances sent by males, when they are the sole migrant in the household, tend to act as insurance. Investment, by contrast, is pursued by both males and females, but only among those migrating to the USA.

Box 9.1 gives the story of one woman's life and the effect of her remittances on her family. This suggests that remittances have had a generally positive impact on gender empowerment, both from the point of view of expanding the employment horizons of females but also by giving females who are the recipients of remittances the possibility to decide how to spend funds transferred to them. The lives of female remitters cannot be easy. Separated from their children and families they must think constantly of the benefits they are creating in their home villages.

Box 9.1 Maria's story

Maria is from Mindanao in the Philippines. In the Philippines she is an accountant, in Ireland she is a domestic worker. Maria has been working in Ireland for over twelve years. Maria was joined in Ireland by her two younger sisters. They too have professional qualifications in the Philippines but work as domestic workers in Ireland. The majority of the earnings Maria has made as a domestic worker in Ireland she sends home to her family in the Philippines. Maria has succeeded in educating her four children and building a property portfolio that includes a new house, plots of land in commercial areas and a coconut farm that should be providing an income of €200 a week within the year.

The foreign-based female domestic workforce is the second-largest source of foreign currency to the Philippines economy. In the Philippines they are seen as 'living heroes'. However, the story is a little more complex than that. Maria and her two sisters are the mothers of young children back in the Philippines. They can manage the balancing act between poverty and subsistence until they have children, then their low wages make it impossible to provide a good education and thus a chance of a stable sustainable future. The women choose to give up their middle-class status in the Philippines in order to make money in Europe.

Maria explains that it was when she had her four children that she and her husband decided that the only way to provide for their future was for her to go abroad. 'I left the house when the children were sleeping and I cried the whole journey to the bus terminal.' When she left, her youngest daughter was just two; it would be two years before she would see her again. 'My hair was cut short when I left the Philippines, when I returned it was long. I met my youngest daughter at the airport, she said, "You are not my mamma, my mamma has short hair," but going home in the bus she began to beat her breast and said "You are my mamma, I know because my heart beats like this." But I know those years I have lost with my children cannot be got back.' Feeling this pain and heartbreak for home and her children I wonder how can Maria face minding the children of Irish parents: 'Minding the children helps you, as it's as if you are minding your own children, but in your subconscious you have a feeling of guilt. Sometimes when I hold their small hand in mine I think of my own children, and it's so hard.'

The influx of remittances into the Philippines has caused problems there. Families used to a subsistence existence now have cheques for €100, €200 and more coming into the house from Ireland each week. This has led to what is described as a 'crisis of abundance', when idle husbands go on spending sprees with the money their wives send home; 'cheapy cheapy wine', other women and jewellery are some of the things they waste the money on.

Of course many domestic workers hope to get home in the shortest length of time. The jewel in Maria's crown of investments is her coconut farm nestled in the foothills of lush Mount Apo. 'When I am in Ireland doing my ironing I think about sitting here on my rocking chair surrounded by my children and crops and looking at the mountain.' But behind the romantic dream of a future at home in the Philippines, there is the nagging doubt that plagues all domestic workers: was the sacrifice of ten and fifteen years spent working in Ireland, out of the lives of their young children and loved ones, worth it?

Remittances and microfinance

Often, initiatives with development potential intersect, and that is the case with remittances and microfinance. With the arrival of the Phase II MFIs and especially the Phase II for-profit MFIs, the search for depositors has intensified in order to provide internal capital to supply the credit market. Remittances represent a growing and relatively stable source of funds. The effects of the financial crisis might still affect the stability of remittance flows as unemployment levels in the developed world and the regional economic powerhouses continue to climb. Rural poor recipients of remittances must therefore seek a safe home for the excess of remittances once their current needs are satisfied. Since a major reason for remittances is insurance, the recipients will save the remittance until needed and will inevitably turn to the banking sector to satisfy this requirement. In general, the connection with the banking sector for the poor is the MFI.[3] The MFIs for their part not only need remittance deposits to offset the need to borrow capital from the markets but by offering savings products can also gain future clients and charge commissions on the transfer of funds.

3 For a general discussion on remittances and MFIs see Peters (2010).

An examination of the literature on remittances and microfinance will not yield startling conclusions. It appears that MFIs involved in the remittances market have a significantly higher level of savings than those not involved in this market. There is a dearth of information on how long the recipients of a remittance hold their funds in a savings account. Also there is little or no information on the profile of the typical client receiving a remittance. One point of note is that once an MFI launches a remittance product the clientele appears to be wealthier (Mata 2011). This may correlate with the fact that remittances tend to favour those better off rather than the chronic poor.

A study carried out in Mexico (Demirgüç-Kunt et al. 2009) found that remittances and migration are strongly associated with the development of the banking sector. However, while this is possible to examine with current data a far more interesting question is posed in the conclusion of the study: will the expansion of banking services caused by the remittances result in additional development in the remittance recipient communities?

Conclusions

Considering that official remittances are at the same level as FDI for developing countries, remittances are an important and growing resource for the poor. When unofficial remittances are taken into account the importance of remittances cannot be overstated. Nevertheless, the financial crisis and its effect on jobs in most Western countries have undoubtedly had an impact on both migration and remittances.

For the recipient countries, two key policy issues must be addressed. First, government needs to have a policy initiative which aims to enhance the amount of remittances, particularly through formal channels. There is evidence that only 50 per cent of remittances are recorded and are remitted through formal channels (Ratha et al. 2011). The informal remittances are often made through networks of money dealers commonly offering a speedier and cheaper means of transfer than the formal channels. There are a number of problems with unofficial transfer channels. First, there is no benefit to the national banking system. Second, the unofficial system may be in the hands of criminal enterprises that use remittances to launder money. Third, unofficial flows cannot be securitized since their exact volume is unknown. Finally, there may be macroeconomic consequences with respect to inappropriate exchange rate movement and tax collection.

The cost of sending remittances remains high and tends to be regressive. Most migrants send small amounts, generally in the range of $200, and the average charge applied by the top three money transfer operators (Western Union, MoneyGram and Dolex) can be as high as $16 for $100 and $18 for $200. The smaller the amount the higher the cost per dollar sent. There is a general consensus that governments of developed countries should assist by lowering the costs and barriers to official remittance channels in order to enhance the level of remittances. In order to reduce such transaction costs, governments should promote new technologies and increase competition in the sector. Much has been done in relation to North–South transfers, and costs have been reduced substantially. However, South–South transfers are still unacceptably high given the very limited resources of the clients at both the sending and the receiving ends. Governments can lower the capital requirements on remittance services and widen formal financial intermediaries' networks. Lowering the cost of transferring remittances will help to increase the poverty-reducing impact of international remittances and will represent a win-win situation for both the host and the home countries.

Second, home governments should develop a policy approach on how to turn remittances into development opportunities. This could be done by the launching of remittance bonds or through government incentive schemes such as the three-for-one system used by the Mexican government whereby communal remittances dedicated to a development activity will be matched by both the national and the regional governments (Burnside and Dollar 2004).

Remittances represent an as-yet-untapped resource for developing countries to finance development initiatives. The history of remittances is longer than the forty-year history of development aid. Many European countries benefited from the remittances sent from the US by their migrants much as today's migrants remit to their home countries. Policy efforts are necessary not only to improve the flow of remittances but also their use.

One suggestion is the establishment of an international body – an 'International Remittances Institute' – that would monitor the flows of labour and remittances and oversee policies to make them easier, cheaper, safer and more productive (Ratha 2009). While the suggestion is noble, the remit is there and there are enough international institutions that could carry out this not too onerous task.

Remittances are certainly an important element in the development process. The levels are significant and can be used to bring families out of poverty, as evidenced by Maria's story. The cost to the migrant is sometimes heavy.

Irrespective of how important remittances are in terms of their volumes, they will still be involved in development with a small *d*. Remittances do not contribute to the structural changes which are at the core of a policy to reduce aid dependency. Individuals can change the situation of their immediate family or friends with a remittance, but they cannot institute change at the macro level.

10 | NON-GOVERNMENTAL ORGANIZATIONS AND PHILANTHROPIC FOUNDATIONS

To give away money is an easy matter and in any man's power. But to decide to whom to give it, and how large a sum, and when, and for what purpose, and how, is neither in every man's power, nor an easy matter. (Aristotle, *The Nicomachean Ethics*)

NGOs, civil society and development: a case of schizophrenia?

One of the major features of the development aid scene since the 1980s has been the proliferation of non-governmental organizations (NGOs) both national and international, which are committed to assisting the poor and the deprived in the developing world. The NGO sector has been one of the fastest-growing of all activities related to development assistance.

NGOs consist of very disparate groups of individuals with diverse agendas such as membership organizations representing specific interests or groups; private sector and professional bodies; and altruistic organizations with agendas for achieving broad humanitarian aid, human rights, environmental and poverty reduction goals. However, the NGO sector does not stop there. To these must be added a large number of influential religious and academic organizations, social movements and campaign networks. As well as true NGOs, there are many quasi-NGOs operating internationally. They include government-operated NGOs (GONGOs), which have been established by and on behalf of governments, quasi non-governmental organizations (QUANGOs) and hybrid organizations such as the International Red Cross, organizations of indigenous peoples and institutions such as the Inter-Parliamentary Union.

The diversity of interests they represent is astonishingly wide. For example, the number of internationally operating NGOs is estimated at forty thousand. National numbers are even higher: Russia has 277,000 NGOs, India is estimated to have had around 3.3 million NGOs in 2009, that is, one NGO for fewer than every 400 Indians, and many times the number of primary schools and primary health centres in that country. Nepal has 20,000 NGOs while the UK has 170,000 registered charities.

Given the wide range of organizations, there has been a good deal of difficulty in coming up with an exact definition of an NGO. The European Convention on the Recognition of the Legal Personality of International Non-Governmental Organizations offers the following:

(...) associations, foundations and other private institutions which satisfy the following conditions: a) have a non-profit-making aim of international utility; b) have been established by an instrument governed by the internal law of a Party; c) carry on their activities with effect in at least two States; and d) have their statutory office in the territory of a Party and the central management and control in the territory of that Party or of another Party. (Council of Europe 1986)

A second definition is provided by NGOs themselves:

A non-governmental organization (NGO) is any non-profit, voluntary citizens' group which is organized on a local, national or international level. Task-oriented and driven by people with a common interest, NGOs perform a variety of service and humanitarian functions, bring citizen concerns to Governments, advocate and monitor policies and encourage political participation through provision of information. Some are organized around specific issues, such as human rights, environment or health. They provide analysis and expertise, serve as early warning mechanisms and help monitor and implement international agreements. Their relationship with offices and agencies of the United Nations system differs depending on their goals, their venue and the mandate of a particular institution.[1]

Despite this valiant attempt to clarify the situation there is no accepted definition of an NGO (Willetts n.d.). Both the definitions quoted above are useful but they do not go the full distance in covering what is a complex array of organizations. In June 2004, a seminal report was published on the relationship between civil society and the United Nations: *We the Peoples: The Role of the United Nations in the 21st Century*. Better known as the Cardoso Report, it was named

---

1 See www.ngo.org/ngoinfo/define.html

after the former Brazilian President Fernando Cardoso, under whose chairmanship it was written. The Cardoso Report (United Nations 2000b) is predicated on a new form of multilateralism based on the inclusion of non-governmental actors (referred to as 'constituencies') in discussions previously reserved for states alone. The report maintains that in the light of globalization, strengthening the participation of civil society will help the UN to respond more effectively to the wishes of its citizens and attract more public support for its activities.

The report contained a number of recommendations including: the establishment of multi-stakeholder partnerships; civil society participation in the UN General Assembly and the Security Council; improving accreditation procedure for NGOs; a fund to increase participation of developing countries' organizations; the creation of an Office of Constituency Engagements and Partnerships. The Cardoso Report was poorly received by all significant political actors: by governments from both the North and the South, by most NGOs, and even by the UN Secretary-General (see United Nations 2004).

The Cardoso Report constituted an attempt to integrate the burgeoning NGO sector into the deliberations of the United Nations proper and not just through their membership of the Economic and Social Council (ECOSOC). While the report did not succeed fully, it did engender change in areas such as NGO registration.

The World Bank has adopted a definition of civil society developed by a number of leading research centres:

> the term civil society refers to the wide array of non-governmental and not-for-profit organizations that have a presence in public life, expressing the interests and values of their members or others, based on ethical, cultural, political, scientific, religious or philanthropic considerations. Civil Society Organizations (CSOs) therefore refer to a wide of array of organizations: community groups, non-governmental organizations (NGOs), labour unions, indigenous groups, charitable organizations, faith-based organizations, professional associations, and foundations.

For the World Bank, NGOs therefore form a subset of civil society. Within the UN a total of 13,000 civil society organizations (CSOs) have registered themselves.

A further complication of an already complicated situation arises when consideration is given to the development aid area. Two different areas of 'development' are being addressed by NGOs. Small *d* development is defined as 'the geographically uneven, profoundly contradictory set of processes underlying capitalist developments' while *D* refers to the 'project of intervention in the third world' (Bebbington et al. 2007). This discussion on the merits of the *d* versus the *D* as the *raison d'être* of the development NGOs is a recurring theme of the literature of the sector. There is division on whether the NGO is an agent of systemic change (*d*), in terms of alternative ways of doing development, or simply an organism that operates as an agent for the donor community in terms of service delivery, or a provider of microfinance or an organization presenting alternative methods of accomplishing development aims. The political versus implementation agency dichotomy comes out most clearly by considering the role of the NGO in strengthening democracy. By definition NGOs should be involved in pluralizing society in an effort to strengthen the institutional arena. After all, this is the principal reason the membership fund them. NGOs should work with grassroots organizations that are often composed of poor and marginalized groups in an effort to promote 'bottom up' democracy. Finally, civil society in general and NGOs in particular should be a check on state power by challenging its autonomy at both national and local level by promoting a systemic change agenda at the level of national and local governance (Mercer 2002).

The countervailing NGO or the operational NGO carries out projects either for government or more generally for either a bilateral or multilateral donor. Virtually all the larger NGOs (OXFAM, Action Aid, Save the Children and Doctors without Borders) receive substantial levels of donor funding in order to accomplish their stated aims. However, a large number of NGOs, including some of those already mentioned, tender to donors to carry out specific projects generally in the areas of education, health, and water and sanitation. It is this element of the NGO operation which has drawn the greatest level of condemnation from their own community. Box 10.1 shows the difference in size and scope of two NGOs – Save the Children and Build It International.

There is no doubt that an NGO managing an educational establishment, a health facility or providing some service that government itself should provide is supplanting it and perhaps supporting the impression that governments of many developing countries do not have the capacity to bring adequate services to their people.

Box 10.1 Two NGOs: Save the Children and Build It International

Eglantyne Jebb, an Oxford-educated teacher and sociologist, founded the Save the Children Fund in England in 1919 to aid children in war-ravaged central Europe. 'We cannot leave defenceless children anywhere exposed to ruin – moral or physical,' she said. 'We cannot run the risk that they should weep, starve, despair and die, with never a hand stretched out to help them.'

Today, in more than fifty countries, including the United States, Save the Children USA is transforming children's lives by providing families and communities with the tools they need to break the cycle of poverty. 'While our programmes are diverse, our mission is singular: to create lasting, positive change in the lives of children in need around the world.' Save the Children sees its role as that of a catalyst in community evolution. 'We favour a multi-disciplinary approach, acknowledging that the problems we address – poverty, illiteracy, poor health – are complex and interrelated. Innovation and experience have been the keys to Save the Children's success.'

Save the Children is a major world NGO and receives $274 million in private gifts (2010), $159 million in grants from the US government and $38 million in child sponsorship. Approximately 90 per cent of all operating funding goes into programmes related to the work of the organization.

Governments are elected by the people to manage resource allocation and to provide the services, particularly in education and health, which the people require. This vital role of government and the connection it provides between the rulers and the ruled should not be compromised by an NGO. This role of the NGO, while welcome to the people receiving the service, is often the bone of contention with government who often view the NGO as a nascent political organization wishing to undermine the capacity of the state by pointing out its shortcomings (Bebbington et al. 2007).

Within the NGO community itself there is a strong reaction to

Build It International was established in 2006 with the aim of supporting the small-scale building sector as a way of creating sustainable employment opportunities and economic growth in low-income countries mainly in Africa. Its vision is a world in which affordable good-quality housing, schools, water systems and other community facilities are available to all.

The legal objects of the charity are:

- the relief of poverty and the improvement of the conditions of life particularly in socially and economically disadvantaged and flood-prone communities;
- the promotion of sustainable means of achieving economic growth and regeneration;
- the enhancement of education, primarily in building construction, of deprived and flood-prone communities;
- the preservation, conservation and protection of the environment and the use of natural resources.

In 2010, BII received a total of £420,057 of which £412,000 was voluntary income. Some 83 per cent of the funding went to operations, 14 per cent to fundraising and 3 per cent to governance.

Source: Save the Children website and annual report 2010 and BII annual reports

the NGO as a purveyor of services. This constituency maintains that NGOs have betrayed their roots by becoming an integral part of a system which, to quote one critic, 'sacrifices respect for justice and rights. They have taken the missionary position – service delivery, running projects that are motivated by charity, pity and doing things for people' (Manji and O'Coill 2002).

Funding the NGOs

The very fragmented nature of the NGO sector makes a calculation of the funding levels extremely difficult. While the larger NGOs

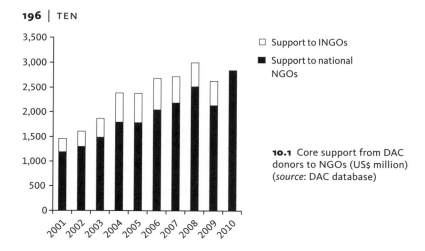

10.1 Core support from DAC donors to NGOs (US$ million) (*source*: DAC database)

issue annual reports detailing their sources and uses of funds, many NGOs are remiss in the area of financial reporting. The DAC donors report annually on their support for NGOs and Figure 10.1 shows the evolution of this support.

Support for NGOs rose steadily in the ten-year period from 2001 to 2010. A slight drop was recorded in 2009 but support recovered in 2010. No support for international NGOs (INGOs) has yet been

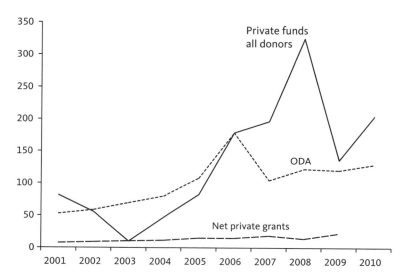

10.2 Private flows, ODA and private grants, 2001–10 (US$ billion) (*source*: DAC database)

recorded for 2010 but the total support to the NGO sector by the DAC donors can be assumed to have exceeded $3 billion. This would only correspond to 2.33 per cent of overall ODA (using the 2010 reported figure). Therefore, while NGOs are seen as an integral part of the development process, they receive very little core support from the DAC donors.

Figure 10.2 shows the private funds flow, ODA and private grant funding reported by the DAC members of the OECD for the period 2001–10. The figure shows that the rise in private grant funding has been steady but nowhere as significant as the flows of private funding or ODA. However, the 2009 figure of $22 billion is significant and represents some 17.18 per cent of the total ODA.

However, the Centre for Global Development hotly contests the figures reported by the DAC. For example, total private UK giving to the developing world through UK charities working in overseas aid and famine relief amounted to $6.3 billion in 2008. This assessment of UK private giving excludes foundations, corporations and churches, so the actual total is higher. The UK government, however, reported only $329 million in overseas private giving to the OECD for 2009.[2]

French private sources gave $1.0 billion in 2008 to developing countries. This includes $468.6 million from individuals, $33.5 million from bequests, and $502.5 million from corporations. France, however, does not report any private funding of development to the OECD.

Italian private giving to the developing world totalled $583.1 million in 2008, substantially more than the $162 million reported by the Italian government to the OECD in 2009. Spanish private giving to the developing world was an estimated $409.2 million in 2007. This included $170.4 million in regular donations and fees; $140.2 million in one-time donations; $47.5 million from private enterprises; $34.4 million from the sale of fair trade products and merchandising; and $16.7 million from other private funds. Spain, like France, does not report any private funding of development to the OECD.

There are similar discrepancies in the figures for all the major DAC countries and this only goes to highlight the extreme difficulty of dealing with a sector which is not totally definable or transparent. The Hudson Institute's overall analysis, based on figures developed by the Centre for Global Prosperity, gives an estimate of the total

---

2 For a more complete analysis see Hudson Institute (2011).

private grant funding of $ 52.5 billion, or 2.3 times the reported DAC figure. If these figures are correct, grant funding from the NGO sector would be almost half that of the official DAC donors. It would be interesting to get some certitude on the higher figures as it would mean that the NGO sector had become an important stakeholder in the development business.

The allocation and management of funding by NGOs

Since the NGOs are to a large extent a black box, the issues of how they allocate the funds which they receive, how they manage those funds, and their accountability are important.

The majority of the DAC donors have a funding cycle which varies from an annual to a five-year review. Country strategy papers (CSPs) are an important directional tool not only in formulating the appropriate bilateral or multilateral country strategy; they are also an important input into the aid efficiency agenda. Individual strategy papers are circulated among the donor community ensuring that each donor present on the ground is aware of the initiatives that the other donors are funding. The exception to this rule are the BRICS and other non-DAC donors and to a large extent the NGOs and civil society organizations (CSOs). Each donor organization has a mechanism for consulting the NGOs and the CSOs during the development of the country strategy papers, but since the NGOs and CSOs are not specifically involved as lead donors in the aid efficiency architecture, coordination of their efforts can fall outside that established architecture. In general the country strategy papers reflect the recipient's priorities as outlined in the National Development Plan or the Poverty Reduction Strategy Programme developed by the recipient in general with the Bretton Woods organizations.

The NGOs and CSOs are free agents in the process of funding allocation since they do not have the same close relationship between themselves and the recipient government in deciding where the funding should go. In general, a major part of DAC ODA goes either directly to government in the form of budget support or to individual government ministries to fund specific government programmes. No NGO funding goes through government, which creates not only a financial accountability problem but also a problem of political accountability.

Since in many countries (and particularly in some African countries with human rights issues), NGOs and CSOs are considered to have a political agenda which often conflicts with the policies of the government, the relationship between the government and the NGOs can be strained. There are many in government who feel that the allocation of NGO funding to specific initiatives is political rather than rational.

This situation has led many countries to implement NGO legislation. Government anxiety regarding NGOs and the proliferation of NGOs has led to the establishment in Uganda in 1989 of the NGO Registration Board requiring NGOs to go through a cumbersome bureaucratic process of annual registration with the board. The Amendment Bill of 2000 further tightened the screw on the NGOs by denying the notion of an NGO–government partnership in development and giving additional powers to the NGO Registration Board to control the activities of NGOs (see Kwesiga and Namisi 2006). This situation is not atypical for Africa.

The question then becomes: given the generally contentious relations between NGOs and recipient governments, does the NGO make its funding allocations on a rational basis? This question becomes even more important if the revised funding figure of approximately $50 billion is factual. The first systematic analysis of privately sourced development aid, raised and allocated by US-based transnational NGOs which fund and run projects to provide or improve education, health care, safe drinking water, sanitation, sewage and emergency relief was reported on in 2009. The authors examined the financial records of 40 of the 47 most prominent NGOs whose funds were spread across 119 countries categorized by the World Bank as low or lower-class income countries. There was no evidence that the allocation of funding was based on anything other than an 'altruistic view, grounded in the constructivist approach, according to which these NGOs allocate private aid based on the recipients' objective need' (Büthe et al. 2009).

A similar exercise looking at allocation decisions was carried out on a dataset of funding allocations made by Swiss NGOs and Swiss ODA. The allocation of self-financed NGO aid was in general similar to the allocation of Swiss ODA. The general conception is that by being closer to the poor, NGO allocations are more poverty-oriented but this was not confirmed by findings. It rather depends on the measurement of recipient need whether NGOs outperformed the government in this respect. The findings supported the view that the poverty orientation of NGO aid would be understated when only measured by average per capita incomes (Nunnenkamp et al. 2008).

It appears that neither the government nor the NGOs followed the World Bank's advice to favour recipient countries offering better institutional conditions for aid to be effective. Instead both NGOs and ODA donors seem to work on the assumption that aid may help improve governance. In the case of Swiss aid, neither official nor NGO donors used aid as a means to promote Swiss exports, but both granted more aid to politically like-minded recipient countries.

The findings of the Swiss study on NGOs acting as agents for ODA are pretty much what might have been expected: the allocation of NGO-administered ODA differs substantially from the allocation of self-financed NGO aid and ODA proper. Public funds channelled through Swiss NGOs appear to be subject to a special set of controls. The question of accountability was not raised in the study but it is an important issue.

There have been calls, particularly from the chief executives of NGOs, that much ODA would be better channelled through the NGOs in order to improve targeting to the poor. This contention has not been borne out by research. The Swiss study cautioned against the view that aid would be better targeted to the needy and deserving if only NGOs had more resources at their disposal and a bigger say on the allocation of aid. The Swiss example rather suggests that the incentives of NGOs to swim against the tide are weaker than widely believed, even when deciding on the allocation of their own resources. Rather than trying to excel by distinguishing themselves from other donors, NGOs may prefer following official aid strategies and allocation rules to get easier access to public funds.

A similar study (Dreher et al. 2007) of the allocation of aid by Swedish NGOs and by the Swedish International Development Agency (SIDA) confirmed the results of the Swiss NGOs study. The study found that the allocation of NGO aid was not superior to ODA. This result may have been a function of the altruistic nature of Swedish ODA which was found to be clearly needs based. The study also concluded that there was no basis for the contention (often made by the leadership of NGOs) that aid delivery through NGOs is superior to aid delivery through official aid agencies. The study concluded that 'aid delivery though NGOs provides no panacea to improve aid effectiveness'. It is therefore safe to conclude that aid delivery through NGOs is similar to (if not the same as) aid delivered by aid agencies.

Despite the evidence to the contrary, the NGO community has persisted in its claims that the failures of development aid can be countered by changing the aid allocation procedure to put NGOs at the centre of the aid delivery mechanism. However, there has been a recognition for some time that NGO strengths do not lie in the provision of large-scale service delivery. Nor do they have a role in creating employment or in social integration. Only government, with its overview of the national situation, is in a position to create the environment for sustainable development (Malhotra 2000).

NGO accountability

The concept of accountability is central to the operation of the state and business in the world today. National constitutions set up the systems whereby state officials at every level must account for their actions. Business must account to the shareholders and the supervisory bodies of the state for the actions they have taken with the funds they have been given by their shareholders. The separation of powers means that each organ of the state has a supervisory power which oversees its operations and holds it accountable.

NGO accountability is not just a technical issue of accounting for funds received; it is also a political issue for many aid recipient governments who see NGOs operating unchecked on their territory. It is normal for governments to legislate for the registration of NGOs, but many countries have tried to go beyond simple registration to govern the operations of the NGOs through administrative provisions.

Technical accountability is a relatively simple issue. NGOs must produce annual reports detailing their sources and uses of funds whether they are major international players such as CARE or Save the Children or relatively small fry like Build It International. These are the legal requirements of the home country of the NGO. Similarly where the NGO is acting as an aid delivery agency for a DAC national aid agency the normal principal–agency relationship holds and the NGO will be accountable to the original funding agency for the implementation of the programme. The role NGOs have played as agents in aid delivery has caused them to develop procedures which have paralleled those used in the business world. This is another issue of conflict within the NGO community, many of whom do not want to see the NGOs adopt the mantle of the business corporation. There are many people working in NGOs who believe that

> increasingly, the model for the 'successful' NGO is the corporation – ideally a transnational corporation – and NGOs are ever more marketed and judged against corporate ideals. As part of this trend, a new development 'scientism' is strangling us with things like strategic framework analysis and results-based management, precisely the values and methods and techniques that have made the world what it is today. The 'realist' ethos holds sway, and Realpolitik justifies all. It is all very pragmatic and utilitarian. (Murphy 2001)

The conflict regarding the structure of the NGO relates to what might be called internal accountability. Purists consider that the NGO should be responsible only to itself in its role as a representative of a constituency whose views it promotes.

The more difficult issue is who are civil society organizations actually accountable to. There is no clear superior authority. There have been some proposals that NGOs should have increased levels of introspection and self-examination. Another proposal is that one NGO should be evaluated by another NGO. The self-regulation approach or the evaluation-by-peer approach may be acceptable to the NGOs themselves, but in the context of undemocratic governments who view the NGOs as their enemies, the self-accountability approach will certainly not be acceptable. The increasing pressure for legislation relating to the oversight of NGO operations in some African countries is clear evidence that governments do not view self-regulation as an acceptable level of accountability.

The future of NGOs in development

The debate on the role of NGOs in little-*d* development or big-*D* Development is bound to continue as NGOs drift further from their original purpose and more into becoming aid delivery agencies.

There are those in the NGO community who wish to see the NGOs return to their original role as the voice of the poor and the dispossessed and to eschew the agency role completely. Others foresee a future for NGOs in occupying the space between the tripolar group of the state, business and civil society. The projected role in this complicated space would be a concentration on the NGO as the arbiter of how a state manages its human rights. Fowler (2000) suggests four important roles for the future NGO:

- (re)-negotiators and trusted mediators between actors and sectors;
- trusted validators of a duty bearer's compliance with rights;
- respected watchdogs of behaviour of duty bearers and claimants, including themselves;
- acknowledged innovators in the public interest, with a constant eye on adoption by bigger and more powerful actors and on enhancing the capacity of claimants.

Relations between government, civil society and business are complex. In a developing country scenario they are more complex than normal. Occupying the space between these three important actors in national development is an attractive proposition for an NGO but it would require a particular skillset which does not appear to be consistent with the current set-up of the NGO. Each NGO has a particular agenda which it pursues with vigour. It rarely negotiates around this agenda and it is the very skills of negotiation and political awareness which are lacking in the skillset of the NGO.

NGOs have played an important role in the development process. A vibrant civil society is a vital adjunct to the checks and balances which are necessary to provide oversight to government activities. The first task of the despot (and this is clear in many African examples) is to dismantle civil society organization and to weaken the institutions of government oversight. Given that evidence shows that NGOs are no better at aid allocation or delivery than aid agencies, their departure from (d)evelopment would not be missed.

The philanthropic foundations

Philanthropic foundations have existed for several hundred years and have their genesis either in religious foundations or in foundations set up by some of the great families of the industrial era in the USA and UK. Most of the early philanthropic foundations were concentrated on the issue of poverty alleviation and the welfare of the poor in the countries in which the foundation was set up. Philanthropic foundations with an international development focus are a relatively recent phenomenon.

The first recorded operations by philanthropic foundations in the area of international development date back to the 1920s, when the

Rockefeller Foundation supported an initiative in the public health sector. Independent, community, and grant-making operating foundations in the United States gave a total of $4.6 billion to developing countries in 2009. A total of 64 per cent of all international grants awarded in 2009 by US foundations were multi-regional grants or grants for unspecified countries. Of the remaining 36 per cent, the single largest recipient of US foundation money was sub-Saharan Africa at 18 per cent (Bebbington et al. 2007). The bulk of this funding was provided by the Bill and Melinda Gates Foundation which gives substantial assistance to international health institutions such as the Global Action for Vaccination and Immunization (GAVI) and the Global Fund against Malaria, Tuberculosis and Aids. While $4 billion is a significant contribution to the development effort it cannot be compared to the $126 billion in ODA, or the $40 billion in remittances from migrants to Africa.

The Gates Foundation is by far the most important private funder of development. Bill Gates has committed $31 billion into his foundation and with the promise of a further $31 billion from Warren Buffett, the Gates Foundation stands ready to become a major player in the field of international development. So far the Gates Foundation has committed $24.8 billion to several causes, among them $3.277 billion to global development, $14.492 billion to global health, with a further $6 billion committed to the United States.[3] The new philanthropic foundations were supposed to preach a businesslike approach and to be lean and mean. The Gates Foundation reports that staff number 927 employees.

But the Gates Foundation is not the only one concentrating on world poverty. A new approach has been the decision by some California-based philanthropists to reach a consensus on how to reduce world poverty. The so-called 'California Consensus' aims to use business processes to attack world poverty through the support of innovation, technology and management methods (see Desai and Kharas 2008). The approach is to invest in drug companies in order to induce them to operate in developing countries. Then the philanthropists would use the thousands of international and local NGOs to create a community of knowledge and privatize aid. The approach described as the 'California Consensus' is not new. Over the years

---

3 www.gatesfoundation.org

there have been other calls to privatize aid as a mechanism to remove the bureaucratic aid agencies from the sector, replacing them with business-oriented aid delivery.[4] The question is whether this initiative would be successful in replacing traditional aid. The whole subject of social entrepreneurship in developing countries has exploded since the beginning of the new millennium as evidenced by the exponential growth in issues-based NGOs and cash-rich philanthropic foundations. Yet despite the addition of billions of dollars allied to the skills of the staff of the NGOs and foundations, there is little evidence of the systemic change that they were created to achieve.[5] It is results that count, and the NGO and philanthropic sector has so far failed to live up to its billing. Books like that of Muhammad Yunus predicting 'a world without poverty' have hyped social entrepreneurship to a level that is not consistent with the results obtained. This latter statement is even true in the case of the Grameen Bank and is relevant to all of the magic bullets presented in this book.

Conclusion

Despite the lack of results, the NGOs and even the new philanthropists are an integral part of the aid development business. Not only are they here to stay: they are proliferating. Their commitment to an issue, a religion or simply as a mechanism for throwing money at a problem in the developing world is beyond debate. What is in question is whether by their presence in the field they add value to the development process. The schizophrenia which the dichotomy between their role as agents of systemic change and their role as simply implementing agents for bilateral or multilateral donors may be part of the reason for their lack of effectiveness. It has been the search for funding outside the traditional national resources which has pushed NGOs into the aid delivery business. The fact that they are no better or no worse than the aid agencies themselves in their allocation decisions or in their management practices is not a valid reason for their existence. The growth of a civil society in the developing world is an issue which is pursued by all the aid agencies. It is important that the tripolar relationship of the state, business and civil society

---

4 'Privatise Foreign Aid', *Wall Street Journal*, 7 July 2007.
5 See 'Bah! Humbug: Why are so many charities ineffective?', *Economist*, 4 December 2007.

be aligned in order to ensure that poverty reduction programmes are successfully pursued.

The development aid space is already overcrowded, and new and small NGOs enter the fray every year. This inevitably puts pressure on the ministries of developing countries to ensure that individual NGO development initiatives conform to the overall national plan. A negative element of the first decade of the twenty-first century was an apparent trend in 'development tourism' whereby local OECD NGOs obtained finance from flush aid agencies in order to move into developing countries. As pressure increases on aid budgets in many DAC countries as a result of the sovereign debt crisis, the development tourists will find that their operations are unsustainable and the funds already disbursed will be wasted. Also the issue of accountability will not go away. Developing countries are nervous of NGOs not for their (D)evelopment activities but because of their (d)evelopment approaches which they consider to be political rather than human-rights-based. Shivji (2007) states it clearly: 'We must choose sides, the side of those who are struggling for a better world against those who want to maintain the existing world. Put simply, we cannot be neutral.'

Can NGOs and philanthropic foundations be made more effective? A study of a successful NGO has developed six practices of high-impact non-profits. The successful NGO will advocate and serve, make markets work, inspire evangelists, nurture non-profit networks, master the art of adaption, and share leadership (see Crutchfield and McLoud Grant 2008). This work parallels in some way a similar study on excellence in for-profit companies carried out in 1988. The precepts for success in the companies surveyed in 1988 did not stand the test of time, and it is likely that the six practices of high-impact non-profits may go the same way, but they are at least an attempt to correct the course of the juggernaut that is the NGO and philanthropic sector. Despite opinions to the contrary, throwing money at the development dilemma is not the answer. An aid strategy and, more important, an aid exit strategy must be concentrated on the development of systemic change which will leave developing countries with the tools to chart their own course to sustainable development.

11 | TOWARDS AN AID EXIT STRATEGY

> An exit strategy from aid dependence requires a radical shift
> both in the mindset and in the development strategy of coun-
> tries dependent on aid and the direct involvement of people in
> their own development. (Benjamin Mkapa, former President
> of Tanzania, foreword to Tandon 2008)

The foregoing ten chapters of this book are intended to give a picture of the aid business since its inception fifty or so years ago. The
modalities of aid have not changed greatly during that time although
there has been some substantial tinkering around the edges.

The last seven chapters have looked at various approaches or
initiatives which held or still hold out some hope of impacting on
the future development and sustainability of the countries which
were carved out of the old colonial empires. You will no doubt have
noticed that I have shied away from discussion on whether aid is
good or bad. Most bookshelves, certainly mine, are groaning under
the weight of books coming out in favour of one side of the argument
or the other. That aid is a big business is undeniable. It deals with
huge sums of money and employs hundreds of thousands of people,
and it is not about to disappear. Also the evidence against it is not
conclusive. The simplistic approach of drawing a graph of overseas
development aid (ODA) versus economic growth as a horizontal line
tell us nothing about the endogenous and exogenous variables which
may have influenced economic growth. Without specific evaluation
tools which can relate the aid situation to the non-aid situation, there
is no way to know definitively whether economic performance in Africa
(for example) would have been better or worse if aid had not existed.

However, all is not well in the aid business. Development aid has
had its ups and downs over the years of its existence, there have
been periods of donor fatigue interspersed with periods of recipient
fatigue. But this time it's different. Both the donors (as exhibited by
the comment of Angela Merkel at the UN which has been echoed by
several other leaders of DAC donor countries) and the recipients (Paul
Kagame and Benjamin Mkapa along with other African leaders) have

expressed their fatigue with a system which seems to have outlived its purpose. The views of President Kagame and former President Mkapa are important since their countries are heavily aid-dependent. ODA as a percentage of gross national income (GNI) for Rwanda was 18 per cent in 2009 and for Tanzania it was 13.7 (World Bank 2011b).

Aside from some small islands in the Pacific, aid dependency is rapidly becoming an African problem. Virtually all the countries of sub-Saharan Africa are heavily aid-dependent. Liberia is the number one, with an ODA/GNI ratio of 78.3 per cent, followed by Burundi, with a ratio of 41.2 per cent. The majority of the countries hover between 10 and 20 per cent, which indicates a heavy dependence on aid.

Aid dependency has been shown to have several negative effects. First, the availability of aid flows gives strong incentives for rent-taking and in most cases weakens democratic institutions. The effect has been described as akin to the 'oil curse' (Djankov et al. 2005). Aid dependency also allows governments to shy away from difficult decisions, using aid to supplement revenues which are difficult to collect.

At the EU Development Days in Stockholm in 2009, Jonathan Glennie gave a speech based on his (2008) book in which he called for the end of ODA. The majority (if not all) of the audience were employed in some capacity in the aid business. At the end of his speech Glennie was roundly applauded. As a spectator I was surprised. Although most people earning their living from aid normally say that their vision is to make themselves redundant, in general they don't really mean it. The applause for Glennie represented a feeling even at grassroots level that something had to change.

The donor community has made several attempts to remedy the faults which have appeared in the development aid model. The Monterrey Conference on Financing Aid concentrated on the provision of finance in a period where the perceived problem with the existing model was the lack of finance. The aid effectiveness conferences in Paris and Accra addressed the 'what' and 'how' of the aid model by endeavouring to increase the effectiveness of donor aid specifically by ensuring greater donor coordination and by setting out a prescription for recipient ownership of the development process. These major conferences were attempts by the donor community and by the symbiotic partners to rectify what they saw to be the factors causing the malaise in the development model.

However, the concentration on the 'what' in terms of additional finance and the 'how' in terms of the methodologies used by the donors stops short of the real change that is necessary in the business model associated with development aid. The three factors that should form the basis of a complete rethink of the development aid model are:

* ending mission creep
* having development aid strategies with an incorporated aid exit strategy, and
* breaking the symbiotic relationship between the donors and the recipients.

A new development model based on these three factors will lead to a new approach to development and create the necessary break with the past.

The elements of an aid exit strategy

There are five elements which may form the basis of a retreat from aid. They are:

* institutional development
* domestic resource mobilization
* economic diversification
* increased global funds
* self-help aid.

All five must be done concurrently since each to a large extent depends on the others. However, the issue of institutional development is of primary importance and therefore has the key position in Figure 11.1.

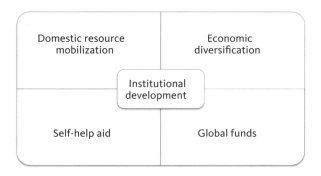

11.1 Elements of an aid exit strategy

Institutional development

It is difficult to generalize on development paths, but an examination of the paths to aid independence of South Korea, Taiwan, Botswana, Mauritius and Namibia throws up at least one area of similarity. All exhibited good governance and had established institutions capable of exerting oversight on the developmental process. Therefore, the first prerequisite for any aid exit strategy is the existence of national institutions of governance which ensure that the state and its organs are properly managed and overseen. One of the principal functions of aid is the creation of formal institutions of state which can ensure that resources are expended in the interests of the nation.

The issue of democratic elections has been more or less settled in most countries of the Third World. Citizens now look at their election process to see whether it has been validated as 'free and fair' (although this phrase is now falling out of use). Despite the acceptance by most countries of the democratic process (at least where elections are concerned), recent events in Kenya and the ongoing farce of elections in Zimbabwe have shown how thin the veneer of acceptance is by the ruling elite for the concept of changes of power being related to elections. The democratic voice of the people is seen as fine so long as it maintains the ruling elite in power.

Donors have been concentrating in the recent past on strengthening the institutions which oversee the democratic process. Electoral commissions, an independent court system, an independent Auditor General's Office and an active legislature composed of legislators from a multi-party political system are all needed if countries are to follow a coherent development path. For the citizens of many Third World countries the existence of such institutions are pie in the sky. To quote Bratton (2007), 'Many (Africans) harbor doubts that elections can bring about alterations of incumbent presidents and ruling parties, while others are realizing that an "electoral" democracy alone does not ensure the presence of a responsive and accountable leadership after elections.'

Rodrik, Subramanian and Trebbi (2002) carried out a study of the respective contributions of institutions, geography, and trade in determining income levels around the world. Their conclusion is clear: the quality of institutions trumps everything. The results of this study would seem to indicate that the development of effective institutions would be a *sine qua non* of any exit strategy.

Without getting into the argument about whether aid is good or bad, the primacy of good governance and the existence of effective institutions in ensuring that donor funds are effective have been demonstrated by Burnside and Dollar (2004). They concluded that 'when South Korea was a low-income country with a large amount of aid in the 1960s, most projects, of many different types, were successful. In Kenya and Zimbabwe in recent decades, on the other hand, many projects of all types have failed, in the sense that they did not provide the services or benefits anticipated from the development.'

Given this result one would think that in order to be more effective aid would be allocated first to those countries that have already established good governance credentials. Alesina and Weber (1999) showed that this was not the case: countries exhibiting levels of corruption were allocated aid at the same level as less corrupt countries. The conclusion is that foreign aid programmes are often unsuccessful because they are not well targeted.

An equally strong case for developing strong institutions before accelerating aid programmes (or indeed any kind of development activities) is made by Djankov et al. (2005), who conclude that 'being dependent on foreign aid seems to result in worsening democratic institutions. The effect is akin to the "curse of oil" effect ...'

The large body of evidence therefore concludes that current modes of development aid are only effective where institutional development has reached a sufficient level to effectively absorb that aid. This result belies the outcome of the Paris and Accra conferences which concentrated on the effectiveness of aid in terms of donor coordination and recipient ownership.

The question becomes one of when has a country achieved an acceptable level of institutional development? The Brookings Institution has developed a Worldwide Governance Index (WGI) which catagorizes countries in respect of their institutional development.[1] This WGI covers six core dimensions of governance:

1   voice and accountability: capturing perceptions of the extent to which a country's citizens are able to participate in selecting their government, as well as freedom of expression, freedom of association, and a free media.
2   political stability and absence of violence/terrorism: capturing

---

1 www.brookings.edu

perceptions of the likelihood that the government will be destabilized or overthrown by unconstitutional or violent means, including politically motivated violence and terrorism.

3 government effectiveness: capturing perceptions of the quality of public services, the quality of civil servants, and the degree of its independence from political pressures, the quality of policy formulation and implementation, and the credibility of the government's commitment to such policies.

4 regulatory quality: capturing perceptions of the ability of the government to formulate and implement sound policies and regulations that permit and promote private sector development.

5 rule of law: capturing perceptions of the extent to which agents have confidence in and abide by the rules of society, and in particular the quality of contract enforcement, property rights, the police, and the courts, as well as the likelihood of crime and violence.

6 control of corruption: capturing perceptions of the extent to which public power is exercised for private gain, including both petty and grand forms of corruption, as well as capture of the state by elites and private interests.[2]

It is perhaps apparent that the WGI list is led by the Nordic countries and New Zealand. The majority of the least developed countries come at the end of the list, and the only sub-Saharan country to appear in the top twenty is South Africa. It is unreasonable to expect that a poorly governed country with a corrupt legislature and judicial system will become like Denmark overnight. The process will be arduous and fraught with danger for those promoting positive change in national institutions. Easterly (2008a) suggests that 'attempts at rapid top down change (in institutions) can even have negative effects' and suggests a gradualist approach to institutional change. However, the development of institutions committed to state development, whether achieved gradually or immediately, is the cornerstone of any strategy which has an aid exit motivation.

A transparent electoral system, an effective parliament and above all a respect for the rule of law are not only important in terms of the receipt and the use of aid; they are also prerequisites for the expansion of foreign direct investment (FDI). A survey of international

---

2 http://brookings.edu/opinions/2010/0924 wgi kaufmann.aspx

investors carried out by Ernst and Young lists five institutional barriers to investment among the six top barriers to FDI.[3] These barriers were: unstable political environment; corruption; weak security; poor infrastructure and logistics; and inefficient regulatory environment.

Domestic resource mobilization

Domestic resource mobilization is not only a mechanism for plugging the gap left by an aid exit strategy. It establishes the relationship between the rulers and the ruled. Through an equitable tax system and the corresponding oversight of the allocation of the funds collected, the government establishes the correct lines of responsibility and accountability between itself and its citizens. A tax system which is seen to favour one section of the community (generally the rich and the well-connected) will only exacerbate inequalities and lead to social disruption. For example, Pakistan, which receives $2.8 billion (2009 figure), collects only 9 per cent of GNI in taxes, which is about half what its neighbour India collects. This low tax collection rate has been attributed to no taxes being paid by the rich. The tax gap, which is a synonym for tax evasion, is the difference between potential and actual tax collection. The potential is the amount of tax the government will collect if everyone fully complies with the tax law. The tax gap has been rising in Pakistan and now stands at 79 per cent. Fewer than 2 per cent of Pakistanis pay any tax at all.[4]

Evidence shows that the tax take of countries in Africa has been falling steadily since independence, from more than 22 per cent of GDP in the mid-1960s to 14–16 per cent of GDP today. This is despite the recent boom in commodity prices, the increase in the numbers of high-net-worth individuals and the growth of the middle class. Two aspects of domestic resource mobilization require attention. The first is the question of reporting. It is important from both a democratic and financial standpoint that the sources of all funds collected by government be available for scrutiny. This would bring an end to secret deals between resource extractors and government and bring into the light the 'sweetheart' arrangements which cost the exchequer millions of dollars. The second area which requires attention is the reporting of the use of budget allocations. This level

---

3 www.ey.com/Publication/vwLUAssets/2011_Africa_Attractiveness_Survey/$FILE/11EDA187_attractiveness_africa_low_resolution_final.pdf

4 Nicholas D. Khristof, 'Our Fantasy Nation', *New York Times*, 4 June 2011.

of reporting should not simply be at parliamentary level but should be available to the communities to whom the allocations have been made. The system employed by the government of Uganda whereby the allocations to community schools and clinics are posted outside the schools and clinics has severely limited the ability of corrupt officials to intercept budget allocations.

Resource-rich countries can obtain advantages from belonging to the Extractive Industries Transparency Initiative (EITI) and by exchanging information with other countries on mechanisms to achieve the highest benefit for the nation from resource extraction. Companies should be obliged to pay taxes locally for resources extracted locally. The use of hedging in mineral agreements should be discontinued.

Tax incentives should only be given where there is substantial proof that the development cannot proceed without them. It is not in the interest of countries to take part in a 'race to the bottom' in terms of tax incentives to secure resource extraction investment. Competition between countries which succeeds in driving down the tax take in order to attract investment will only increase the profits of the companies at the expense of the state. In general it is advisable to have a policy of no tax incentives since they do not work in practice (see Chapter 4).

Illicit capital flows cost African countries each year $25–30 billion. This corresponds to more than 50 per cent of the total ODA ($47 billion) disbursed by the DAC donors in 2009.[5]

A final area for attention is the taxation of the informal sector which in many poor countries is an important employer. Taxing the informal sector will not be easy or popular, but if it is combined with a series of tax measures aimed at reducing inequality and a reallocation of resources towards the poor then it should be more acceptable.

Recent major conferences in Monterrey, Paris and Accra called on all developing countries to accept ownership of their development process. The best mechanism to accomplish this aim is to ensure that all those who benefit from the provisions provided by the state should pay to the limit of their means for the provision of such services. Since development benefits every citizen in the state, every citizen should contribute (again to the limit of his or her means) to the

---

5 OECD, Paris accessed at www.oecd.org/document/11/0,3746,en_2649_34447_2002187_1_1_1_1,00.html

developmental process. It is plainly ridiculous that aid should replace domestic resource mobilization and permit errant countries to establish unequal tax regimes which permit vested interests to benefit from the provision of aid by paying less tax. Aid is a culprit in the area of poor collection of tax. Allen Kagina, the Commissioner General of Uganda's Tax Authority, in an interview with the BBC said, 'The URA has been lax in collecting (tax). If the donors cut off (funds) we'd have to collect 100 per cent. We don't have the capacity to do that just yet.' She added that she believed that it was achievable for the URA to fund the national budget.[6] It has even been posited that aid supplied to Uganda permitted the president of that country to buy a $30 million top-of-the-range Gulfstream G550 private plane.[7] Yet Uganda's transport system is chronically underfunded and has been in crisis for some time. We can assume that the Ugandan situation is mirrored elsewhere.

Therefore ownership of the development process (which was loosely defined by Paris and Accra as the recipients managing aid funds themselves) can best be accomplished by establishing *real* ownership of the development process by establishing equitable tax systems and by improving the collection of taxes. Assistance from the donors should be concentrated on helping less developed countries to mobilize the maximum amount of their domestic resources.

Economic diversification

All least developed countries got a bad deal from the Uruguay Round. The trade agreement dealt with services – but not unskilled, labour-intensive services; it dealt with subsidies – but not agricultural subsidies (the subsidies that really matter to the least developed countries); it dealt with intellectual property rights, which are of little or no interest to developing countries. Overall 70 per cent of gains from the Uruguay Round accrued to developed countries.

The 48 least developed countries were actually left worse off. Africa has neither resources nor education to take advantage of new opportunities presented by trade liberalization. With only 2 per cent of world trade, Africa was sidelined during and after the conclusion

---

6 'Africans on Africa', BBC News, 7 July 2005, accessed at http://news.bbc. co.uk/2/hi/africa/4657139.stm

7 *Daily Mail*, 10 June 2011.

of the Uruguay Round. Some 80 per cent of Africa's external trade is in primary commodities, principally oil, gas and minerals. Only South Africa in the sub-Saharan region has a diversified economy capable of trading at the world level.

Africa has already missed the globalization boat which has lifted the economies of China, India and much of South East Asia. The principal reason is that it has been left without the education, technology, and resources to take advantage of the few trade opportunities that exist.

Open trade regimes such as 'Everything but Arms' and the African Growth and Opportunity Act (see Chapter 5) present opportunities for African countries to export to the EU and the USA, but it is clear that you cannot export what you do not produce. If the least developed countries are to improve their industrial output through the acquisition of machinery, it stands to reason that they must first earn foreign currency through exports in order to finance the purchases. The resource-rich less developed countries can afford this luxury through their earnings from oil, gas or mineral exports. Others are not so fortunate. African states are constrained in terms of financial capital and human capital in developing their industrial capacity and diversifying their economies. They are also hampered by other constraints relating to other factors of production such as the infrastructural deficit and the communications deficit.

Therefore despite trade liberalization being put at the head of the list of strategic options (Mills 2011), the bottom line is that in the short term it will not work. There are several reasons for this conclusion. The first is that most least developed countries do not produce the goods and services which are required on the world market. Where export markets have boomed, for example exports to China, there has been a concentration on primary products. Increases in exports of oil, gas and minerals may look good in statistical terms and no doubt add to the profits of the extraction industries, but the benefit rarely trickles down to the ordinary citizens. Second, most less developed countries (certainly the sub-Saharan ones) do not have the infrastructural capability to get goods to market efficiently. Infrastructure includes not only the road system but also ports and airports. An example of this has been the virtual collapse of the flower export industry in Zambia. During the period when the now-defunct Zambia Airways flew daily to Europe it was possible for flower growers in Zambia to compete with their counterparts in Kenya and

Ethiopia. With the demise of the national airline, Zambian growers were forced to ship their flowers south to Johannesburg in order to link with flights to Europe. The additional shipping costs allied to the longer time between cutting and delivery to Europe meant the death knell of the industry in Zambia.

Given the overall construction of the economies of the least developed countries, which are in the main built around a peasant economy of smallholders, the most obvious area of economic expansion is the agricultural sector. The figures here are stark. Thirty-eight out of forty-eight African countries import food. This does not mean that they are incapable of producing their own food; it simply means that their agricultural sectors are operating at suboptimal levels. Added to this suboptimal performance is the fact that world food prices are increasingly putting even more pressure on those countries that are net food importers. As Jacques Diouf of the Food and Agriculture Organization has remarked, 'The food situation in Africa has the potential for social tension, leading to social reactions and eventually even political problems.'

The suboptimal performance of sub-Saharan Africa in the area of cereal yields is typical of the sector. East Asia and the Pacific had a yield of 1,300 kg/ha in 1961 but had increased this to 4,500 kg/ha in 2005, an increase of 246 per cent. The relevant figures for Latin America are 1,300 kg/ha in 1961 and 3,400 kg/ha in 2005, an increase of 150 per cent. The figures for sub-Saharan Africa are 800 kg/ha in 1961 and 1,100 kg/ha in 2005 or a measly increase of 37 per cent.[8]

African agriculture has tremendous potential for development but is hindered not only by the enormous subsidies paid to EU and US farmers but also by inadequate agricultural policies and an industry structure which is based on smallholder farmers. Inadequate veterinary services complete the dismal picture. McKinsey Global Institute (2010) estimates that African agriculture could be an $880 billion business by the year 2030. This potential market will not be achieved without a huge effort on the part of the governments of the region. Most of the countries of sub-Saharan Africa have signed the compact for the NEPAD-inspired Comprehensive African Agricultural Development Programme (CAADP) which aims to take African agriculture to a new level and not only contribute to increased trade in agricultural

---

8 www.thebrenthurstfoundation.org/files/Brenthurst-Choices-for-Africa.pdf

products but also make a major improvement in the food security of the continent.

It would therefore appear that the path to economic diversification must begin with agriculture and the agro-food industries. This diversification process will not only create a series of new industries with ready markets but will also act as a driver to up-skill the people as they move from work on the land to industrial endeavour.

Tandon (2008) has developed a seven-step approach to end aid dependency which has important application to the area of economic diversification. The seven steps are:

1   adjusting the mindset;
2   budgeting for the poor not for the donors;
3   putting employment and decent wages upfront;
4   creating the domestic market and owning domestic resources;
5   plugging the resource gap;
6   creating institutions for investing national savings; and
7   limiting aid to national democratic priorities.

For cultural reasons associated with the histories of least developed countries being bound to peasant and thereby subsistence farming and associated with large swathes of land being taken over by political interests, there is resistance to overhaul of the agricultural sector. What is needed is indeed a major adjustment of the mindset. This will not be easy in many societies since changes in mindset involve overturning many culturally accepted norms. The role of tribal customs along with the very substantial power of tribal chiefs in land issues are a factor which will require major changes in mindset to instigate change. Other impediments to redress the suboptimal performance of sub-Saharan Africa in agriculture are issues pertaining to land tenure and the role of women in agriculture. Finally, the interference of the state in land allocation over and above the rule of law can have serious effects on agricultural production. The example of the demise of the Zimbabwean agricultural sector following the land reform policies of the ZANU-PF government needs no elaboration. The allocation of land on the basis of political affiliation and not expertise in farming has been shown to be a policy devoid of sense.

The change in mindset must also be applied to agricultural policies, which up to now favour the large farmers at the expense of the poor farmers. Fertilizer support programmes are important if yields are to be improved. However, in many cases these support programmes are a source of corruption whereby large farmers who can afford to buy unsubsidized fertilizer are the major recipients of programmes intended to support subsistence farmers. A recent examination by the World Bank of a fertilizer support programme in Zambia has shown that instead of improving agricultural yields, the programme actually has a negative impact on those it purports to serve.

While agriculture presents the primary path for economic diversification for most less developed countries, those countries lucky enough to be endowed with natural resources have another diversification path available to them. In general, less developed countries export primary commodities whether oil, gas, minerals or indeed agricultural commodities such as cocoa or cotton. In many cases less developed country governments import value-added goods based on primary commodities which they have already exported. It is inconsistent with the concept of national development for countries to continue to export primary commodities without considering how to establish industries based on adding value to their natural resources.

The concept of economic diversification is very much in the hands of government itself and has up to now not received much attention from the development aid community. And nor should it. Investment in economic diversification, whether in agriculture or in valued-added goods or services, is the domain of the private sector. The important element in this process is the policy context. In Chapter 3 I looked at the performance of many least developed countries on the World Bank's Doing Business league. The majority of developing and less developed countries are at the foot of the league principally because of the sometimes labyrinthine procedures which have been developed by predatory regimes in order to extract rent from would-be entrepreneurs or to corner sectors of the economy for their clients – procedures that have succeeded in impeding economic development and thereby economic diversification.

Countries are recognizing that improving their position on the Doing Business table is an important factor in attracting foreign direct investment and in encouraging entrepreneurship. Setting up one-stop shops for establishing businesses with minimal licensing and in reduced time are a feature of the industrial strategy of most countries.

This is another area which requires a change in the mindset of government and where the concept of good governance is at the core of change. The purpose of the labyrinthine procedures and the granting of exclusive monopolistic rights to individuals over areas of the economy was a policy developed by the elite to continue their control of the national means of production. A government committed to national development and an open economy will reduce regulation to the minimum or suppress monopolistic licences in order to accelerate economic activity.

While countries can do much to diversify their own economies, trade regimes must be established which give African countries the ability to compete in areas where they have a competitive advantage. This is particularly true for the agricultural sector.

Much has been accomplished in less developed countries since the year 2000 in terms of macroeconomic stability. In many cases budgets have been balanced and inflation has been held to single figures. Perhaps more important, many less developed countries have avoided the contagion which has spread through the world economic system. All these factors give them the opportunity to benefit from the potential of their natural resources of mineral wealth, land and labour without an input from the international aid system.

Developing countries have shown that they can master the macro-economic environment. The remarkable progress made by Rwanda in moving up the Doing Business league table shows that if the mindset of the government is geared towards improving the business climate, it can be very successful. Other sub-Saharan countries have witnessed the success of Rwanda and are anxious to replicate it. This will inevitably lead to a virtuous cycle where countries currently languishing at the foot of the Doing Business table will be vying with each other in a race to the top. Inevitably, economic diversification is an issue for the government rather than the donors. Government officials in developing countries have shown themselves to be adept at managing the economy from a financial perspective and have also proved during the Doha Development Round to be skilled negotiators. With a mindset aimed at removing the traditional impediments and corruption from private-sector activities, there is no reason why the potential estimated by McKinsey particularly in the agricultural sector cannot be achieved.

A Global Fund for Infrastructure

The success of the Global Fund and Global Action for Vaccination and Immunization (GAVI) in mobilizing the entire donor community to contribute to a concerted effort to solve the problems associated with the major health issues of the developing world stands as an example of what can be achieved when funds are directed at a specific development problem. The success of the fight against HIV/AIDS, tuberculosis and malaria as well as the immunization of children suggests that the model used by the Global Fund and GAVI needs to be examined and perhaps extended to other sectors.

The Paris and Accra Conferences concentrated on mechanisms required to improve aid efficiency. The outputs included the concept of division of labour and a coordinated national strategy by the group of mainly DAC donors. The division of labour suggests that donors should concentrate their efforts on specific sectors and allow other colleagues to withdraw from a particular sector and concentrate their effort elsewhere. For example in country X, donor A may withdraw from the education sector and concentrate all its aid on the health sector. This allows other donors to withdraw from the health sector and concentrate on education. The purpose of this manoeuvre was to develop a concentration by specific donors on specific sectors where they displayed a 'competitive advantage'. Government would benefit by having to deal with a smaller group of donors in each sector and would avoid the problems inherent in the traditional aid model. Since the objective of Paris and Accra was to improve aid efficiency, it stands to reason that the outputs in terms of division of labour would indicate a recognition by the aid business that the traditional model of aid agencies spreading themselves across a wide spectrum of developmental sectors was no longer effective.

The Global Fund model consists of a small central organization which collects donations from individual donors, NGOs and in particular philanthropic foundations, then launches a call for tender among developing countries and selects the best proposals of national campaigns to fight disease and finally issues funds to the successful tenderers. There are no national Global Fund offices in each country receiving grants and the programmes are carried out by health organizations in the recipient countries. During the life of the programme, audits are carried out to ensure financial rigour and programme direction. In many ways the Global Fund has many of the attributes of the Marshall Plan. The organization is small, the mission is defined, there is a proven technology to accomplish the mission, funding is delivered directly to the national agencies who are then responsible for carrying out the programme. The time-consuming (and sometimes ineffective) meetings between donors and government are eliminated and the programme managers are permitted to get on with the job at hand.

While the Paris and Accra agendas did succeed in part and in many countries the number of donors in any given sector has been trimmed, there are generally at least three donors who consider that they have sufficient 'comparative advantage' to remain in a given sector. One of the group is generally nominated as the 'lead donor' and speaks for the group in discussions with the government. This begs the question of why the Paris and Accra Conferences did not go the full distance by suggesting that only one donor should be present in each sector. The outcome of Paris and Accra is typical of the incremental changes which have been a feature of the laborious progress of change in the traditional aid model. If one were to take the results of Paris and Accra to their logical conclusion, one might have ended up with something very similar to the Global Fund model itself. Say, for the sake of argument, that the output of the conferences had been one single donor per sector in country X. Add to this conclusion that the same donor was considered to have 'comparative advantage' in this sector in every other country, then we would have a sector-specific donor. This result would be remarkably close to the Global Fund model. Of course, a large international conference with every donor having a seat at the table might have had considerable difficulty in reaching such a conclusion. That would have required many aid agencies voting for their own demise – an unlikely occurrence. The aid business glorifies the Marshall Plan as one of the great successes in its history but has become loath to replicate it in effect.

Considering that the model of the Global Fund has had considerable success in pursuing its mission, what other sector would benefit from a concerted approach?

The one major constraint which must be overcome if Africa is to free itself from aid dependency is the infrastructural deficit. The absence of road and rail links, the deplorable state of the existing ports, the power deficit which leads to the cutting off of vital industry and the lack and cost of communications all stifle the business community. The power situation is critical with more than thirty countries facing power shortages or facing high costs for the provision of emergency power. It has been estimated that Africa's infrastructure sector needs $93 billion per year, one third of which is needed for maintenance. The majority of the DAC donors have been involved in the infrastructure sector and total DAC grants for infrastructure (transport and energy) amounted to $850 million in 2009.[9] This represents 0.5 per cent of the $93 billion annual requirement. It is apparent from these figures that aid funding alone cannot come anywhere near the requirements for infrastructural spending. However, the level of funding from the DAC donors for infrastructure represents only 8.5 per cent of overall DAC aid funding to Africa. Some 45 per cent of DAC funding goes to the social sectors.

Responding to the infrastructure needs would require either a major reallocation in aid budgets or an innovative approach. Since most infrastructure projects have a revenue model (this is especially true for power and communications), there is a strong incentive to bring the private sector on board in infrastructure projects and to use donor funding as catalytic funding in order to get projects off the ground. This is the approach which has been used by the EU–Africa Infrastructure Trust Fund which receives pledges from EU member states and uses those pledges to cover some or all of the initial requirements to establish the viability of an infrastructure project. The fund is managed by the European Investment Bank which has the capacity to bring together a consolidated group of investors to fund the actual programme. Among the projects supported by the fund were the EASSy underwater cable and the Kaprivi Interconnector.[10]

I have already given the example of the North–South Corridor project which received more than $1 billion worth of pledges during the launch conference in Lusaka in 2009. Unfortunately, since that date little progress appears to have been made. However, an innovative project funded by the European Development Fund, the European Investment Bank and the African Development Bank will, beginning in 2011, rehabilitate a large section of the North–South Corridor running through Zambia.

The success of the EU–Africa Infrastructure Trust Fund, the novel and positive approach from some funders and development banks to come together on funding, and the success of funds such as GAVI

---

9 OECD/DAC statistics.
10 See details at www.eu-africa-infrastructure-tf.net/

and the Global Fund indicates that a Global Fund to develop African infrastructure would be a viable way forward in addressing the funding requirements for infrastructure. The fund would be global, accepting pledges from all donors. Projects involving the connection of two or more countries would be vetted and the initial risk associated with feasibility and design would be covered by the fund. After passing this stage the fund would step aside and the project funds would be obtained from a wide range of investors including government, the private sector, development banks and investment institutions. A special investment vehicle could be set up to manage each project and a revenue model would provide the return to the investors and would provide funds to cover the maintenance of the facility. These types of arrangements are conventional for all investment entities.

It is worth mentioning the role of China in the area of African infrastructure. The very substantial loans made by China to Angola and Congo are predicated on the use of the funds to invest in infrastructure which will be concentrated on assisting the transport both by land and sea of oil, gas and mineral resources. A global approach to the problem of Africa's infrastructure would allow a coordination of the ongoing efforts of China and other non-DAC donors into such a global initiative.

The ambitious nineteenth-century British project initiated by Cecil Rhodes to link Cape Town to Cairo has left a series of as-yet-unfinished links in a chain which could join the continent from South to North. The vast size of Africa provides enormous challenges in providing the links which will spur economic development and assist external trade.

Self-help aid

Ngozi Okonjo Iweala, former Nigerian Finance Minister and current Managing Director of the World Bank, speaking at a conference 'Africa the Next Challenge', mentioned that Ireland and Spain had received development aid from the EU and were not ashamed of it.[11] The statement itself is of interest only because of the veiled reference to the Social and Cohesion Funds of the EU. There is one feature of the Marshall Plan which has been replicated in the Social and

---

11 The full speech is available at www.ted.com/index.php/talks/ngozi_okonjo_iweala_on_aid_versus_trade.html

Cohesion Funds of the EU and that is the concept of 'matching funds'. This concept means that the recipient must put up the same or an equivalent amount of funding (measured either as money, labour or materials) towards any project as the donor. This concept of matching funds can be equated to ownership or self-help.

The history of development aid has been one of the North carrying out development projects in the South. Typically a group of experts (or a construction company) would arrive, carry out the development project and then leave. In many cases the project, if an economic investment, would stumble along for a couple of years before falling apart. Infrastructure projects (specifically roads) would be constructed and the maintenance would be left to the relevant government department, with the result that no maintenance would be done and the road would fall to pieces. Along would come the same donor or another donor and the road would be 'rehabilitated' back to its former glory only to start disintegrating again within a few years. This was not only the experience of the DAC donors. Brautigam (2011) recounts the experience of the Chinese setting up factories in Africa. After they handed over the factories to the local management, production fell and the factories started to decline. The new wave of Chinese assistance consisted of going back and reviving the initial project. Only this time the Chinese managers stayed on. The concept of an industrial enterprise or infrastructure as a national asset did not exist in many African countries. On a visit I made with the former President of Zambia, Levy Mwanawasa, to a recently constructed market (financed by the EU) in Lusaka he consistently reiterated to the television cameras that this was a national asset which should be kept in good condition and maintained by those using it.

This problem of the non-maintenance of donor-funded projects has led to donor efforts to insist that recipients accept ownership of projects and programmes. The whole question of ownership formed the core of the recommendations to aid recipients from the Paris Conference on Aid Efficiency. Ownership in this case means the relevant ministry being the project manager of the programme being undertaken by the donor in their area of competence. This idea of ownership reaches its zenith in the case of programme sector budget support or general budget support where the ministry or the government has total control over the disposition of donor funding. The latter was not only intended to confer ownership on the recipient but was also intended to respond to the needs of the recipient and not what the donors thought should be done.

There is now a certain level of disquiet with the concepts of programme and general budget support related in the main to worries about governance and corruption which are seen as a primary consideration for this aid modality. Experience on the Marshall Plan and with the Social and Cohesion Funds of the EU may not be readily transferable to the development aid business in Africa. Both those experiences took place in situations where governance was not in question and neither was the commitment of the recipients. Given that there might be a degree of difficulty in replicating these experiences in the context, the concept of matching funds or self-help might certainly improve the psychological barriers associated with the getting of something for nothing.

Donors should therefore begin to develop programmes particularly in the social sectors of education and health where donor funding is matched exactly by a government effort. This would cover the ideas of ownership and the national assets in one fell swoop. This approach would also prepare governments in a better fashion to take over fully the funding of the sector as aid is gradually withdrawn.

Does this aid exit strategy respond to the problem of long-term aid?

The old adage 'If it's not broken don't fix it' certainly applies to the aid business, which has been recognizably broken for some time now. There are reasons why the business model has not evolved and they are related to the very political nature of aid. If aid were simply a business activity then there is little doubt that substantial evolution would have occurred. However, aid has been politicized whether in terms of extraordinary sums being allocated to political allies (as is the case with Pakistan) or in the maintenance of predatory but friendly regimes during the Cold War proxy wars. The political nature of aid has diminished since the end of the Cold War but risks being revived if aid is seen as a tool to combat terrorism. Aid from the BRICS, specifically aid from China, is not so much political (although all recipients of Chinese aid must support the 'One China' policy) but is specifically aimed at resource capture or market creation.

The conferences in Monterrey, Paris and Accra were a recognition by the OECD/DAC donors that problems existed in the business model. However, the attendees did not have the political courage (or perhaps simply not the political backing of their governments) to propose the root-and-branch reform which was necessary. Countries in all parts of the world have exited from aid. Some, such as South Korea, stand out as prime examples of how a country can not only graduate but can become a world leader in a relatively short space of time. The objective of the aid industry should be to dissect the elements which have led to the success of South Korea and to disseminate and replicate the elements of success in less developed countries. It all begins with government and economic reform, whether the country is South Korea or China. Therefore it begins with institutions. The first action of the despot is to destroy the institutions of state. A corrupt administrative branch assisted by a corrupt judiciary and impotent oversight institutions are the despot's greatest allies. Therefore governance, both administrative and financial, is core to success in graduating from aid.

What of the three criteria I have established earlier as being the basis of a rethink of the development aid model? Does the strategy I have set forth respond to the problems of mission creep, lack of exit strategy and the breaking of the symbiotic relationship? Each of the five elements of the aid exit strategy has a defined mission. Although measurements of institutional performance are notoriously difficult the Worldwide Governance Index can be used to measure how effective countries are at improving their institutional capacity. There is an exit strategy built in so that when a country has reached a target WGI the assistance can be stopped. There is no symbiotic relationship since the onus is on government to improve its performance and the assistance can be in the form of expertise. Similarly the domestic resource mobilization has a defined target, whether it be the OECD figure of 27 per cent of GDP or another independently set figure. The exit strategy is built in so that when the tax administration is operating efficiently assistance can be removed. The symbiotic relationship does not exist since expertise is being provided only in the period to ensure desired performance. Economic diversification is an issue for the government alone although it will be important to supply policy assistance in order to set up the environment in which business can flourish. The least developed country governments are well aware that their position in the Doing Business league and their governance record are the factors which will spur economic diversification. The proposal for a Global Fund for Infrastructure has the mission of bringing together the many different sources of funding which can make infrastructural projects a reality. The mission is clearly defined although it may be longer term because of the nature of large infrastructural projects. The funds necessary would be drawn from development banks, financial institutions, government and the private sector and are anyway beyond the scope of the aid agencies. It is important that the fund would consider those projects which have a revenue model which will be attractive to private investment. The symbiotic relationship is broken because the fund simply organizes the funding for a Private Investment Vehicle (PVI) which manages the project. Finally, the self-help element of the strategy can use the methodologies developed on the EU's Structural Funds and Social Funds and would reach their conclusion when a set level of GDP per capita had been attained. Again, since government would have complete ownership of the development process, the relationship between the donors and the recipients would be broken.

Does the proposed model go too far?

Any proposal to exit from aid will be considered by the aid industry to be going too far. This can be evidenced by the tinkering around the edges which has been a factor of the evolution of the business model over the past ten years or so. While I do not want to enter the argument which has raged over the usefulness of aid, there is no doubt that the contribution of some of the authors on the negative side has concentrated the minds of the donor community on the 'why' of development aid and on not simply adjusting the 'what' and the 'how'. Unfortunately the results of Monterrey, Paris and Accra show that the industry is still obsessed by the 'what' and the 'how' of development aid. The answer from Monterrey was that more funding was required (this is a typical 'what' solution) while Paris and Accra concentrated on aid efficiency (a typical 'how' solution).

Undoubtedly, the proposal for an aid exit strategy is a radical step for an industry which refuses to grapple with the endemic and systemic problems associated with development aid. However, a logical withdrawal from aid is less radical than the proposal for dismantling the aid system completely by announcing to recipients that all aid will stop in five years. Denmark was considered radical when it announced its aid exit strategy for eleven countries in early 2011. Danish aid to

Benin, Bolivia, Cambodia, Nicaragua, Vietnam and Zambia was immediately phased out when Denmark announced a cut in its number of partner countries from 26 to 15. Phasing-out will end when current programmes finish or in 2013 at the latest.

Instead of grasping the nettle that is development aid, the aid industry has contented itself in tinkering around the edges and embarking on a search for the magic bullet which would solve the development aid problem. In chapters 4 to 10, I have looked closely at seven so-called magic bullets and have concluded that only one – domestic resource mobilization – has the potential to contribute in the short term to an aid exit strategy. There is no doubt that trade liberalization and the larger markets created by regional integration will inevitably lead to improved economic performance in many less developed countries. However, the contribution of trade liberalization will be dependent on the less developed countries developing products and services which are sought on the global market. At this time few less developed countries are in this happy position. Their trade is dominated by commodity trade which may benefit the few but does not appear to trickle down to the poor. The cumulative revenues from oil in Africa rose from almost zero in 1965 to $300 billion in 1999; during that period cumulative revenues per capita rose from almost zero to $3,000 in 1999 while GDP per capita in US$ remained constant at about $250.[12] These figures show that even a burgeoning trade in oil has had no real effect on the living standards of the average African.

Regional integration holds out some hope for improvements in inter-regional trade which should allow companies in less developed countries to develop their products to the stage of acceptance on the global markets. The success of regional organizations in expanding trade has been well documented with the EU as the prime example. The rules-based approach of the EU to issues of product quality and the protection of intellectual property rights is sometimes lacking in regional organizations with a high number of less developed country members. The loose rules related to membership and the lack of enforcement mechanisms for decisions taken at regional level will inevitably weaken the ability of the regional organizations to fully contribute to economic development.

The claims made for microfinance as the magic bullet that would

---

12 www.thebrenthurstfoundation.org/files/Brenthurst-Choices-for-Africa.pdf

eventually eliminate poverty appear to be greatly exaggerated. A close examination of the mechanism shows that far from moving people from poverty there is a propensity to move them into debt which they cannot sustain. The microfinance phase 2 organizations with their concentration on profit and high interest rates bear a striking comparison to the sub-prime lenders in the United States which have wreaked such havoc on the financial system. Whatever the final outcome, microfinance will not be the vehicle which eliminates poverty.

Remittances will continue to play a role in developing individuals who benefit from remittances. However, their overall role in development will be limited because of the fact that they apply to the few and not the many. Individual families will benefit through the purchasing power which remittances give them and there will inevitably be a trickledown effect as the money circulates in the local community. However, despite the large volumes, remittances will always be a bit player in development.

Whatever the future for ODA, the NGOs and the philanthropic foundations are here to stay. They represent the collective decision by individuals and by extremely wealthy individuals to fund initiatives in developing countries. Their contribution is very important but the existence of a clinic in province X has very little effect on the population in province Y. The contributions of the large philanthropic foundations to the Global Fund and to GAVI represent perhaps their greatest impact on development. This kind of financial support avoids the setting up of parallel organizations and assists in the concentration of funding to solve particular problems. This approach is completely in line with the aid efficiency agenda. NGOs for their part have an important role in assisting civil society in least developed countries to play their role in institutional development.

Finally, the BRICS have been the most lauded new entrant into the development aid space. It is perhaps incongruous that three of the BRICS (India, China and South Africa) are the recipients of substantial aid themselves. While the volume of aid from the BRICS is small and the motivation behind it is not always concentrated on development, they are an important new element in the development equation. They are important because they represent South–South cooperation and they act as models for less developed countries who aspire to emulate their economic development. However, they are far from the magic bullet that they appeared to be.

Is the time right for an aid exit strategy?

The history of aid is replete with occasions when either the donors or the recipients have suffered from 'aid fatigue'. Some of the comments used as chapter headings in this book show that there is now a constituency consisting of major European figures like Angela Merkel, young Africans such as Paul Kagame and even former presidents like Benjamin Mkapa who are of the opinion that development aid in the form of ODA should be wound down.

This constituency obviously includes many aid workers themselves, if the response of the audience in Stockholm to Glennie is to be believed. However, despite a constituency including major European and African politicians and some aid workers themselves, why is there still lots of rhetoric but very little action in developing an aid exit strategy?

One reason could be that aid has become a juggernaut which just keeps on churning out money to the least developed countries to either waste or use as is their normal practice. Turning the prow of the juggernaut is just too difficult and can only be accomplished by making minute changes in course like those of Paris and Accra.

A less charitable explanation is given by Glennie when he says that aid represents good value for money for the North. It is much easier politically to keep the aid tap pumping away than to give the less developed countries the trade concessions they need in agriculture to grow their economies. Therefore, aid must continue.

Another explanation is that there is a residual guilt among the former colonists for their behaviour during the colonial period. For some, aid is a mechanism for maintaining good diplomatic and trade relations with developing countries and for others, like David Cameron, it is simply that they saw Live Aid in 1985 and committed themselves at that point to help the poor. Whatever the reason for continuing aid (and the explanations above are only donors' reasons for continuing aid), there is a vested interest in most less developed countries in a future where they are in full control of their developmental process. The world has moved on since the days of European or American hegemony. The rise of China, India and Brazil along with the East Asian Tigers is slated to change the world order. The least developed countries want to gain their place in that new world order. As the generation of freedom fighters fades away, their replacements are looking at creating real nation-states capable of holding their heads up in the world community. Aid dependency is inconsistent with these national desires. The real challenge is accepting these changes and taking the appropriate steps.

The future of aid

Faced with a sovereign debt crisis in the major donor countries, diatribes that the current aid model is not working and fatigue on both the supply and the demand side, the real question may be whether aid has a future at all. The virtual tsunami which aid is facing may be sufficient to bring the current, though long-lived, phase of development to an end. That would be a pity for the citizens of the many countries that have failed to take the initiative in weaning themselves off aid. An aid exit strategy should not punish people who have for many decades had no part in the running of their own country and who have suffered poverty and deprivation at the hands of ineffective or predatory leaders. A new model of development aid incorporating an aid exit strategy must be applied with compassion or it will be ineffective. It must be time-bound but the time given to each country should be related to their baseline of aid dependency.

The Economist magazine, which once described Africa as a 'basket case', in December 2011 lauded the economic progress of the continent with a front page headlined 'Africa Rising'. Despite this optimism, there have been many false dawns in the progress of development and we must hope that this is not just one more in a long line. Sub-Saharan Africa still has a major democratic deficit. The predatory despots still try to pass on to their progeny (either natural or political) their control over the lives of their oppressed citizens. The Arab Spring has certainly affected the equation of continued hegemony in the countries which still cannot get rid of the 'Big Man'. North Africa was the most developed part of the continent and many in sub-Saharan Africa now look north and wonder how long it will be before the examples of Bengazi and Cairo will be followed.

Security is still a major issue and the bands which roam the enormous countries created by the colonists leaving havoc in their path will inevitably delay the development process. New communications technologies are making their impact on public opinion and will be among the forces for change.

The forces arraigned in support of the current model are strong. They have a vested interest in keeping developing countries weak and exploitable. Unfortunately, many of these forces come from the developed world. The game to date has been played by the rules of those who set the rules in the beginning. The environment in which those rules were set is changing. Perhaps in a strange way the tsunami facing the development aid business will have the positive effect of forcing change on a model which has outlived its usefulness. Tinkering at the edges is no longer an option.

BIBLIOGRAPHY

Adams, Richard Jr and John Page (2005) 'Do International Migration and Remittances Reduce Poverty in Developing Countries?', *World Development*, 33(10): 1,645–99.

African Development Bank (2010) 'Domestic Resource Mobilisation across Africa: Trends, Challenges and Policy Options', Committee of Ten Policy Brief, 2/2010.

— (2011a) 'India's Economic Engagement with Africa', *Africa Economic Brief*, 2(6), 11 May.

— (2011b) 'Russia's Engagement with Africa', *Africa Economic Brief*, 2(7), 11 May.

African Development Bank and Development Centre of the OECD (Organisation for Economic Co-operation and Development) (2010) *African Economic Outlook: Trade Policies and Regional Integration in Africa 2010*, Paris: OECD Publishing.

African Union (n.d.) APSA Factsheet. Available from African Union.

Aggarwal, Reena, Asli Demirgüç-Kunt and Maria Soledad Martinez Peria (2006) 'Do Workers' Remittances Promote Financial Development?' Washington, DC: World Bank.

Alacevich, Michele (2009) 'The World Bank's Early Reflection on Development: a Development Institution or a Bank?' *Review of Political Economy*, 21(2): 227–44.

Alden, C. (2007) *China in Africa*, London: Zed Books.

Alesina, Alberto and David Dollar (2000) 'Who Gives Foreign Aid to Whom and Why?', *Journal of Economic Growth*, 5(1): 33–63.

Alesina, Alberto and Beatrice Weber (1999) 'Do Corrupt Governments Receive Less Foreign Aid', National Bureau of Economic Research Working Paper 7108, accessed at www.nber.org/papers/w7108

Anderson, Kym, Joe François, Tom Hertel, Bernard Hoekman and Will Martin (2000) 'Potential Gains from Trade Reform in the New Millennium'. Paper prepared for the Third Annual Conference on Global Economic Analysis, Monash University, June 2000.

Arpac, Ozlem, Graham Bird and Alex Mandilaras (2008) 'Stop Interrupting: An Empirical Analysis of the Implementation of IMF Programmes', *World Development*, 36(9): 1493–513.

Arvind Ashta, Saleh Khan and Philipp Otto (2011) 'Does Microfinance Cause or Reduce Suicides?' Unpublished paper accessed at www.microfinancegateway.org/gm/document-1.9.49964/Does%20Microfinance%20Cause.pdf

Asian Development Bank (2000) *The Role of Central Banks in Microfinance in Asia and the Pacific*, accessed at www.adb.org/Documents/Books/Central_ Banks_Microfinance/Overview

Babatunde, Raphael O. and Enrica C. Martinetti (2010) 'Impact of Remittances on Food Security and Nutrition in Rural Nigeria', University of Pavia, accessed at www.unipv.eu/on-line/en/Home/.../CICOPS/documento5711.html

Bahl, Roy W. and Richard M. Bird (2008) 'Subnational Taxes in Developing

Countries: The Way Forward', Institute for International Business Working Paper no. 16. Available at SSRN: http://ssrn.com/abstract=1273753 or http://dx.doi.org/10.2139/ssrn.1273753

Bateman, Milford (2010) *Why Doesn't Microfinance Work?*, London: Zed Books.

Baunsgaard, Thomas and Michael Keen (2005) 'Tax Revenue and Trade Liberalisation', IMF Working Paper 05/112, Washington, DC: IMF.

Bebbington, A., S. Hickey and D. Mitlin (2007) *Can NGOs Make a Difference?*, London: Zed Books.

Berenbach, Shari and Craig Churchill (1997) 'Regulation and Supervision of Microfinance Institutions: Experience from Latin America, Asia and Africa.' MicroFinance Network Occasional Paper No. 1, Washington, DC.

Bergsman, Joel (1999) 'Advice on Taxation and Tax Incentives for Foreign Direct Investment'. Unpublished paper available at www.ifc.org/ifcext/fias.nsf/AttachmentsByTitle

Berkman, Steve (2008) *The World Bank and the Gods of Lending*, West Hartford, CT: Kumarian Press.

Berthelemy, Jean-Claude (2011) 'China's Engagement and Aid Effectiveness in Africa'. Working paper no. 129, Tunis: African Development Bank. Accessed at www.afdb.org

Bird, R. M. (2008) 'Tax Challenges Facing Developing Countries', inaugural lecture of the Annual Public Lecture Series of the National Institute of Public Finance and Policy, New Delhi, India, 12 March.

Bolton, Giles (2008) *Aid and Other Dirty Business*, London: Ebury Press.

Boudreaux, Karol and Tyler Cowen (2008) 'The Micromagic of Microcredit', *Wilson Quarterly*, Winter.

Brandt, Willy (1980) *North–South: A Programme for Survival*, London: Pan Books.

Bratton, Michael (2007) 'Formal Versus Informal Institutions in Africa', *Journal of Democracy*, 18(3), July.

Braude, Wolfe, Pearl Thandrayan and Elizabeth Sidiropoulos (2007) 'Emerging Donors in International Development Assistance: The Case of South Africa', International Research Development Centre paper, http://publicwebsite.idrc.ca/EN/Documents

Brautigam, Deborah (2007) 'China's Foreign Aid in Africa: What Do We Know?' Paper prepared for the Conference on 'China in Africa: Geopolitical and Geo-Economic Considerations', 31 May–2 June, John F. Kennedy School, Harvard University.

— (2011) *The Dragon's Gift: The Real Story of China in Africa*, Oxford: Oxford University Press.

Brennan, Zoe (2010) 'How can a nation ring fence foreign aid but slash defence? We reveal how your money is misspent ... and even makes poverty worse', *Daily Mail*, 18 September.

Brown, William (2009) 'Reconsidering the Aid Relationship: International Relations and Social Development', *The Round Table*, 98(402): 285–99.

Buckoke, Andrew (1992) *Fishing in Africa: A Guide to War and Corruption*, London and Basingstoke: Picador.

Bulíř, Aleš and Hamann, A. Javier (2005) 'The Volatility of Development Aid: From the Frying Pan into the Fire', International Monetary Fund, February.

Burgess, Stephen (2010) 'The African Standby Force, Sub Regional Commands and African Militaries', US Air War College. Accessed at www.au.af.mil/awc/africom/.../BurgessSubregionalCommands.pdf

Burnside, Craig and David Dollar (2004) 'Aid Policies, and Growth: Revisiting the Evidence', World Bank Policy Research Paper 3,251.

Büthe, T., S. Major, and A. de Mello e Souza (2009) 'The Politics of Private Development Aid: Serving Recipient Or Donor Interests?' Paper presented at a Research Seminar at the Centre for Research on International and Global Studies, University of California at Irvine, January.

Cabral, L. and J. Weinstock (2010) 'Brazilian Technical Cooperation for Development: Drivers, Mechanics and Future Prospect', Overseas Development Institute paper. Accessed at www.odi.org.uk/resources/docs/6137.pdf

Cai, Phoenix X. F. (2008) 'Aid for Trade: A Roadmap for Success', *Denver Journal of International Law and Policy*, 36(3/4), Summer/Fall.

Calderisi, Robert (2007) *The Trouble with Africa*, New Haven, CT: Yale University Press.

Cargill, Tom (2010) 'Our Common Strategic Interests: Africa's Role in the Post G8 World', Chatham House Report, London: Royal Institute of International Affairs.

Chami, Ralph, Connel Fullenkamp and Samir Jahjah (2003) 'Are Immigrant Remittance Flows a Source of Capital for Development?', IMF Working Paper WP/03/189.

Chang, Ha-Joon (2006) *Kicking the Ladder Away: Development Strategy in Historical Perspective*, London: Anthem Press.

— (2008) *Bad Samaritans*, London: Random House.

Channa, D. (2009) 'India as an Emerging Donor', *Economic and Political Weekly*, XLIV(12): 11–14.

Cheston, Susy and Lisa Kuhn (2001) 'Empowering Women through Microfinance', research sponsored by the Women's Opportunity Fund, accessed at www.microcreditsummit.org/papers/empowerment.pdf

Christian Aid (2008) *Death and Taxes:* *the True Toll of Tax Dodging*, London: Christian Aid.

— (2009) *Breaking the Curse: How Transparent Taxation and Fair Taxes Can Turn Africa's Mineral Wealth into Development*, London: Christian Aid.

CIA (n.d.) The World Factbook. Accessed at www.cia.gov/library/publications/the-world-factbook/

Cirera, X., D. Willenbockel and R. Lakshman (2011) 'What is the Evidence of the Impact of Tariff Reductions on Employment and Fiscal Revenue in Developing Countries?' Technical report, London: EPPI-Centre, Social Science Research Unit, Institute of Education, University of London.

Cobham, Alex (2005) 'Tax Evasion, Tax Avoidance and Development Finance'. Paper prepared for the International Policy Dialogue: New Sources of Development Finance, Frankfurt/Main, 24 August.

Collier, Paul (2005) 'Is Aid Oil?: An Analysis of Whether Africa Can Absorb More Aid'. Paper produced for the Centre for the Study of African Economies, Oxford University.

— (2007) *The Bottom Billion: Why the Poorest Countries are Failing and What Can be Done About It*, Oxford: Oxford University Press.

Collier, Paul and David Dollar (2002) 'Aid Allocation and Poverty Reduction', *European Economic Review* 46: 1475–500.

Collier, Paul and Tony Venables (2008) 'Trade and Economic Performance: Does Africa's Fragmentation Matter'. Paper produced at Oxford University.

Commission for Africa (2005) *Our Common Interest: An Argument*, London: Penguin Books.

— (2010) *Still Our Common Interest: Report of the Commission for Africa*, Commission for Africa. Accessed at www.commission forafrica.info/2010-report

Copson, Raymond W. (2007) *The United States in Africa: Bush Policy and Beyond*, London: Zed Books.

Costa Vaz, A. and C. Inoue (2007) 'Emerging Donors in International Development Assistance: The Case of Brazil'. Paper, International Development Research Centre, Canada.

Council of Europe (1986) European Convention on the Recognition of the Legal Personality of International Non-Governmental Organisations, Strasbourg, 24.IV.1986, accessed at http://conventions.coe.int/Treaty/EN/Treaties/Html/124.htm

Crutchfield, Leslie R. and Heather McLoud Grant (2008) *Forces for Good: The Six Practices of High Impact Nonprofits*, London: John Wiley and Sons.

CSFI (2008) 'Underbanked Consumer Overview and Market Segments Factsheet', Centre for the Study of Financial Innovation, June.

Danaiya Usher, Ann (2010) 'Donors Lose Faith in Zambian Health Ministry', *The Lancet*, 376, 7 August.

Davies, Ken (2009) 'While Global FDI Falls, China's Outward FDI Doubles', *Columbia FDI Perspectives*, no. 5, 26 May. Reprinted with permission from the Vale Columbia Center on Sustainable International Investment, www.vcc.columbia.edu

De Gucht, Karel (2010) 'Open Trade Open Minds', speech to the Civil Society Trade Seminar, Prague, 24 March.

De la Brière, Bénédicte, Elisabeth Sadoulet, Sylvie Lambert and Alain De Janvry (2000) 'The Role of Destination, Gender, and Household Composition in Explaining Remittances: An Analysis for the Dominican Sierra', University of California. Accessed at http://are.berkeley.edu/~sadoulet/papers/Migration7.pdf

Demirgüç-Kunt, Asli, Ernesto Lopez Cordova, Maria Soledad Martinez Peria and Christopher Woodruff (2009) 'Remittances and Banking Services: Evidence from Mexico', World Bank Policy Research Paper, WPS4983, June.

Deressa, Yonas (1988) 'Subsidising Tragedy: The World Bank and the New Colonialism', speech to the Heritage Foundation, 28 July.

Desai, Raj and Homi Kharas (2008) 'The California Consensus: Can Private Aid End Global Poverty', *Survival*, 50(4), August–September: 155–68.

DEVEX (2010) 'Proposal for India's new central aid agency scrapped', 8 June, www.devex.com/en/blogs/49/blogs_entries/67765

Diamond, Larry (2008) 'The Rule of Law versus the Big Man', *Journal of Democracy*, 19(2).

Diamond, Peter and Marc Plattner (2010) *Democratization in Africa: Progress and Retreat*, Baltimore, MD: Johns Hopkins University Press.

Dichter, Thomas (2007) *What's Wrong with Microfinance*, UK: Practical Action Publishing.

Di Renzio, Paolo (2005) 'Increased Aid vs Absorptive Capacity: Challenges and Opportunities Towards 2015', *IDS Bulletin*, 36(3): 20–7.

— (2006) 'Briefing: Paved with Good Intentions? The Role of Aid in Reaching the Millennium Development Goals', *African Affairs*, 106(422): 133–40.

Djankov, S., J. G. Montalvo and M. Reynal-Querol (2005) 'The Curse of Aid', *Journal of Economic Growth*, 13: 169–94.

Dowden, Richard (2008) *Africa: Altered States, Ordinary Miracles*, London: Portobello Books.

Draper, Peter (2010) 'Rethinking the (European) Foundations of Sub-Saharan African Regional Economic

Integration: A Political Economy Essay', OECD Development Centre, Paris, September.

Dreher, Axel (2006) 'IMF and Economic Growth: The Effects of Programmes, Loans and Compliance with Conditionality', *World Development*, 34(5): 769–88.

Dreher, Axel, F. Mölders and P. Nunnenkamp (2007) 'Are NGOs the Better Donors: A Case Study of Aid Allocation for Sweden', Kiel WP 1383, Kiel Institute for the World Economy.

Eade, Deborah and Ernst Ligteringen (2001) 'NGOs and the Future: Taking Stock, Shaping Debates, Changing Practice', in Deborah Eade and Ernst Ligteringen, *Debating Development: NGOs and the Future*, Oxfam, 2001. Accessed at www.development inpractice.org/book/debating-development-ngos-and-future

EAGER (2001) 'An Aid Exit Strategy for African Countries', Equity and Growth through Economic Research Policy Brief, no. 59, Alexandria, VA: EAGER Publications.

Easterly, William (2007) *The White Man's Burden: Why the West's Efforts to Aid the Rest Have Done So Much Ill and So Little Good*, Oxford: Oxford University Press.

— (2008a) 'Design and Reform of Institutions in LDCs and Transition Economies', *American Economic Review*, 98(2): 95–9.

— (2008b) *Reinventing Foreign Aid*, Cambridge, MA: MIT Press.

— (2009) 'Can the West Save Africa?', *Journal of Economic Literature*, XLVII, June: 373–447.

Edwards, Michael and David Hulme David (1996) *Beyond the Magic Bullet: NGO Performance and Accountability in the post-Cold War*, Hartford, CT: Kumarian Press.

Elliott, Larry and Heather Stewart (2009) 'Tories Plan to Reduce Aid to Non-Commonwealth Countries', *Guardian*, 12 July.

Environmental Performance Index 2010 at http://epi.yale.edu

Ernst and Young (2011) 'It's Time for Africa', Ernst and Young's 2011 Africa attractiveness survey, accessed at www.ey.com/Publication/vwLU Assets/2011_Africa_Attractiveness_ Survey/$FILE/11EDA187_ attractiveness _africa_low_resolution _final.pdf

European Commission (2000) 'Integration of Food Security Objectives within a Poverty Reduction Framework'. Concept paper, Brussels, February, accessed at http:// ec.europa.eu/development/services/ dev-policy-proposals_en.cfm.

— (2007) 'Everything but Arms' at http://ec.europa.eu/trade/ wider-agenda/development/ generalised-system-of-preferences/ everything-but-arms/

— (2008) *Budget Support: an Effective Way to Finance Development*, Brussels: EuropeAid Cooperation Office.

— (2010a) 'Aid for Trade Monitoring Report 2010', COM(2010) 159, Brussels, European Commission.

— (2010b) EU–ACP Economic Partnership Agreements: State of Play at June 2010, at http://trade.ec.europa. eu/doclib/docs/2010/june/tra-doc_146263.pdf

Exim Bank (2010) Annual Report 2010, Chairman's statement, www.exim-bankindia.com/anro910.pdf

Faíña Medín, José Andrés et al. (2010) 'International Organizations and the Theory of Clubs', *Revista de Metodos Cuantitativos para la Economia y la Empresa*, 9: 17–27.

Ferguson, Niall (2008) *The Ascent of Money*, London: Penguin Books.

Finger, M. (2000) *The WTO's Special Burden on the Less Developed Countries*, Cato Institute, 19(3).

— (2001) 'Implementing the Uruguay Round Agreements: Problems for Developing Countries', *World Economy*, 24: 1097–108.

— (2006) 'Aid for Trade: How We Got Here, Where We Might Go', Background Brief No. 10, ILEAP, September.

— (2008) 'Aid for Trade: How We Got Here, Where We Might Go', in D. Njinkeu and H. Cameron, *Aid for Trade and Development*, Cambridge: Cambridge University Press.

Fjeldstad, O.-H., and M. Moore (2007) 'Taxation and State-Building: Poor Countries in a Globalised World', WP 2007:11, Christian Michelsen Institute.

— (2009) 'Revenue Authorities and Public Authority in Sub-Saharan Africa', *Journal of Modern African Studies*, 47(1).

Forbes (2007) 'The Top 50 Microfinance Institutions', accessed at: www.forbes.com/2007/12/20/micro finance-philanthropy-credit-biz-cz_ms_1220microfinance_table.html

Foster, V. and C. Briceño-Garmendia (2010) *Africa's Infrastructure: A Time for Transformation*, Washington, DC: World Bank.

Fowler, Alan (2000) 'NGO Futures, Beyond Aid: NGDO Values and the Fourth Position', *Third World Quarterly*, 21(4): 589–603.

Frankel, Jeffrey A. and David Romer (1999) 'Does Trade Cause Growth?' *American Economic Review*, June.

Fraser, Alastair and John Lungu (2008) 'For Whom the Windfalls: Winners and Losers in the Privatisation of Zambia's Copper Mines', Civil Society Trade Network of Zambia/Catholic Centre for Justice, Development and Peace. Available at www.liberationafrique.org/IMG/pdf/Minewatchzambia.pdf

Games, Dianna (2010) 'Renaissance Fund's Random Spending Should be More Strategically Focused', Africa@Work, 13 December 2010, accessed at www.africaatwork.co.za/?author=2

Garrett, Laurie (2007) 'The Challenge of Global Health', *Foreign Affairs*, January/February: 14.

German Development Institute (2009) 'India's Development Cooperation – Opportunities and Challenges for International Development Cooperation', Briefing Paper 3/2009.

Gill, Bates and James Reilly (2007) 'The Tenuous Hold of China Inc. in Africa', *Washington Quarterly*, 30(3): 37–52.

Glennie, Jonathan (2008) *The Trouble with Aid: Why Less Could Mean More for Africa*, London: Zed Books.

— (2011) 'Is It Time for Mali to Plan an Exit Strategy from Aid', Overseas Development Institute paper, 2011.

Goldberg, Steven (2009) *Billions of Drops in Millions of Buckets: Why Philanthropy Doesn't Advance Social Progress*, New Jersey: John Wiley and Sons.

Grice, Andrew (2009) 'G8 Admits Its Failure to Meet Gleneagles Aid Pledges', *Independent*, 11 July.

Guest, Robert (2005) *The Shackled Continent – Africa's Past, Present and Future*, London and Basingstoke: Pan Books.

Hancock, Graham (1994) *The Lords of Poverty*, London: Grove Press.

Helble, M., C. Mann and J. S. Wilson, (2009) 'Aid for Trade Facilitation', Policy Research Working Paper 5064, Washington, DC: World Bank.

Hollingshead, Ann (2010) 'The Implied Tax Revenue Loss from Trade Mispricing, Global Financial Integrity'. Report, accessed at www.gfintegrity.org/.

Hubbard, R. Glenn and William Duggan (2009) *The Aid Trap: Hard Truths about Ending Poverty*, New York: Columbia University Press.

Hudson Institute (2011) 'Global Index of Philanthropy and Remittances 2011', Washington, DC.

IBSA website, www.ibsa-trilateral.org/

IDEA/SIDA (2007) 'Evaluating Democracy Support – Methods and Experiences', International Institute for Democracy and Electoral Assistance, Sweden.

IEA 2010 Key World Energy Statistics, www.iea.org/textbase/nppdf/free/2010/key_stats_2010.pdf

IFAD (2009) 'Sending Money Home to Africa: Remittance Markets, Enabling Environment and Prospects'. Paper presented at the Global Forum on Remittances, Tunis, October 2009.

IGAD (2004) Draft Protocol for the Establishment of the Eastern Africa Standby Brigade (EASBRIG), Jinja, Uganda, 13–17 February, accessed at www.issafrica.org/AF/RegOrg/unity_to_union/pdfs/igad/easbrig-feb04prot.pdf

ILEAP (2006) The Financial Architecture of Aid for Trade, April. Paper, accessed at www.odi.org.uk/resources/docs/4215.pdf

IMF Staff (2001) 'Global Trade Liberalization and the Developing Countries', Washington, DC: IMF.

International Development Committee (2009) Aid Under Pressure: Support for Development Assistance in a Global Economic Downturn, Fourth Report of Session 2008–09, vol. 1, Stationery Office.

Iyoha, Milton A. (2005) 'Enhancing Africa's Trade: From Marginalisation to an Export-Led Approach to Development', Economic Research Working Paper no. 77, August 2005.

Jager, N. (2010) 'Failing Aid: India's Cooperation with Fragile States: The Case of Sudan', paper, Leuphana University, 2010.

Jongwanich, Juthathip (2007) 'Workers' Remittances, Economic Growth and Poverty in Developing Asia and the Pacific Countries', UNESCAP Working Paper WP/07/01, January.

Jordan, Lisa and Peter Van Tuijl (2006) NGO Accountability: Politics, Principles and Innovations, London: Earthscan.

Joseph, Richard and Alexandra Gillies (2009) Smart Aid for African Development, London: Lynne Rienner.

Kagame, Paul (2009) 'Africa Has to Find Its Own Road to Prosperity', Financial Times, 7 May.

Kaldor, Nicholas (1963) 'Will Underdeveloped Countries Learn to Tax', Foreign Affairs, 41(2): 410–20.

Kar, Dev and Devon Cartwright-Smith (2009) 'Illicit Financial Flows from Developing Countries 2002–2006', Global Financial Integrity paper, Washington, DC.

Kar, Dev, Devon Cartwright-Smith and Ann Hollingshead (2010) The Absorption of Illicit Financial Flows from Developing Countries: 2002–2006, Global Financial Integrity. May.

Karlan, Dean, Jonathan Morduch and Sendhil Mullainathan (2010) 'Take-Up: Why Microfinance Take-Up Rates Are Low and Why It Matters', Financial Access Initiative, June.

Kassa, Yigrem (2010) 'Regulation and Supervision of Microfinance Business in Ethiopia'. Paper presented at International Conference on Microfinance Regulation, 15–17 March, Dhaka, Bangladesh.

Keen, Michael and Mario Mansour (2010) 'Revenue Mobilisation in Sub-Saharan Africa: Challenges from Globalisation', Working Paper WP/09/157, International Monetary Fund, Washington, DC.

Khan, Mustaq H. (2010) 'Governance, Growth and Development', Department of Economics, SOAS.

Killick, Tony (2005) 'Don't Throw Money at Africa', IDS Bulletin, 36(3): 14–19.

Klein, Michael and Tim Harford (2005)

The Market for Aid, Washington, DC: International Finance Corporation.

Kragelund, P. (2008) 'The Return of Non-DAC Donors to Africa: New Prospects for African Development', *Development Policy Review*, 26(5): 555–84.

Kumar, Kabir, Claudia McKay and Sarah Rotman (2010) 'Microfinance and Mobile Banking: The Story So Far', Global Call for Action Against Poverty Focus Note no. 62, July.

Kwesiga, J. B. and H. Namisi (2006) 'Issues in Legislation for NGOs in Uganda', in L. Jordan and P. Van Tuijl (eds.), *NGO Accountability: Politics, Principles and Innovations*, London: Earthscan.

Lancaster, Carol (2007) 'The Chinese Aid System', Centre for Global Development, June, accessed at www.cgdev.org/content/publications/detail/13953/

Liedo, Victor, Aaron Schneider and Mick Moore (2004) 'Governance, Taxes and Tax Reform in Latin America', Institute of Development Studies paper.

Luft, G. (2004) 'Fueling the Dragon: China's Race into the Oil Market, Institute for the Analysis of Global Security'. Paper accessed at http://www.iags.org/china.htm

Lyimo, B. and E. M. Sungula (2008) 'Lessons from Tanzanian Experience in Trade Capacity Building', in D. Njinkeu and H. Cameron (eds), *Aid for Trade and Development*, Cambridge: Cambridge University Press.

McKinsey Global Institute (2010) *Lions on the Move: The Progress and Potential of African Economies*, McKinsey Global Institute.

McPherson, Malcolm (n.d.) 'A New Course for Western Aid to Africa', accessed at http://www.atlantic-community.org/index/articles/

Mahmoud, Simeen (2003) 'Actually How Empowering is Microcredit?' *Development and Change* 34(4): 577–605.

Malhotra, Kamal (2000) 'NGOs without Aid: Beyond the Global Soup Kitchen', *Third World Quarterly*, 21(4): 655–68.

Malkin, Elisabeth (2008) 'Microfinance's Success Sets Off a Debate in Mexico', *New York Times*, 5 April.

Manji, F. and C. O'Coill (2002) 'The Missionary Position: NGOs and Development in Africa', *International Affairs*, 78(3): 567–83.

Manning, Richard (2006) 'Will Emerging Donors Change the Face of International Cooperation?' *Development Policy Review*, 24(4): 371–85.

Martens, Jens (2006) 'What if Developing Countries Could Finance Poverty Eradication from Their Own Public Resources', Global Policy Forum paper.

Mata, Ritha Sukadi (2011) 'Microfinance Institutions (MFIs) on the Remittance Market: Money Transfer Activity and Savings Mobilization'. Working Paper CEB 09-022.RS, ULB, Universite Libre de Bruxelles.

Matin, Imran, David Hulme and Stuart Rutherford (2002) 'Finance for the Poor: From Microcredit to Microfinancial Services', *Journal of International Development*, 14: 273–94.

Mercer, C. (2002) 'NGO's, Civil Society and Democratisation: A Critical Review of the Literature', *Progress in Development Studies*, 2.1: 5–22.

Meredith, Martin (2006) *The State of Africa: A History of Fifty Years of Independence*, London: Free Press.

Mills, Greg (2011) *Why Africa is Poor: and What Africans Can Do about It*, Johannesburg: Penguin.

Mitlan, Diana, Sam Hickey and Anthony Bebbington (2006) 'Reclaiming Development? NGOs and the Challenge of Alternatives', Global Poverty Research Group paper.

Mohapatra, Sanket, Dilip Ratha and Ani Silwa (2011) 'Outlook for Remittance Flows 2011–13', Migration and Development Brief 16, World Bank, 23 May, accessed at http://siteresources. worldbank.org/EXTDECPROSPECTS/ Resources/476882-1157133580628/ MigrationandDevelopmentBrief16. pdf

Moran, Michael (2009) 'New Foundations, the New Philanthropy and Sectoral "Blending" in International Development Cooperation'. Paper presented to the Australian Political Studies Association Conference, September.

Morduch, Jonathan (2000) 'The Microfinance Schism', World Development, 28(4): 617–29.

Morris, Jan (2003a) Heaven's Command: An Imperial Progress, London: Faber and Faber.

— (2003b) Pax Britannica: The Climax of an Empire, London: Faber and Faber.

Moss, Todd, Vijaya Ramachandran and Scott Standley (2006) 'Why Doesn't Africa Get More Equity Investment?' Paper presented for African Economic Research Consortium Biannual Research Workshop, Nairobi, December.

Moyo, Dambisa (2010) Dead Aid: Why Aid is Not Working and How there is Another Way for Africa, London: Penguin.

Muhumuza, William (2005) 'Unfulfilled Promises? NGOs' Micro Credit Programmes and Poverty Reduction in Uganda', Journal of Contemporary African Studies, 23(3): 391–416.

Murphy, B. (2001) 'International NGOs and the Challenge of Modernity', in Deborah Eade and Ernst Ligteringen (eds), Debating Development: NGOs and the Future, Oxfam.

Mutambara, Arthur (2009) 'The Paradox of Foreign Aid', http://arthur-mutambara-zimbabwe.blogspot. com/2009/04/arthur-mutambara-paradox-of-foreign-aid.html

Mutume, Gumisai (2007) 'Africans Fear "Ruin" in Europe Trade Talks', African Renewal, 21(2), July.

NABARD Task Force (1999) 'Regulation and Supervision of MFIs', National Bank for Agriculture and Rural Development, accessed at www. nabard.org/pdf/publications/ reports/Regulation_and_Super vision_of% 20mFIs.pdf

Naim, M. (2007) 'Rogue Aid', Foreign Policy, Washington DC, March/April.

Njinkeu, Dominique (2009) 'Africa, Trade and the Crisis: A Stimulus Package for Africa', ILEAP (International Lawyers and Economists against Poverty). Accessed at www.ileap-jeicp.org/

Njinkeu, Dominique, John Wilson and Bruno Powo Foss (2009) 'Expanding Trade within Africa: The Impact of Trade Facilitation', ILEAP (International Lawyers and Economists against Poverty). Accessed at www. ileap-jeicp.org/

Nunnenkamp. P., J. Weingarth and J. Weisser (2008) 'Is NGO Aid Not So Different After All? Comparing the Allocation of Swiss Aid by Private and Official Donors', Kiel WP 1405, Kiel Institute for the World Economy, March.

OECD (annual) Development Aid at a Glance, Statistics by Region, Africa, Paris: OECD.

— (2003) 'Philanthropic Foundations and Development Co-operation', offprint of the DAC Journal, 4(3).

— (2009) 'Transfer Pricing Guidelines for Multinational Enterprises and Tax Administrations', Centre for Tax Policy and Administration, Paris.

— (2011) 'The Impact of Trade Liberalisation on Jobs and Growth: Technical Note', OECD Trade Policy Working Papers, No. 107,

OECD Publishing. http://dx.doi.org/10.1787/5kgj4jfj1nq2-en

Osaki, Keiko (1999) 'Economic Interaction of Migrants and Their Households of Origin: Are Women More Reliable Supporters?' *Asian and Pacific Migration Journal*, 8(4): 447–71.

Page, Sheila (2003) 'Developing Countries: Victims or Participants: Their Changing Role in International Negotiations', Overseas Development Institute, London. Accessed at www.odi.org.uk/resources/download/1735.pdf

Page, Sheila, Massimiliano Cali and Willem te Velde Dirk (2008) 'Development Package at the WTO? What Do Developing Countries Want from the Doha Round?' UK Overseas Development Institute.

Peters, Bram (2010) 'Remittances as an Opportunity for MFIs: an Analysis Framework', August, accessed at www.microfinancegateway.org

Peters, Tom and Robert Waterman (1988) *In Search of Excellence: Lessons from America's Best Run Companies*, New York: Grand Central Publishing.

Pfeiffer, Lisa Marie, Susan Materer Richter, Peri Fletcher and J. Edward Taylor (2007) 'Gender in Economic Research on International Migration and Its Impacts: A Critical Review', in A. R. Morrison, Maurice Schiff and Mirja Sjöblom (eds), *The International Migration of Women*, Washington, DC: World Bank.

Polman, Linda (2011) *War Games*, London: Penguin Books.

Rahman, A. (1999) 'Micro Credit Initiations for Equitable and Sustainable Development: Who Pays?', *World Development*, 27(1): 67, 82.

Ramachandran, V. (2010) 'India Emerges as an Aid Donor', Centre for Global Development, ttp://blogs.cgdev.org/globaldevelopment/2010/10/india-emerges-as-an-aid-donor.php

— (2011) 'South Africa to Launch Development Aid Agency', Centre for Global Development, accessed at http://blogs.cgdev.org/globaldevelopment/2011/01/south-africa-to-launch-development-aid-agency.php

Rashid, Lila (2010) 'Microfinance Regulations in Bangladesh: Development and Experiences'. Paper presented at the International Conference 'Microfinance Regulation: Who Benefits?' arranged by the Micro Credit Regulatory Authority of Bangladesh, 15–17 March, 2010, in Dhaka. Accessed at www.mra.gov.bd/conference/images/speakers/paper/Bangladesh-MRA.pdf

Ratha, Dilip (2009) 'Dollars without Borders: Can the Global Flow of Remittances Survive the Crisis?' Accessed at www.foreignaffairs.com/articles

Ratha, Dilip, Sanket Mohapatra and Sonia Plaza (2008) 'Beyond Aid: New Sources and Innovative Mechanisms for Financing Developments in Sub-Saharan Africa', World Bank Policy Research Working Paper 4609.

Ratha, Dilip, Sanket C. Mohapatra, Aglar Özden, Sonia Plaza, William Shaw and Shimeles Abebe (2011) *Leveraging Migration for Africa: Remittances, Skills, and Investments*, Washington, DC: World Bank.

Reinikka, Ritva and Jakob Svensson (2004) 'Local Capture: Evidence from a Central Government Transfer Programme in Uganda', *Quarterly Journal of Economics*, 119(2): 679–705.

Riddell, Roger C. (2007) *Does Foreign Aid Really Work?* Oxford: Oxford University Press.

Rist, Gilbert (2008) *The History of Development: From Western Origins to Global Faith*, 3rd edn, London: Zed Books.

Rodrik, D., A. Subramanian and F. Trebbi (2002) 'Institutions Rule: the Primacy of Institutions over Geography and Integration in Economic Development', National Bureau of Economic Research, NBER Working Paper No. 9305.

Rotberg, Robert I. (2008) *China into Africa – Trade, Aid and Influence*, Washington, DC: Brookings/World Food Program.

Rutherford, Stuart (2002) 'Money Talks: Conversations with Poor Households in Bangladesh about Managing Money', Institute for Development Policy and Management, University of Manchester.

Sachs, Jeffery (2005) *The End of Poverty: How We Can Make It Happen in Our Lifetime*, New York: Penguin.

Salidjanova, Nargiza (2011) 'Going Out: an Overview of China's Outward Foreign Direct Investment', US–China Economic & Security Review Commission, USCC Staff Research Report, 30 March. Accessed at www.uscc.gov/researchpapers/2011/GoingOut.pdf

Schlager, C. (2007) *Challenges for International Development Cooperation: The Case of Brazil*, Bonn: Friedrich Ebert Stiftung, 3 March.

Sen, Amartya (2001) *Development as Freedom*, Oxford: Oxford University Press.

Severino, Jean-Michel and Olivier Ray (2009) 'The End of ODA: Death and Rebirth of Global Public Policy', Centre for Global Development , Working Paper 167.

Sharer, Robert (1999) 'Trade an Engine of Growth for Africa', *Finance and Development*, 36(4), December, accessed at http://www.imf.org/external/pubs/ft/fandd/1999/12/sharer.htm

Shaxon, Nicholas (2011) 'Treasure Island: Tax Havens and the Men Who Stole the World', London: Bodley Head.

Shivji, Issa (2007) *Silences in the NGO Discourse: The Role and Future of NGOs in Africa*, Nairobi and Oxford: Fahamu.

Shleifer, Andrei (2009) 'Peter Bauer and the Failure of Foreign Aid', *Cato Journal*, 29(3): 378–90.

Smith, Phil and Eric Thurman (2007) *A Billion Bootstraps: Microcredit, Barefoot Banking and the Business Solution for Ending Poverty*, New York: McGraw Hill.

Söderbaum, Fredrik (2010) '"With a Little Help from My Friends": How Regional Organizations in Africa Sustain Clientelism, Corruption and Discrimination'. Paper, School of Global Studies, University of Gothenburg.

Somavia, Juan (2011) 'The Challenges of Growth, Employment and Social Cohesion'. Paper presented at the International Monetary Fund (IMF) and World Bank annual meetings.

South Centre (2010) 'The Impact of the Global Economic Crisis on Industrial Development of Least Developed Countries', Research Paper 28.

Stiglitz, Joseph (2002) *Globalization and Its Discontents*, London: Penguin Books.

Stiglitz, J. and A. Charlton (2006) *Fair Trade for All: How Trade Can Promote Development*, Oxford: Oxford University Press.

Tandon, Rajesh (2001) 'Riding High or Nosediving: Development NGOs in the New Millennium', in Deborah Eade and Ernst Ligteringen (eds), *Debating Development: NGOs and the Future*, Oxford: Oxfam.

Tandon, Yash (2008) *Ending Aid Dependence*, Nairobi and Oxford: Fahamu Books.

Taylor, J. Edward, Jorge Mora, Richard Adams and Alejandro Lopez-Feldman (2005) 'Remittances, Inequality and Poverty: Evidence from Rural Mexico' Working Paper 05-003, Department of Agricultural and Resource Economics, University of California, Davis, June.

Therkildsen, O. (2004) 'Autonomous Tax Administration in Sub-Saharan Africa: The Case of the Ugandan Revenue Authority', *Forum for Development Studies* 31(1): 59–88.

UNCTAD (2008) *World Investment Directory*, Geneva: UNCTAD.

— (2010) *World Investment Report 2010*, Geneva: UNCTAD.

— (2011) *World Investment Report 2011*, Geneva. Accessed at www.unctad-docs.org/files/UNCTAD-WIR2011-Full-en.pdf

UNIDO, Supply Side Constraints on the Trade Performance of African Countries, 2007. Background Paper No.1, accessed at www.unido.org/fileadmin/media/documents/pdf/tcb_supply_side_constraints.pdf

UNINSTRAW (2008) 'Gender, Remittances and Local Rural Development: The Case of Filipino Migration to Italy'. United Nations International Research and Training Institute for the Advancement of Women paper. Accessed at www.fidafrique.net/IMG/pdf/PhilippinesReportFinal.pdf

United Nations (2000a) Improving Tax Administration in Sub-Saharan Africa: The Potential of Revenue Agencies and Electronic Service Delivery, ST/SG/2000/L.3 13 September, at http://unpan1.un.org/intradoc/groups/public/documents/un/unpan004712.pdf.

— (2000b) *We the Peoples: The Role of the United Nations in the 21st Century*, New York: UN Department of Public Information,.

— (2003) *Monterrey Consensus on Financing for Development*, United Nations Department of Public Information.

— (2004) Report of the Secretary-General in response to the report of the Panel of Eminent Persons on United Nations-Civil Society Relations, UN Doc. A/59/354, 13 September.

Van Langenhove, Luk and Philippe De Lombaerde (2007) 'Regional Integration, Poverty and Social Policy', *Global Social Policy*, 7(3): 379–85.

Van Rooy, Alison (0000) 'Good News! You May Be out of a Job: Reflections on the Past and Future 50 Years for NGOs', *Development in Practice*, 10(3): 300–18.

von Drachenfels, Christian and Matthias Krause (2009) 'Fostering Economic Development in Sub-Saharan Africa: What Role for Reforming Business Relations?', German Development Institute paper, Bonn.

Wacziarg, R. and K. Horn (2004) 'Trade Liberalisation and Growth: New Evidence', Centre on Democracy, Development, and the Rule of Law, Stanford Institute of Internatonal Studies, No. 7, August.

Wang, Jian-Ye (2007) 'What Drives China's Growing Role in Africa?' Working Paper, IMF, Washington, DC.

Walsh, Conal (2005) 'Uproar at BAT's Tiny UK Tax Bill', *Observer*, 2 October.

Willetts, Peter (n.d.) 'What is a Non-Governmental Organisation?', in the UNESCO Encyclopaedia of Life Support Systems accessed at www.staff.city.ac.uk/p.willetts/CS-NTWKS/NGO-ART.HTM

World Bank (2002a) *Foreign Direct Investment Survey*, Washington, DC: World Bank.

— (2002b) 'Globalization, Growth and Poverty: Building an Inclusive World Economy', IBRD, Washington DC. http://econ.worldbank.org/external/default/main?pagePK=64165259&theSitePK=475520&piPK=64165421&menuPK=64166093&entityID=000094946_0202020411335

— (2003) *World Development Report 2003*, Washington, DC: World Bank

— (2004) 'Good Practice in Trade

Facilitation: Lessons from Tunisia', *PremNotes*, no. 89, July.

— (2006a) 'Global Economic Prospects: Economic Implications of Remittances and Migration', paper, Washington, DC: World Bank.

— (2006b) 'Governance Matters VI: Aggregate and Individual Governance Indicators 1996–2006', World Bank Policy Research Working Paper 4280.

— (2006c) *Mining Royalties: A Global Study of Their Impact on Investors, Government, and Civil Society*, Washington, DC: World Bank.

— (2008a) *World Development Index 2008*, Washington, DC: World Bank.

— (2008b) 'Finance for All: Policies and Pitfalls in Expanding Access', World Bank Policy Research Report, Washington. Accessed at http://siteresources.worldbank.org/INTFINFORALL/Resources/4099583-1194373512632/

— (2011a) *Doing Business 2011: Making a Difference for Entrepreneurs*, Washington, DC: World Bank.

— (2011b) *World Development Report 2011*, Washington, DC.

World Bank/FAO (2009) *Awakening Africa's Sleeping Giant*, Washington, DC: World Bank.

World Economic Forum (2011) *The Global Competitiveness Report 2010–2011*.

Wraight, Christopher D. (2011) *The Ethics of Aid and Trade: Development, Charity or Waste?*, London: Continuum.

WTO (World Trade Organization) (2001) Doha Ministerial Declaration, Ministerial Conference Fourth Session, Doha, 9–14 November 2001, WT/MIN/(01)/DEC/1, 20 November.

— (2005) Ministerial Declaration adopted on 18 December 2005 WT / MIN (05)/DEC 22 December 2005, Doha Work Programme, Geneva, www.wto.org/english/thewto_e/minist_e/min05_e/final_text_e.htm

— (2006) Recommendations of the Task Force on Aid for Trade, WT/AFT/1, 27 July, Geneva http://aric.adb.org/aid-for-trade-asia/pdf/WT%20AFT%201.pdf

— (2010) 'Aid for Trade: Is It Working?' Factsheet accessed at www.oecd.org/dataoecd/30/36/45581702.pdf

Yunus, Muhammad (2003) *Banker to the Poor: The Story of Grameen Bank*, London: Aurum Press.

— (2008) *Creating a World without Poverty: Social Business and the Future of Capitalism*, London: PublicAffairs.

Zhao, Shelly (2011) 'The China–Angola Partnership: A Case Study of China's Oil Relations in Africa', 25 May. China Briefing accessed at www.china-briefing.com/news/2011/05/25/the-china-angola-partnership-a-case-study-of-chinas-oil-relationships-with-african-nations.html

INDEX

About Zed Books

Zed Books is a critical and dynamic publisher, committed to increasing awareness of important international issues and to promoting diversity, alternative voices and progressive social change. We publish on politics, development, gender, the environment and economics for a global audience of students, academics, activists and general readers. Run as a co-operative, Zed Books aims to operate in an ethical and environmentally sustainable way.

Find out more at:

www.zedbooks.co.uk

For up-to-date news, articles, reviews and events information visit:

http://zed-books.blogspot.com

To subscribe to the monthly Zed Books e-newsletter, send an email headed 'subscribe' to:

marketing@zedbooks.net

We can also be found on **Facebook**, **ZNet**, **Twitter** and **Library Thing**.